Acclaim for

DANA PRIEST and **WILLIAM M. ARKIN'S**

TOP SECRET AMERICA

"This is an invaluable book, a breathtaking investigative account of America's vast new secret world....It offers an indispensable guide to anyone who worries about the explosive growth of what the authors call America's terrorism-industrial complex since September 11....Priest and Arkin explain better than Congress ever has the staggering waste and ineptitude that inevitably have followed."
—Bob Drogin, *Los Angeles Times*

"Ambitious... *Top Secret America* makes the team's investigations available in detail to those of us who live beyond the Beltway.... Since Priest and Arkin themselves lack security clearances, part of the interest of their book is how they acquired so much secret information." —Richard Rhodes, *Washington Post*

"The authors' report is mind-boggling...necessary and impressively thorough." —Ronald Goldfarb, *Washington Lawyer*

"One of the many strengths of *Top Secret America* is that Priest and Arkin take nothing for granted. They ask basic, even faux-naïve questions about the purpose, accountability, and effectiveness of the acronym soup of covert programs, companies, and Pentagon commands created or expanded after September 11. Their analysis is neither naïve about the threat posed by al-Qaeda and similar groups, nor credulous about the generals, spies, and bureaucrats who have so dramatically expanded the country's defenses in response to September 11." —Steve Coll, *New York Review of Books*

"Priest and Arkin fully flesh out how the Byzantine security maze actually works, breaking down its components....The authors' arguments are compelling."

—Lydia DePillis, *Washington City Paper*

"Despite the sobering subject matter, *Top Secret America* makes for lively reading. It is full of the authors' remarkable insights, anecdotes and encounters."

—Steven Aftergood, Secrecy Blog of the Federation of American Scientists

"An important book....Priest and Arkin...blow the whistle on how, since 9/11 and the adoption of the Patriot Act, the government and its contractors use classification and security screens to conceal expenditures that have failed to enhance national security."

—*Publishers Weekly*

"As carefully documented by Priest and Arkin in their new book....no one—not even the government itself—has any real idea how much money's being spent or who's doing what in these new agencies; and worse, they are so secretive, duplicative, and inefficient that they simply don't work."

—Chip Pitts, Madison.com

TOP
SECRET
AMERICA

ALSO BY DANA PRIEST

The Mission: Waging War and Keeping Peace with America's Military

ALSO BY WILLIAM M. ARKIN

Divining Victory: Airpower in the 2006 Israel-Hezbollah War

*Code Names: Deciphering U.S. Military Plans, Programs,
and Operations in the 9/11 World*

Operation Iraqi Freedom: 22 Historic Days in Words and Pictures
with Marc Kusnetz, Gen. Montgomery Meigs (USA, Ret.),
and Neal Shapiro

*The U.S. Military Online: A Directory for Internet Access
to the Department of Defense*

Encyclopedia of the U.S. Military
with Joshua Handler, Julie A. Morrissey, and Jacquelyn Walsh

Nuclear Weapons Databook, Volume IV: Soviet Nuclear Weapons
with Thomas B. Cochran, Robert S. Norris, and Jeffrey I. Sands

*Nuclear Weapons Databook, Volume III: U.S. Nuclear Warhead
Facility Profiles* with Thomas B. Cochran, Milton M. Hoenig,
and Robert S. Norris

*Nuclear Weapons Databook, Volume II: U.S. Nuclear Warhead
Production* with Thomas B. Cochran, Milton M. Hoenig,
and Robert S. Norris

Nuclear Battlefields: Global Links in the Arms Race

*Nuclear Weapons Databook, Volume I: U.S. Nuclear Forces and
Capabilities* with Thomas B. Cochran and Milton M. Hoenig

Research Guide to Current Military and Strategic Affairs

TOP
SECRET
AMERICA

THE RISE OF THE NEW AMERICAN SECURITY STATE

DANA PRIEST and **WILLIAM M. ARKIN**

BACK BAY BOOKS
Little, Brown and Company
New York   Boston   London

Copyright © 2011 by Dana Priest and William Arkin

All rights reserved. In accordance with the U.S. Copyright Act of 1976, the scanning, uploading, and electronic sharing of any part of this book without the permission of the publisher constitute unlawful piracy and theft of the author's intellectual property. If you would like to use material from the book (other than for review purposes), prior written permission must be obtained by contacting the publisher at permissions@hbgusa.com. Thank you for your support of the author's rights.

Back Bay Books / Little, Brown and Company
Hachette Book Group
237 Park Avenue, New York, NY 10017
littlebrown.com

Originally published in hardcover by Little, Brown and Company, September 2011
First Back Bay paperback edition, September 2012

Back Bay Books is an imprint of Little, Brown and Company. The Back Bay Books name and logo are trademarks of Hachette Book Group, Inc.

The publisher is not responsible for websites (or their content) that are not owned by the publisher.

The Hachette Speakers Bureau provides a wide range of authors for speaking events. To find out more, go to hachettespeakersbureau.com or call (866) 376-6591.

ISBN 978-0-316-18221-8 (hc) / 978-0-316-18220-1 (pb)
Library of Congress Control Number 2011933644

10 9 8 7 6 5 4 3 2 1

RRD-C

Printed in the United States of America

From Dana: To Bill, Nick, Haley, Shirley,
and Ken for their love and humor, and to the late Banksy Priest
for keeping me company for so many hours every day

From Bill: To Rikki and Hannah,
and Luciana, my love with no time line

CONTENTS

GLOSSARY OF TERMS
AND ACRONYMS

CENTCOM (Central Command): A unified command of the Defense Department, headquartered at MacDill AFB. CENTCOM manages U.S. troops and military operations in the countries of the Middle East, North Africa, and Central Asia.

CIA (Central Intelligence Agency): The CIA, headquartered in McLean, Virginia, collects, evaluates, and disseminates information on political, military, economic, scientific, and other developments abroad. Its spies collect intelligence on threats to U.S. interests, among them terrorism, weapons proliferation and development, international drug trafficking and criminal syndicates, and foreign espionage.

CIPFIN (Defense Critical Infrastructure Program for Finance): A database and element of the Defense Critical Infrastructure Program that identifies and assesses the security of physical assets, cyberassets, and infrastructures in the public and private sectors that are essential to national security.

DHS (Department of Homeland Security): Established by the Homeland Security Act of 2002, DHS came into existence on January 24, 2003. It is in charge of developing and coordinating a comprehensive national strategy to strengthen the United States against terrorist threats or attacks. It includes the Transportation Safety Administration and Immigration and Customs Enforcement (formerly the INS).

DIA (Defense Intelligence Agency): The largest producer and manager of foreign military intelligence for the Department of Defense. It is one of sixteen members of the U.S. intelligence community. The DIA director is the primary adviser to the defense secretary and the chairman of the Joint Chiefs of Staff on military intelligence matters. It manages the Defense Attaché program.

DNI (Director of National Intelligence): A cabinet-level position, the DNI is a sort of intelligence czar whose role is to coordinate all sixteen agencies and departments that make up the intelligence community. The DNI is the principal adviser to the president and the National Security Council for intelligence matters related to national security. The DNI also oversees and directs the implementation of the National Intelligence Program. In reality, the power of the DNI has depended less on the definition given in the legislation than on the title holder's relationship to the president and to the heads of the various intelligence agencies.

DoD (Department of Defense): An executive department headed by the secretary of defense. The DoD is responsible for providing, organizing, and managing the military forces needed to prevent and fight wars and protect the security of the United States. The major elements of these forces are the army, the navy, the Marine Corps, and the air force, consisting of about 1.3 million men and women on active duty. They are backed, in case of emergency, by the 825,000 members of the reserves and National Guard. In addition, there are about 600,000 civilian employees in the DoD.

DOHA (Defense Office of Hearings and Appeals): A component of the Defense Legal Services Agency of the Defense Department that provides legal adjudication and claims decisions in personnel security clearance cases for contractor personnel doing classified work as well as for the Defense Department and twenty other federal agencies and departments.

FBI (Federal Bureau of Investigation): The primary federal law enforcement agency responsible for counterterrorism investigations and federal crimes within the United States. Its director holds a cabinet–level position.

FISD (Federal Investigative Services Division): Carries out background investigations used by government agencies to determine individuals' suitability for employment and security clearances. In 2005, the Defense Security Service transferred the DoD personnel security investigative function (and about sixteen hundred personnel) to FISD. Most of the major agencies of the intelligence community outside the DoD are responsible for their own security investigations and clearance programs.

GAO (Government Accountability Office): Established in 1921, GAO is an independent budget and accounting agency that works for Congress. GAO investigates how the federal government spends taxpayer dollars, and the head of GAO is the comptroller general of the United States.

GEOINT (Geospatial Intelligence): Consists of imagery, imagery intelligence, and geospatial (mapping, charting, and geodesy) information concerning the physical features of Earth and underground. Prior to 9/11, the U.S. Geologic Survey was responsible for producing imagery and geospatial data for the United States.

IO (Information Operations): Information operations, sometimes called influence operations, are primarily engaged in influencing foreign perceptions and decision making. During armed conflict, they also include efforts to achieve physical and psychological results in support of military operations. Military IO includes psychological operations (PSYOP), military deception, and operations security (OPSEC), which are measures to protect the security of U.S. operations and information and further their goals.

JCITA (Joint Counterintelligence Training Academy): Located in Elkridge, Maryland, JCITA is the primary training organization specializing in advanced counterintelligence. Established in 2000, it is a part of the Defense Intelligence Agency. JCITA provides training to over ten thousand military and defense agency personnel around the world through in-residence, mobile training, and distance learning.

JCS (Joint Chiefs of Staff): The senior staff of military officers who advise the president, the defense secretary, and the National Security Council on military matters. It is made up of the chairman of the Joint Chiefs of Staff (CJCS), the vice chairman of the Joint Chiefs of Staff (VCJCS), and the chiefs of the army, navy, air force, and Marine Corps, all appointed by the president following Senate confirmation. Headquartered in the Pentagon, the JCS has no operational authority but has become increasingly important in planning the strategy and tactics of the military's counterterrorism efforts.

JSOC (Joint Special Operations Command): JSOC was created in 1980 as a hostage rescue force. It was revamped by army general Stanley McChrystal in 2003 to become a proficient offensive military force engaged largely in killing and capturing top terrorist leaders in Iraq, Afghanistan, the Philippines, Yemen, and elsewhere.

JTAC (Joint Terminal Attack Controller): Air force personnel on the ground helping to guide pilots in the air to hit their targets.

JTTF (Joint Terrorism Task Force): Under the direction of the FBI, a JTTF brings together federal, military, state, and local law enforcement entities to investigate, analyze, and develop sources on terrorism within the United States. From 35 on 9/11—the first was established in New York City in 1980—the number of JTTFs grew to 106 by 2011. The largest, in New York, Washington, and Los Angeles, include hundreds of employees and liaison officers from other agencies; the smallest are no larger than a dozen or so people.

NCTC (National Counterterrorism Center): Established by the Intelligence Reform and Terrorism Prevention Act of 2004, NCTC integrates and analyzes all intelligence on terrorism and counterterrorism and designs strategic counterterrorism plans. It is a subordinate organization of the Office of the Director of National Intelligence. It maintains the Terrorist Screening Database (TSDB), an authoritative list fed by two primary sources: international terrorist information from NCTC and domestic terrorist information from the FBI.

NGA (National Geospatial-Intelligence Agency): A Department of Defense combat support agency that provides geospatial intelligence in support of national security. NGA also develops imagery and map-based intelligence solutions for U.S. national defense, homeland security, and safety of navigation. Headquartered in Bethesda, Maryland, NGA has major facilities in Washington, northern Virginia, and St. Louis.

NIEs (National Intelligence Estimates): Produced by the interagency National Intelligence Council, NIEs are the authoritative overall future assessments of the intelligence community, usually produced at the top secret classification level. Subjects can range from projections of Russian and Chinese nuclear forces to the national security impact of climate change.

NIMA (National Imagery and Mapping Agency): Renamed the National Geospatial-Intelligence Agency in 2003.

NORAD (North American Aerospace Defense Command): A U.S.-Canadian military organization charged with warning of attacks against the United States from missiles, aircraft, or spacecraft. It controls airspace over North America. The commander is responsible to both the U.S. president and the Canadian prime minister.

NRO (National Reconnaissance Office): The NRO was established in September 1961 as a classified agency of the Department of Defense and declassified only in 1992. Headquartered in Chantilly, Virginia, NRO manages the design and construction of the nation's reconnaissance satellites, which are the main collection assets for geospatial intelligence source data. Most of its activities are undertaken by contractors.

NSA (National Security Agency): Established in 1952, the NSA eavesdrops around the world. Its mission is also to protect U.S. national security information systems and to collect and disseminate foreign signals intelligence (called SIGINT, or intercepts). Its areas of expertise include cryptanalysis, cryptography, mathematics, computer science, and foreign language analysis. It is part of the Department of Defense and is staffed by civilian and military personnel.

ONI (Office of Naval Intelligence): The navy's lead intelligence center, it is headquartered at the National Maritime Intelligence Center (NMIC) in Suitland, Maryland. It produces maritime intelligence and analyzes and assesses foreign naval capabilities, trends, operations, and tactics, global civil maritime activity, and an extensive array of all-source analytical products.

OPSEC (Operation Security): Measures taken to prevent documents, technology, and plans from being disclosed to unauthorized personnel.

OSD (Office of the Secretary of Defense): The OSD formulates general defense policy and policy related to the DoD. It is organized primarily through a set of undersecretaries: undersecretary for acquisition, technology, and logistics; undersecretary for intelligence; undersecretary for personnel and readiness; and undersecretary for policy.

SECDEF (Secretary of Defense): Under the president, who is commander in chief, the defense secretary exercises authority and control over the Department of Defense. The department is composed of the Office of the Secretary of Defense; the military departments and the military services within those departments; the chairman of the Joint Chiefs of Staff and the Joint Staff; the combatant commands; the defense agencies; DoD field activities; and such other offices, agencies, activities, and commands as may be established or designated by law or by the president or the defense secretary.

SOCOM (Special Operations Command): SOCOM was activated on April 16, 1987, in response to congressional action in the Goldwater-Nichols Defense Reorganization Act of 1986 and the Nunn-Cohen Amendment to the National Defense Authorization Act of 1987. Congress mandated a new four-star command to prepare special operations forces (SOF) to carry out assigned missions and, if directed by the president or the secretary of defense, to plan for and conduct special operations.

SOF (Special Operations Forces): A term used to describe elite military units proficient in counterinsurgency, training foreign military forces, civil affairs, and psychological operations. They are more highly qualified, both physically and mentally, and better equipped than conventional forces. They operate in small teams and are made up of the army's Special Forces; otherwise known as Green Berets; U.S. Navy SEALs; and the air force's special operations airmen.

SPACECOM (Space Command): Established in 1984 and shut down in 1992, SPACECOM was previously one of the unified joint commands with functional rather than geographic responsibilities—military operations, weapons, exercises, plans, and strategy related to space. Headquartered at Peterson AFB, its commander was "triple-hatted," serving also as commander in chief, North American Air Defense Command, and commander, Air Force Space Command.

TOSA (Technical Operations Support Activity): A clandestine intelligence, surveillance, and reconnaissance (ISR) organization that supports special operations, JSOC, and other short-term intelligence collection efforts that demand close-in presence. Formerly known as the Intelligence Support Activity, The Activity, and Grey Fox.

USD(I) (Undersecretary of Defense for Intelligence): This individual serves as the principal staff assistant and adviser to the defense secretary and the deputy defense secretary on all military intelligence, counterintelligence, security, and other intelligence-related matters. The USD(I) provides oversight and policy guidance for all DoD intelligence activities, but also manages a few select operations. See DPAO, chapter 4.

INTRODUCTION

A Perpetual State of Yellow

Though she could barely walk anymore at age seventy-six, Joy Whiteman remained calm as she fumbled to remove her new white tennis shoes, lift herself out of her wheelchair, and grab the side of the X-ray machine. She teetered slowly, in socks, through the security scanner at the Boise Airport in Idaho. Airport security guards folded her wheelchair and rolled it through the scanner, keeping an eye on the frail woman in a bright flowered jacket.

"Can you make it without pain?" a guard asked her.

"Oh, sure," she replied.

Whiteman followed instructions, lifted her hands above her head, emptied her pockets of crumpled pieces of paper, then apologized for having left her driver's license in her purse rather than having it in hand for the guards to examine with her plane ticket. The line slowed behind her. Some people sighed at the inconvenience. Others smiled in sympathy at the awkward sight. I grimaced. What were the odds that she was a terrorist?

But Whiteman didn't mind at all. "I have no problem with it. I don't want to blow up," she said when I asked about the hassle. "I could be carrying a gun or something."

"Yeah," her husband, Bill, 72, said. "These people are always one step ahead of us."

Whiteman's smile faded. "Last time, they wheeled me through without looking at the X-ray," she said. "I could have had a bomb or explosives."

A decade of terrorism warnings about possible attacks in the United States had convinced Whiteman that she had much to fear. Walking through a body scanner without her wheelchair was a small price to pay for safety. Never mind that no terrorist had ever fit her profile or been foiled walking through a security scanner. Never mind that the Department of Homeland Security, which was responsible for setting airport security policy, was ridiculed by people at every other intelligence agency because it hadn't learned to hone its focus and still saw threats everywhere.[1]

The scene of Joy Whiteman holding herself up with the walls of the body scanner while a crew of security guards, paid by taxpayers, made sure she didn't fall, seemed a perfect metaphor for what has transpired in the United States over the past ten years. Having been given a steady diet of vague but terrifying information from national security officials about the possibility of dirty bombs, chemical weapons, biotoxins, exploding airliners, and suicide bombers, a nation of men and women like the Whitemans have shelled out hundreds of billions dollars to turn the machine of government over to defeating terrorism without ever really questioning what they were getting for their money. And even if they did want an answer to that question, they would not be given one, both because those same officials have decided it

---

[1] Never mind that last time President Obama's former national security adviser James Jones went through the Tel Aviv airport, he had asked the security guards, "Don't you want my shoes?" Jones, who had read top secret assessments of terrorism every day for nearly two years, certainly didn't think the Israelis were lax on security. He had realized again how conditioned he had become to U.S. practices, even if he actually believed they were an overreaction.

would gravely harm national security to share such classified information—and because the officials themselves don't actually know.

In the panic-filled chaos of late 2001 through 2002, this dragnet approach to terrorism was understandable, given how little the CIA, the FBI, and military intelligence agencies knew then about al-Qaeda. But in ten years, they have made vast strides in technical surveillance capabilities and intelligence analysis. They have killed so many al-Qaeda operatives that only hundreds are left in the world (in addition to the organization's post-9/11 affiliates). The dragnet approach no longer makes much sense.

One reason America is stuck at Yellow Alert[2]—"Significant Risk" of terrorist attack accompanied by no specific information—and stuck with such an enormous complex of organizations and agencies trying to defend the country is that being wrong is too costly for politicians in Washington. "Who wants to be the guy that says we don't need this anymore and then three weeks later something happens?" asked Obama national security adviser James Jones, former commandant of the Marine Corps. "I don't think you can ever get it back" to a smaller size.

We believe the primary reason for this is that the government has still not engaged the American people in an honest conversation about terrorism and the appropriate U.S. response to it. We hope our book will promote one.

Many people in the intelligence community wish this book were not being published at all. Before publishing our initial series on Top Secret America in the *Washington Post* in July 2010, we showed the government a database of government organizations and private companies working at the top secret level, assembled over several years as part of our research. We described how the data had been culled from publicly available information, and asked to hear any national security concerns. After detailed discussions

---

[2] The Department of Homeland Security ended the color-coded alerts in April 2011, but many airports and other government facilities continued to use them.

with most of the sixteen agencies of the intelligence community,[3] the Office of the Director of National Intelligence, which is supposed to lead those agencies, returned with a surprising request: don't publish the database. It might harm national security, we were told. The office declined to offer specifics and issued a warning to contractors about the impending publication of the series. The *Post*, meanwhile, had already begun to identify possible national security issues, and executive editor Marcus Brauchli ordered appropriate changes.

We are grateful to Little, Brown for allowing us to put this case before readers in much greater detail.

Despite all the unauthorized disclosures of classified information and programs in scores of articles since September 11, 2001, our military and intelligence sources cannot think of an instance in which security has been seriously damaged by the release of information. On the contrary, much harm has been done to the counterterrorism effort itself, and to the American economy and U.S. strategic goals, by allowing the government to operate in the dark, by continuing to dole out taxpayer money to programs that have no value and to employees, many of them private contractors, who are making no significant contribution to the country's safety. Allowing outsiders like us to signal shortcomings is one of the great protections the U.S. Constitution gives to the media.

Calling the reaction to al-Qaeda's 9/11 attack a "war" ensured that the government could justify classifying everything associated

---

[3] The U.S. intelligence community, or IC, consists of sixteen agencies and organizations within the Executive Branch: Air Force Intelligence, Army Intelligence, the Central Intelligence Agency, Coast Guard Intelligence, the Defense Intelligence Agency, the Department of Energy's intelligence arm, the Department of Homeland Security's intelligence arm, the Department of State's Bureau of Intelligence and Research, the Department of the Treasury's intelligence arm, the Drug Enforcement Administration, the Federal Bureau of Investigation, Marine Corps Intelligence, the National Geospatial-Intelligence Agency, the National Reconnaissance Office, the National Security Agency, and Navy Intelligence. The Office of the Director of National Intelligence is the seventeenth member of the intelligence community; and some consider the Department of Defense another member; but by executive order, the IC consists of sixteen agencies.

with fighting it. Under President George Bush, journalists' efforts to figure out how the United States was waging this war against al-Qaeda were often criticized by senior administration leaders, members of Congress, cable television pundits, even the public. Many of those journalists hoped that would change under the presidency of Barack Obama. It is true the president and his cabinet members have not publicly disparaged the news media as much as his predecessor did. But behind the scenes, the situation is actually much worse. President Obama's Justice Department has taken a more aggressive tack against the unauthorized disclosure of classified information by pursuing more so-called leak investigations than the Bush administration. Recent indictments were issued against a former CIA employee who allegedly talked to book author James Risen, a *New York Times* reporter, about a botched attempt to slip faulty nuclear plans to Iran; and a former National Security Agency official, Thomas Drake, who helped a *Baltimore Sun* reporter detail the waste of billions of dollars at his agency. In early June 2011, the government was forced to offer Drake a deal because its lawyers said they did not want to reveal classified information related to the case in court. Drake accepted the prosecution's offer to plead guilty to a single misdemeanor of misusing a government computer to provide information to an unauthorized person. He is expected to serve no prison time. Then there is the case of former Justice Department official Thomas Tamm. In August 2007, eighteen FBI agents, some with their guns drawn, burst into his home with only his wife and children present, to raid his files during an investigation into his alleged role in helping the *New York Times* develop its seminal warrantless surveillance story in 2004. The government dropped his case nearly four years later, in April 2011, after Tamm's career had been ruined and he faced financial peril.

The Justice Department is also mulling an indictment on espionage charges against WikiLeaks founder Julian Assange for publishing tens of thousands of pages of classified U.S. diplomatic cables and war-related field reports, some of them allegedly provided by a young army private first class, who is also under arrest. Regardless of Assange's publicly stated bias against U.S. policies and the allegations against his personal behavior, this unprecedented trove of material has allowed reporters around the world to write some of the most insightful and revealing stories of our time. In some cases those revelations even fueled brave public protests against undemocratic, corrupt regimes, developments the U.S. government says it supports in the name of promoting democracy.

Congress has jumped on the secrecy bandwagon, too. Maryland senator Benjamin Cardin—whose state is home to the National Security Agency, the nation's eavesdroppers—introduced a bill in 2011 making it a felony to disclose classified information to an unauthorized person. This legislation expands considerably the current law that makes it illegal to disclose information on nuclear codes, cryptography, electronic intercepts, nuclear weapons designs, and the identities of covert agents. But most important, it places even greater power into the hands of the executive branch to just declare something classified rather than to have to demonstrate that harm would be done if the information were to be made public.

Had Cardin's law been on the books shortly after 9/11, newspapers would have had a much harder time publishing stories about the CIA's covert prisons and waterboarding and other harsh treatment of detainees. Journalists may have been kept from revealing that many of the captives held at the military prison in Guantánamo Bay, Cuba, turned out not to be terrorists at all; that U.S. Army soldiers were abusing Iraqi prisoners at the Abu Ghraib prison; that the National Security Agency was collecting communications of people living in the United States without the required permission; and even that in 2011 Pakistan had rounded up men in their country they believed had helped U.S. authorities find Osama bin Laden.

The laws under consideration also would have made it illegal for government employees to help reporters research articles in 2002 and 2003 about the weakness of evidence surrounding Iraq's alleged weapons of mass destruction or, seven years later, the stunning admission by the key one-time German intelligence source, code-named Curveball, that his story was entirely fabricated.

Another piece of legislation now under consideration would criminalize the disclosure and publication of information about human intelligence—spies and informants. That law may have made it illegal for newspapers to have published articles about Canadian citizen Maher Arar, whom U.S. authorities turned over to the infamously inhumane Syrian police in 2002 after mistakenly deciding he was a terrorist. Or the CIA's bungled operation in Macedonia, where case officers mistook German citizen Khalid al-Masri for someone else and disappeared him for months, something that has cost him his sanity. He is a broken man today, one without even a public apology from the United States.

This book offers a counterproposal: that only more transparency and debate will make us safe from terrorism and the other serious challenges the United States faces. Terrorism is not just about indiscriminate violence. As its name suggests, it is about instilling paranoia and profound anxiety. It aims to disrupt economies and inspire government clampdowns. It is time to close the decade-long chapter of fear, to confront the colossal sum of money that could have been saved or better spent, to remember what we are truly defending, and in doing so, to begin a new era of openness and better security against our enemies.

A Note on Methodology

Our investigation focused on top secret work because the staggering amount of work classified one rung below, at the secret level, was simply too large to accurately track. We conducted several hundred interviews with current and former military, defense, and intelligence officials and private contractors, and visited at least a hundred places where top secret work is carried out.

To create a database of organizations and private companies working with top secret clearances involved compiling hundreds of thousands of public records about government organizations and private-sector companies over a period of two and a half years. These records included government documents, contracts and task orders, corporate and government job descriptions, property and budget records, corporate and social networking websites, corporate databases, and other material.

The people in this book are referred to by the title or rank they held when they were interviewed. Our reporting cannot be more fully described without breaking the promises of confidentiality requested by the vast majority of current and former officials who agreed to answer our questions and offer their observations and assessments of this hidden universe. Most of those who helped us did so with the knowledge that they were breaking some internal agency rule in doing so; they proceeded anyway because they wanted us to have a more complete picture of the inner workings of the post-9/11 world we sought to describe and because they, too, believe too much information is classified for no good reason. They spoke because they, too, were alarmed that one of the greatest secrets of Top Secret America is its disturbing dysfunction.

Our anonymous sources come in a couple of varieties: people interviewed with the approval of the government on the condition that they not be identified; people who agreed to explain things and give their assessments without official approval on the promise that they not be named. Some of the latter also requested that their military branch, agency, rank, and/or particular office be kept private. In most cases, anecdotes and other facts shared by anonymous sources were verified by at least one other person and often by several others. Many government offices were also contacted for comment and input. Most responded. A few declined.

We have carefully considered the national security implications of our work and have left out some information. The point of describing this overgrown jungle of top secret organizations and corporations is to enhance national security and the public's understanding of it.

TOP
SECRET
AMERICA

Liberty Crossing, in McLean, Virginia, houses the headquarters of the Office of the Director of National Intelligence and the National Counterterrorism Center. (Michael S. Williamson/*Washington Post*)

CHAPTER ONE

Top Secret America

Small fires were still smoldering under the rubble of the Pentagon crash site when President George Bush's senior staff approached Congress for emergency money for cleanup and retaliation. The first request was bolder than anything anyone on Capitol Hill could ever remember receiving: "...and such sums as necessary for an indefinite period of time." Scott Lilly, then Democratic minority staff director for the House Appropriations Committee, which under law helps Congress decide what executive branch programs to fund and in what amount, likened the first post-9/11 supplemental budget to "a repeal of the Constitution." While the committee members knew the administration would have to come back to them for more money, in the dazed shock that followed the attacks, no one questioned that a war against al-Qaeda would necessarily involve a massive infusion of funds.

Negotiations were brief, given the nation's state. Emergency preparations to respond to another attack were under way throughout Washington and it was considered unsafe to be on Capitol

Hill, rumored to be the one target al-Qaeda had missed that day. Authorities had quickly simulated what various types of explosives would do to the nation's most recognizable buildings. In the case of the Capitol, of particular concern were the panes of nineteenth-century glass. One powerful bomb could easily cause three thousand deaths as a result of the shrapnel of flying glass. Other scenarios were just as devastating and prompted the closing of streets around the area.

In a matter of days, a bipartisan group of leaders approved an additional $40 billion—two-thirds of total federal spending for education that year and twice as much as Bush had ended up requesting—to counter the attack. Wisconsin representative David R. Obey, Lilly's boss and the top Democrat on the House Appropriations Committee, called the measure "a down payment" on a "long twilight struggle against terrorism. This is going to be a very nasty enterprise."

Less than three weeks later, by the end of the month, congressional leaders approved another $40 billion. Some of the money was devoted to quickly reconstructing the Pentagon, and cleaning up the World Trade Center site, as well as to fortifying the Capitol and other federal buildings. "We were single-minded," said Jim Dyer, Republican House Appropriations Committee staff director. "We were going to show the bad guys how quickly we could respond, that we were strong enough to take a hit and bounce right back."

Three weeks later, envelopes of deadly anthrax emptied the Capitol and adjoining office buildings. Members and staff of the House and Senate Appropriations Committees, locked out of their offices, spent their days at the CIA, the FBI, the Department of Energy, and the other agencies that were most immediately involved in the response. The displaced House Appropriations members added items not on the White House list: protection for the Statue of Liberty; a remote backup computer server site for the FBI, which had none at the time; preparation for mass vaccine production; more equipment and personnel for the National Security Agency

(NSA), the nation's electronic surveillance agency;[1] and much more money for domestic nuclear security. The list, anxiously compiled, was long. By December, Congress passed another supplemental spending bill. Supplementals are funds not included in the normal fiscal year budget of any department, and they would become a way of life for the federal government following the 2001 attacks. When the buildup to the war in Iraq began just a year later, massive infusions of cash again were requested and approved. Much of the new money, on top of the already existing multi-billion-dollar budgets of the intelligence community and the military agencies, went into classified budget annexes under a new catch-all category called "GWOT" (pronounced Gee-Watt), for the Global War on Terror.[2] Given the fact that the country was now actively at war in Afghanistan, barely a member could speak out against more GWOT funds. "These were massive amounts no one could check," said Lilly. "It got so huge it overwhelmed the system. There was no way we could keep track of it. You'd no sooner be finished with one bill and you'd be given a request for a supplemental." Keeping tabs on the deluge of money was all the harder because much of the spending was also hidden from public view in what became a routine classified no-man's-land dealing with counterterrorism and homeland security, where it remains today.

The expansion of the classified portion of the federal budget reflected what was happening in the operations of the defense and intelligence agencies. On September 17, Bush signed a nearly

---

[1] The National Security Agency, established in 1952, eavesdrops around the world. Its mission is to protect U.S. national security information systems and to collect and disseminate foreign signals intelligence (called SIGINT, or intercepts). Its areas of expertise include cryptanalysis, cryptography, mathematics, computer science, and foreign language analysis. It is part of the Department of Defense and is staffed by civilian and military personnel.

[2] The official term of the Department of Defense is the Global War on Terrorism, though the GWOT is often referred to by many as the Global War on Terror. President Bush established the GWOT Expeditionary Medal for members of the armed forces by Executive Order 13289 of March 12, 2003. The EO serves as the only formal definition, referring to "operations to combat terrorism in all forms throughout the world."

open-ended Presidential Finding,[3] a document legally required in order to authorize covert activities by the CIA and other intelligence agencies. (The term *covert*—as opposed to clandestine or secret—means the activities are supposed to remain concealed so that the United States could plausibly deny its involvement if necessary. *Clandestine* and secret activities are concealed, but, if they are discovered, their U.S. sponsorship can be acknowledged. Under law, military operations, even the most carefully concealed, are not meant to be covert.)[4] As reported first by Bob Woodward for the *Washington Post,* Bush's Presidential Finding on al-Qaeda directed the CIA to undertake the most sweeping and lethal covert action since the agency was founded in 1947. The objective was to attack bin Laden's organization and to kill or capture those responsible for the 9/11 attacks and their supporters. Bush immediately gave the agency $1 billion and instructed the military to help the CIA in any way it could.

From the Presidential Finding grew dozens of frenzied programs to beef up the spy agency's paramilitary capabilities and

---

[3] A Presidential Finding (formally called a Memorandum of Notification) for covert action under the National Security Act, as amended, requires the president to explain why a covert action is necessary to support a foreign policy objective. "The finding must: be in writing; not retroactively authorize covert activities which have already occurred; specify all government agencies and any third party that will be involved; not authorize any action intended to influence United States political processes, public opinion, policies or media; not authorize any action which violates the Constitution of the United States or any statutes of the United States. Notification to the congressional leaders must be followed by submission of the written finding to the chairmen of the intelligence committees and the intelligence committees must be informed of significant changes in covert actions. Any department, agency or entity of the executive branch may not spend funds on a covert action until there has been a signed, written finding" (Joint Explanatory Statement of the Committee of Conference, HR 1455, July 25, 1991, quoted in Alfred Cummings, "Covert Action: Legislative Background and Possible Policy Questions," Congressional Research Service Report, April 6, 2011).

[4] Sometimes there was actually little difference between the two, as Leon Panetta told the Senate Armed Services Committee in June 2011 in response to questions during his confirmation hearing for the post of secretary of defense. Panetta admitted that "as a practical matter" the line between covert actions and clandestine military operations "has blurred" (U.S. Congress, Senate Armed Services Committee, Questions for the Record, Nomination of the Honorable Leon E. Panetta, n.d. [2011]).

support infrastructure around Afghanistan. Each one of them flew by the desk of John Rizzo, the CIA senior deputy legal counsel, for review.

"There was a flood of money and also a flood of authorities, a flood of responsibilities that we were directed to undertake, obviously immediately," said Rizzo, who by then had already spent a quarter-century at the agency. "It overwhelmed the infrastructure that was in place."

I had met Bill Arkin ten years before, during a much simpler operation: Desert Storm, the 1991 U.S. invasion of Iraq, the first Gulf War. Arkin was a meticulous chronicler of the military and the national security establishment, writing about the nuclear arms race during the cold war and, later, about the airpower era of the 1990s. He conducted assessments on the ground in Iraq and the former Yugoslavia and then persuaded the air force to give him detailed bomb damage assessment data to develop authoritative accounts of accidental civilian deaths, known as collateral damage, inflicted during air campaigns.

From his converted office barn in Vermont, the former army intelligence analyst wrote books on how to research the military and how to use the Internet to unearth government secrets. In the 1980s, using only publicly available information, such as telephone books, Arkin had located the secret U.S. nuclear weapons sites in Europe, infuriating the Defense Department and causing a firestorm in Europe but also showing the government what a poor job it did keeping secrets.

To understand any national security question, he collected and cataloged troves of documents: budgets, contracts, military directives, program descriptions, hearing transcripts, job listings, phone directories, audits, and a brain-pickling list of other sources.

Shortly after September 11, Arkin began to notice numerous changes in the budgets, hearings, and military directives he had discovered. Colorfully random two-word titles began to appear, nonsensical phrases like Busy Lobster, Fervent Archer, and Scarlet Cloud. The names of military operations, such as Brave Warrior, Justice Assured, and Freedom Eagle, all made a statement about political purpose and resolve. But Titrant Ranger? What did that mean?

Arkin's way of dealing with this proliferation of code names was to pull them into detailed computer files and study them as a whole. He had collected more than 3,500 of these odd phrases. To analyze them, he created a three-tiered classification system, a secrecy pyramid. At the base were designations that he already knew, and which were commonly used nicknames for military exercises and hardware and the like, phrases like Desert Storm and Enduring Freedom. The next level contained classified names that could only be vaguely definable by cross-referencing them with a budget line, a contract, a cryptically written directive. (Anything associated with the Nimble Elder program, for example, turned out to have something to do with weapons of mass destruction and counterterrorism.) Then there was the upper layer, the 5 percent of names that appeared rarely and without any description and were probably associated with the most secret and compartmentalized activities.

After years of analysis, Arkin figured that his voluminous research on code names had excavated only the tip of the pyramid, but he was still surprised at the number of new code names that were being manufactured every day. As he began matching code names to other references he had kept over the years, he discovered a giant flaw in the government's security system. A lot of the code names, even those near the top of the secrecy pyramid, showed up in the descriptions on job-listing websites of positions available to candidates who held security clearances. He was surprised, and delighted, to see classified NSA program names among them, such as this first job announcement he collected from the Windermere Group, an obscure intelligence consulting company, which was looking for a "Senior Analytic Support Specialist" based in Columbia, Maryland, to work on "at least two of the following: ANCHORY, OCTAVE, SKYWRITER, SEMESTER, JAGUAR, ARCVIEW, e-WorkSpace, PINWALE, or HOME-BASE."

As massive online job boards such as Monster.com replaced job listings that had appeared in newspapers, an astonishing number of these notices became searchable in their totality for the first time. Arkin began to catalog from four hundred to six hundred new job postings a day from the federal government and private companies looking for top secret–cleared workers with very specific skill sets. At any one time, he could find as many as 15,000 listings for very specialized positions that required a top secret clearance. Between 2006 and 2010 he cataloged 182,000 such job announcements in his files. As he did so, Arkin started to count government organizations and private companies working at the "secret" level of classification. Something is classified secret[5] if its unauthorized disclosure would cause "serious damage" to national security. For instance, many of the State Department cables published by WikiLeaks are classified secret because they provide candid assessments of foreign leaders and agreements. Routine field reports from military units are also classified secret on the theory that they might provide useful tidbits to an enemy. He was quickly overwhelmed by the volume. There were simply too many organizations and companies to track. Had he been looking prior to September 11, he would have expected to see evidence of a significant number of such programs, but the post-9/11 quantity was mind-boggling.

Given the huge number of secret programs, he decided to track

---

[5] Executive Order 12356 says a classification of secret "shall be applied to information, the unauthorized disclosure of which reasonably could be expected to cause serious damage to the national security." What exactly that means is a judgment call, but examples of serious damage include "disruption of foreign relations significantly affecting the national security; significant impairment of a program or policy directly related to the national security; revelation of significant military plans or intelligence operations; and compromise of significant scientific or technological developments relating to national security."

only those classified top secret. A classification of top secret[6] meant that public disclosure would lead to "exceptionally grave harm" to national security. The classification generally went to intelligence sources and special capabilities, particularly those involving nuclear weapons or special operations. Top secret information might reveal sources who were secretly passing information to U.S. authorities, or sophisticated technologies used to listen in on the conversations of adversaries, or the content of those conversations. Virtually everything concerning spy satellites and the methods of NSA monitoring is classified top secret, whereas most of what the conventional military does during war is classified secret. Cross-referencing and reading the fine print of job announcements in the summer of 2008, when we first joined forces, he had a list of two hundred companies that did top secret work; several weeks later he had five hundred—and not just their names but their addresses, as well as specific program titles and descriptions that corresponded with those locations.

Code names linked companies and agencies and activities, and the number of locations doubled again, quadrupled, and then doubled again. Unknown locations appeared; obscure agencies emerged; organizations that neither Arkin nor I had ever heard of went from the few to the dozens to the scores.

As the focus shifted to organizations, Arkin shifted much of his research to contracts. All that money meant that the government was also the nation's largest buyer. It purchased things, from toilet paper to computer equipment to the niftiest surveillance devices and drones. It contracted for services, from architectural design and construction to intelligence analysis, and augmented staff for

---

[6] Executive Order 12356 says a classification of top secret "shall be applied to information, the unauthorized disclosure of which reasonably could be expected to cause exceptionally grave damage to the national security." Examples of exceptionally grave damage include armed hostilities against the United States or its allies, disruption of foreign relations vitally affecting the national security, the compromise of vital national defense plans or complex cryptologic and communications intelligence systems, the revelation of sensitive intelligence operations, and the disclosure of scientific or technological developments vital to the national security.

even the most sensitive activities. The most secret would use cover names and intermediaries, but Arkin matched addresses and phone numbers and fake names on government procurement announcements, he found out how the agencies purchased their fuel oil and electricity, and he was able to map a full picture of the life and diet of a giant, growing entity.

The bloom of code names and job listings and addresses wasn't meaningful just for its own sake but for something much larger. Just as the most significant thing about a spiking count of white blood cells was what the blood test couldn't see—the infection that prompted the white cells to multiply in the first place—the top secret jobs and companies, and the government organizations they worked for, pointed to something unprecedented that had yet to be identified in the body politic. We call this Top Secret America.

CHAPTER TWO

All You Need to Know

Top Secret America, its exponential growth and ever-widening circle of secrecy, had been set in motion by one overwhelming force: the explosion in the number of covert and clandestine operations against al-Qaeda leaders and people suspected of supporting them. These operations had become larger, and involved more American and foreign operatives, than any secret undertaking in the nation's history. John Rizzo, the man who approved all those operations after 9/11, told me after he retired from thirty-four years at the CIA that "the cumulative number" of covert operations during the cold war "pales in comparison to the number of programs, number of activities the CIA was asked to carry out in the aftermath of 9/11 in the counterterrorism area."

By design, this unprecedented expansion was invisible to the American people. But hints of what was happening began to leak out in whispered conversations. People inside the government began to tell stories about enemy fighters in Afghanistan who would arrive at American battlefield detention facilities having been kneecapped on the trip in, or of detainees who had been punched, kicked, and stuffed in small, hot boxes under the blazing summer sun to get them to talk to interrogators. Others were being denied food, shackled to the walls, and kept standing or crouching for hours on end. These measures were all part of a panicked attempt to get the prisoners to tell the Americans what they knew about Osama bin Laden and coming attacks against the United States.

Other sources described a detention site at Bagram Airfield controlled by an organization other than the U.S. Army, which ran the base. Even regular American soldiers weren't allowed to enter. Eventually I found a former U.S. Navy SEAL who was also trained as an interrogator. He put a name to the list of interrogation methods other sources had been telling me about—"stress and duress" techniques: Standing for long periods of time. Imprisonment in cramped quarters. Limited diet. Sleep deprivation. I had covered the military for many years, and I knew this sort of thing had not been done in the decades prior to 9/11.

I called up the White House's National Security Council spokesman for a comment about the stress and duress techniques and the existence of the mysterious facility. He said, for the record, "The United States is treating enemy combatants in U.S. government control, wherever held, humanely and in a manner consistent with the principles of the Third Geneva Convention of 1949." It sounded like a complete denial. But how could all these sources be wrong? Or how could the White House believe that those interrogation methods conformed with the Geneva Conventions?

In the middle of investigating these strange tales, the administration offered an official hint about what was going on. On September 26, 2002, the House and Senate Intelligence Committees invited Cofer Black, former head of the CIA's Counterterrorism Center, to testify. A decade earlier, Black had helped capture Carlos the Jackal, one of the most infamous terrorists of his time. Black had been given the CIA counterterrorism job before 9/11, when it was a low-profile assignment; now he led the agency's war. He had CIA director George Tenet's ear and the president's attention. He didn't really even need to report to his immediate boss, the CIA director of operations.

The CIA, Black told Congress that day, had been granted new forms of "operational flexibility" in dealing with suspected terrorists. Then, his voice deepening with drama and arrogance, he told the intelligence committee, "This is a very classified area. But I have to say that—all you need to know—there was a before 9/11, and there was an after 9/11. After 9/11 the gloves come off." Most people focused on the references to the gloves coming off, which was certainly an enticing statement. But I couldn't forget that other phrase, "all you need to know."

Why was it up to this civil servant, no matter how well respected he was among his colleagues, to decide what anyone else, even the elected representatives he was addressing, did and did not need to know about the deadliest enemy facing the United States? Obviously details about the timing and location of operations, the exact technologies used, and the particular sources involved would need to remain secret. But why would anyone just simply trust the government with all that power and responsibility? It seemed almost un-American that a small group of people at the White House and within the CIA could decide that only they should know how the world really worked, while the rest of the citizenry was expected to assume that they would figure out how to defeat such an elusive foe all on their own, do the right thing, and then tell the truth if they messed up. Black's phrase would ring in my ears for years.

Just a week after Black's testimony, the public got a sample of what "the gloves…off" meant. On November 3, 2002, using a Predator drone armed with two five-foot-long Hellfire missiles, the CIA killed several people in a car driving through the desert in Yemen, a country with which the United States was not at war. The dead were an al-Qaeda leader, Abu Ali al-Harithi, who was suspected of masterminding the 2000 attack on the USS *Cole*, and a naturalized U.S. citizen from Yemen, Ahmed Hijazi.

The CIA was ecstatic. Its new secret weapon had worked. Not

only had it killed a single terrorist in a remote location before he ever heard the buzzing of the drone engine, but it gave the White House confidence that it could wage war covertly in any part of the world and deny its involvement if necessary. But not this time. Despite their habit of hiding in the shadows, senior CIA leaders were so proud of what had happened that they wanted to share it with the public, a decision that would become quite controversial within the rank and file.

Some sources inside government, and former military officials and lawyers in particular, had questions about the legality of the drone attack. "Wasn't that assassination?" I asked the cranky CIA spokesman, William Harlow, knowing that assassination had been outlawed decades ago. "They attacked us, remember?" he yelled over the phone. "Don't you get it?"

Not everyone was so sure, however, that the missile attack was a justified response to 9/11. Even solid supporters of the CIA questioned it. "This ought to be a last resort for the United States," Jeffrey H. Smith, a former general counsel at the CIA, told me. The preferable route, he said, would be to capture and try terrorists, and share the evidence of guilt with the world. "To the extent you do more and more of this, it begins to look like it is policy," he said. After a while, such pinpoint targeting of individuals might "suggest that it's acceptable behavior to assassinate people.... Assassination as a norm of international conduct exposes American leaders and Americans overseas."

The existence of armed Predators had been hidden deep down in layers of government secrecy. Before 9/11, unarmed surveillance Predators had been flown by air force pilots operating under the conventional rules of war. Lethal strikes by manned aircraft in all wars, including the last one in Kosovo, had been an armed services responsibility, too.

Over lunch, another source outlined how the target in an attack like the one in Yemen would be selected. There was a process, he explained. It involved lots of people. There was a list. It was hard to get on. Those on it—high-value targets, or HVTs, in official lingo—were either killed or captured; those captured by the CIA were apparently providing good information, the source said, critical leads in preventing new attacks.

Were the high-value targets in Afghanistan?

Not all of them, he said, before changing the subject.

I called a former agency analyst for a more detailed explanation. He said my lunch date was probably referring to "renditions." Renditions had started under President Clinton and had been "very helpful," he said. Suspected, detained terrorists or fugitives found in one country would be secretly transported by the CIA back to their own countries, where they were wanted by the courts or internal intelligence agencies. The CIA rendered these people "to the bar of justice": to the courts in a third country, the source said, even if the court were in Saudi Arabia or Egypt, where fair trials for terrorist suspects were rare and torture was routine.

Renditions, another person said, came with lots of legal review. The third country usually needed an arrest warrant for the person. Many of the renditions carried out during the Clinton administration involved sending members of the religiously extreme Muslim Brotherhood and Egyptian Islamic Jihad to Egypt, which had outlawed both groups. Egyptian Islamic Jihad had carried out the assassination of former president Anwar al-Sadat; in its ranks was the man who would become al-Qaeda's number two, Ayman al-Zawahiri. It was reported that the Egyptian intelligence services tortured many of these prisoners during interrogations, including Zawahiri.

Another man with lots of experience in the secret world was helpful, too. At a dark restaurant, over a bowl of vegetable soup and saltine crackers, I asked whether these current renditions were like those carried out in the Clinton administration.

"Not exactly."

"In what way 'not exactly'?"

They are "extraordinary renditions," the source said. "The CIA needs to get information from them. It's completely, 100 percent legal. It's an ongoing war. The EITs [enhanced interrogation techniques—another new acronym I'd never heard] have been approved by a zillion lawyers." When I asked him for some examples of EITs, he replied, "Can't say exactly," and we moved on in the conversation.

A few weeks later, I found myself sitting on a broken park bench in a seedy part of Washington, DC, with another source. "EITs," I said. "What are those?"

"You know I can't tell you that. It's classified. I won't tell you anything that's classified."

Okay.

"Everything's medically supervised," the source said.

"By doctors? That makes sense," I responded.

"Yeah."

"By agency doctors?" I asked.

"From OMS."

We were both whispering.

"Must be hard on them."

"They've been cleared psychologically."

"Makes sense."

"You wouldn't believe the kinds of things I hear...cigarette burns on the hands...reminds me of Nazi Germany."

"Who used cigarettes?"

"I told you, I'm not going to tell you anything classified."

I Googled "OMS" when I got back to the office. "Office of Medical Services, CIA" popped up. I typed in "CIA.gov" and began looking around the website.

Career Opportunities, Medical Officer: Are you up to the challenge? The Office of Medical Services is hiring individuals with medical degrees and board certification in primary care specialties to provide medical care and advice to Agency employees, dependents and assets. Positions are available for overseas assignments.

Salary: $127,542

All applicants must successfully complete a thorough medical and psychological exam, a polygraph interview and an extensive background investigation. US citizenship is required.

Important Notice: Friends, family, individuals, or organizations may be interested to learn that you are an applicant for or an employee of the CIA. Their interest, however, may not be benign or in your best interest. You cannot control whom they would tell. We therefore ask you to exercise discretion and good judgment in disclosing your interest in a position with the Agency. You will receive further guidance on this topic as you proceed through your CIA employment processing.

With these nuggets, I pulled my car up to the curb outside a local deli. A new source got in. We drove around the corner and parked. He was worried about the legality of things going on at the agency but didn't say what he meant by that. He fretted about the damage to the CIA and its people. "We'll be hung out to dry." We talked for an hour, and although he didn't say much then, I could tell he really wanted to say more.

The CIA is the president's personal sword of power in foreign lands if all else fails, one he can use without asking Congress first. If the president asked, the agency would attempt to overthrow governments, as it tried but failed to do in Cuba, North Vietnam, Nicaragua, and Angola, and successfully did in Chile, Guatemala, the Congo, Iran, and, twice, in — of all places — Afghanistan.

The CIA is the one agency in the U.S. government that was created by law (the National Security Act of 1947 and Title 10 of the U.S. Code) to do things overseas that no other agency in government is allowed to do: CIA operatives blackmail foreign bureaucrats into stealing state secrets, or bribe them with money, sex, alcohol, medical care for ailing relatives, or a private school education for their children; or they appeal to their sense of a greater good. They steal secrets themselves, using spy gear that can distinguish the words typed on a computer keypad from faint differences in keystroke sounds. They covertly help one foreign political party over another, hoping to ensure that the "right" people gain power.

To facilitate these covert actions required help from many of the code-named programs Arkin was discovering. The deep layers of secrecy were to keep terrorists, foreign spies, and reporters away. We were in terrible company and often treated accordingly, especially by President Bush's cabinet members, conservative members of Congress, and cable television pundits who especially liked to label us traitors.

Even the government officials whose job was to deal with the media often weren't any better. Harlow, the CIA's spokesman, often lost his temper when I asked for direct access to people doing secret things. Having traveled the world with the military, I just didn't understand why I was failing to progress with the CIA. Maybe I wasn't using the right terminology or phrases, or hadn't found the right people to ask. But the obvious answer was made clear to me one day when Harlow finally got tired of the badgering and let me have it, explaining in a very loud voice why, for the umpteenth time, he had no comment to my questions. "This is a goddamn secret organization! That's why!"

So, like other intelligence beat reporters trying to describe the post-9/11 world, I had to use more indirect methods. For example, when I had gathered half a dozen specific leads, I would run them by a couple of good sources I had known for many years. "I've always said you were an accurate reporter," is the only response I would get back. It wasn't much, but it told me I was on the right track.

Over the next four years, as more sources became willing to provide pieces of the puzzle, a portrait of the CIA's most deeply buried covert action program began to emerge. It was code-named Greystone.

Greystone had hundreds of subcomponents, including post-9/11 detention, interrogation, and rendition programs, and all the required logistics, from airplanes used to fly detainees around the world to fake names for the secret prisons overseas where detainees were kept in isolation, sometimes for years.

Greystone was one of the big reasons the CIA's relatively small portion of Top Secret America had grown so quickly and involved so many private contractors. It included hundreds of CIA employees and hundreds of officials in foreign intelligence services, though only a handful knew any more than their tiny slice of the pie.

Greystone was executed in a series of countries where the CIA and its counterparts overseas believed al-Qaeda, its followers, and new affiliates were located. Originally, this included Afghanistan, Pakistan, Indonesia, Malaysia, Thailand, the Philippines, Uzbekistan, Somalia, Germany, France, Italy, Kosovo, and Macedonia. It did not include Iraq, because al-Qaeda was not there.

In the beginning, no one outside the small circle of people executing the operations knew the program existed, and even those people didn't know every single subprogram under the larger Greystone umbrella. By White House design, that small circle did not include Secretary of State Colin Powell, who was supposed to be in charge of U.S. relations with foreign countries, or his general counsel, William Taft. Nor did it include the four-star regional commanders who managed U.S. military relations and operations in different parts of the world, or the members of the House and Senate Intelligence Committees, who were supposed to oversee every major operation undertaken by the CIA.

Such limitation and compartmentalization were applied to programs like Greystone, which was called, in CIA parlance, a Controlled Access Program (CAP). The Pentagon's version of one is called a Special Access Program (SAP). They exist to give the CIA and the Pentagon extra protection against unauthorized disclosure.

By 2002, President Bush was ordering war preparations in Iraq, too, based on the belief that Iraqi leader Saddam Hussein was building a biological, chemical, and nuclear weapons capacity that he might one day share with al-Qaeda or use himself against the United States.

The information on Iraq's weapons of mass destruction was another one of the secrets so well buried beneath so many layers of classification that very few people in the CIA or Pentagon had actually seen the evidence themselves to support the assertion that such weapons existed.

Only the congressional intelligence committees and the defense appropriations subcommittees that drew up the budget for the intelligence agencies were privy to regular classified briefings. This gave these congressional groups a special role in overseeing intelligence activities, a role unlike that assumed by any of the other congressional committees. As war with Iraq became likely, members of Congress clamored for more information and for the intelligence community to get together and produce what is known as a National Intelligence Estimate (NIE), an analysis by the National Intelligence Council with input from all the intelligence agencies.[1] It is considered the most authoritative work on a particular question, in this case, Does Iraq possess WMD, and how likely is Saddam Hussein to use them against the United States? But when the NIE arrived on Capitol Hill, no more than six senators, and only a handful of House members, ever actually bothered to read beyond the five-page executive summary of the ninety-two-page document laying out the government's information on Iraq's weapons capabilities.

Reviewing all the intelligence was exceptionally arduous and inconvenient. Because the NIE was so highly classified, members of Congress couldn't have a copy delivered to their offices or sent to them via email. Instead, they had to walk over to one of the secure reading rooms and sit alone. They could not enlist the help of an aide, and they were not allowed to take notes. The document was dense, "like the Brahms of music," as Democratic West Virginia senator John D. Rockefeller IV described it to me after he

---

[1] National Intelligence Estimates (NIEs), produced by the interagency National Intelligence Council, located at CIA headquarters, are the authoritative overall future assessments of the intelligence community, usually produced at the top secret classification level. Before the creation of the position of director of national intelligence (DNI) in 2004, they were delivered by the director of Central Intelligence (DCI), who was also the director of the CIA. Subjects can range from projections of Russian and Chinese nuclear forces to the national security impact of climate change. Unclassified summaries of NIEs are occasionally prepared for Congress and the public, but these mostly lose the detail and the nuance of actual NIEs, which are often lengthy and contain numerous footnotes and appendixes laying out analytic disagreements among the various intelligence agencies.

had read it. It contained many qualifying footnotes that even the most dedicated reader might miss, including an important dissenting opinion from the State Department Intelligence and Research branch that cast great doubt on the NIE's overall assertions that Iraq probably possessed chemical and biological weapons and was well on its way to developing nuclear ones, too.

Congress's oversight of intelligence was unlike any other job it performed. Since just about everything in the realm of terrorism was classified, members of Congress were the only outsiders allowed to know what was happening inside, and they played their role badly. Even when a select few members were briefed on President Bush's controversial counterterrorism tactics—warrantless wiretaps by the National Security Agency, targeted killings by the agency or military, extreme interrogations, which were the EITs my sources were raising questions about—any concerns they had were muted by extreme secrecy, and they could not go public given nondisclosure agreements that even these elected officials were made to sign. When it came time for members of Congress to analyze whether the risk from Iraq warranted going to war, they seemed too busy with other things—like keeping up with annual budget requests and their constituents back home—to study the information that was available. After all, even Colin Powell, respected on both sides of the aisle and seen as honest, had confirmed that the WMD were there and that something had to be done.

None of the top secret code names and job descriptions that Arkin was finding were for the congressional staffers on the intelligence committees who were supposed to do all the work to monitor the phenomenal growth in Top Secret America. Two committees do the lion's share of the intelligence oversight: the House and Senate Permanent Select Committees on Intelligence and the House and Senate Appropriations Subcommittees on Defense. Yet the number of staffers on each has not grown much at all in the decade since the 9/11 attacks. The number of staffers with knowledge of and experience with the most costly and technologically complex agencies, the National Security Agency and the National

Reconnaissance Organization, which manages multi-billion-dollar eavesdropping and spy satellite programs, actually declined. On the authorization committees, which set policy and design budgets, there were no more than four staffers dealing with the NSA and the NRO.

The leaders of the House and Senate Intelligence Committees, who often were the only members briefed by the CIA on covert action, were not allowed to consult with their lawyers or the specialized staff members steeped in the issues, even if they had the appropriate security clearances. Instead, these members of Congress were left on their own to make sense of highly technical issues such as surveillance of fiber-optic cables in the Internet communications grid structure, or the legal interpretations, history, and nuances of a particular regulation in the law governing electronic searches and seizures.

The poor quality of congressional oversight wasn't just a matter of money and staff, though. When members voted to approve the use of military force against Iraq, which in effect approved the presumptive deaths of thousands of U.S. men and women in uniform, they didn't do it after studying the best information available or conducting exhaustive hearings; they simply took President Bush and his well-qualified national security team at their word.

So much information hidden away in compartments like Greystone created a government system that became distorted by its own secrecy. Take, for instance, the German intelligence source codenamed Curveball, an Iraqi living in Germany whose stories about Saddam's biological weapons so greatly influenced thinking at the top of the U.S. government. Because his identity was so closely held, in a compartment within a compartment, it wasn't vetted in a rigorous manner and, as a result, his lies were not publicly revealed until long after the war began. And only in February 2011 did he confess publicly, in an account published by the *Guardian* newspaper in Britain. Rafid Ahmed Alwan al-Janabi, who was Curveball in flesh and blood, admitted that he had fabricated stories for intelligence officers about mobile bioweapons trucks and clandestine bioweapons laboratories in an effort to bring down Saddam Hussein. "I had a chance to fabricate something to topple the regime. I and my sons are proud of that and we are proud that we were the reason to give Iraq the margin of democracy."

Had more doubts been aired about Curveball's credibility early on, maybe Powell would have had doubts about his presentation to a rapt audience at the United Nations a month before the 2003 invasion. "We have firsthand descriptions of biological weapons factories on wheels," Powell said. "The source was an eyewitness— an Iraqi chemical engineer who supervised one of these facilities. He actually was present during biological agent production runs. He was also at the site when an accident occurred in 1998. Twelve technicians died." None of that was true.

To understand how far the government has fallen into the bottomless well of official secrets, step into William Bosanko's stately pale-yellow office at the National Archives on Pennsylvania Avenue, not far from the White House. With only twenty-three employees, his agency, the obscure Information Security Oversight Office (ISOO), is supposed to ensure that the entire government classifies and protects its documents properly. But since 2001, the number of newly classified documents has tripled to over 23 million, while his staff has barely grown. Bosanko said that with so few resources, ISOO has not even attempted to gain access to the government's Special Access Programs.

Bosanko's office has studied how much the federal government spends just to keep secrets secret. The price tag: $10 billion a year.

"Today the classification system is in crisis," said Bosanko. "We are failing at the most basic requirements," including training officials not to overclassify documents and periodically assessing whether some material can be declassified. But does that make us any less safe?

"Yes, absolutely," he said, "because the real secrets don't get the right protection."

Curveball's identity and the information he gave German intelligence, which they shared with the U.S. Defense Intelligence Agency, was handled using the authority conferred by Executive Order 12958, signed by President Clinton in April 1995. The order updated similar ones going back to President Truman establishing a system of national security information and designated classes of information: confidential, secret, and top secret. The order gave permission for certain top intelligence and defense officials to create vaults of information to which only a few people would have the combination.

These vaults—the aforementioned SAPs and CAPs—are distinguished from all other classified information by their "BIGOT" lists.[2] A BIGOT list is the list of specific individuals who have access to each compartment. Anyone not on the list, no matter how highly cleared, must not be told what's inside.

The intelligence community itself still doesn't have a complete picture of all its CAPs and SAPs. In late 2010, a friendly man in charge of a new Controlled Access Program Coordination Office (CAPCO) in the Office of the Director of National Intelligence began compiling a database of these programs. The database itself, the man explained to me, is a compartmented secret, a mystery box that contains itself.

After years of work, CAPCO's database contained the barest basics: code names, rationale for compartmentation, any significant changes since inception. It does not include the substance of the programs and it does not include most of the Defense Department's relevant programs, which means it is missing a lot.

How much? When the names of the Defense Department's SAPs are printed out and delivered to the leadership of the congressional

---

[2] The odd term dates from the secret preparations for the D-Day invasion in World War II; it refers to the invasion planners coming over from the North African campaign by way of Gibraltar. BIGOT is TOGIB—for "to Gibraltar"—backwards.

defense committees every March 1, the list is three hundred pages long—and those are just the names of the programs. The database doesn't include two other categories of deep secrets: "waived SAPs" and "unacknowledged SAPs," neither of which the full committees have to be briefed on. Nor does it contain the many Special Access Programs that can be hosted within the other federal agencies, a list that includes the Departments of Homeland Security, State, Justice, and Energy. And it only really contains the top-level program of an entire genealogical tree of programs. "Let's say you have a dresser in your bedroom—that's the top-level thing," explained the man. "Within that dresser you have twelve drawers we call 'compartments.' Now, each of those drawers you might open, and let's say one of them is a sock drawer. You have a divider in there for all your socks. Well, those are 'subcompartments.'"

The compartments are sealed so tightly that even officials above someone in the reporting and command chain may not be aware of what's going on below.

The secrecy surrounding these compartments and sock drawers is so dense that even the people who supervise the system don't understand the terminology or use it correctly. Or, as the man in charge of the database described it: "Someone will be giving a briefing and they'll say, 'Subcompartment,' and three guys will go, 'That's not a subcompartment.'" I later interviewed an even more senior official in charge of reviewing the database man's work, and he wasn't sure what CAP stood for, either, much less what was included in, and what was excluded from, that category of secrets.

Greystone, for example, is a dresser. Renditions is a compartment. Contract airplanes is a subcompartment. Renditions to a particular country—say, Thailand—is a sock drawer.

In all, the CAPCO says that there are 212 dressers, or Control Systems—the top layer—in the intelligence world. But not only does this not count all the drawers in each of the dressers or all the compartments within each drawer, it doesn't reach across all agencies and departments.

Only the most senior intelligence officials are allowed to look inside all the Control Systems, but they really don't have the time to do that. Likewise, at the Defense Department, where more than two-thirds of all intelligence programs reside, only a handful of "Super-Users" are allowed to see all the Special Access Programs. But while the president, the director of national intelligence, the national security adviser, and anyone else the president designates are allowed to see everything, they would never have the time or the inclination to get that far down into the details.

"There's only one entity in the entire universe that has visibility on all SAPs—that's God," James R. Clapper, then director of Pentagon intelligence programs, told me.

The Super-Users at the Defense Department have access to all the department's secrets and to many, but not all, of the intelligence agencies' secrets. Some Super-Users, including the defense secretary and the chairman of the Joint Chiefs of Staff, are included by law in the elite group; the defense secretary determines who else may have access. When Donald Rumsfeld ran the Pentagon, his disdain of the military was symbolized by the fact that he took Super-User status away from several positions to which it was attached previously, including the J2 (the intelligence chief on the Joint Chiefs of Staff). Rumsfeld's successor, Robert Gates, immediately restored the J2's access.

Two Super-Users told me there was simply no way they could keep up with so much sensitive work. "I'm not going to live long enough to be briefed on everything," was how one put it. The other recounted that for his initial briefing, he was escorted into a tiny, dark room, seated at a small table, and told he couldn't take notes. Reports of program after program after program began flashing on a screen until in frustration he yelled, "Stop!" "I wasn't remembering any of it," he said.

When Rumsfeld's successor, Robert Gates, asked retired army lieutenant general John R. Vines to examine the method for tracking the Defense Department's most sensitive programs, he was stunned by the size and scope of what fell under his review. Vines was familiar with complex organizations—he had commanded 145,000 troops in Iraq. But he found the system for tracking sensitive programs too complex and confusing even for people on the inside to understand, and inaccessible to the CIA and other agencies that needed to coordinate with the department. He couldn't find anyone, except the secretary of defense, who had access to all the department's programs, and the secretary certainly wouldn't have the time to keep up with even a sliver of what was available to him.

"I'm not aware of any agency with the authority, responsibility, or a process in place to coordinate all these interagency and commercial activities," Vines said in an interview. "The complexity of this system defies description."

The complexity and lack of accountability made it impossible, he said, to tell whether the country was safer because of all this spending and because of the particular programs the money was spent on. Yes, you could give the system credit for the lack of big attacks, Vines mused, but who really knew whether that was because these programs had stopped serious plots? There could be some other reason. And if the prevention of major terrorist attacks was due to just one or two of the existing programs, how could those few successes be singled out?

Michael Hayden, the former director of the CIA and the NSA, had a different view of the complexity. "I was in government service for forty years; most of that was in intelligence," he told PBS's *Frontline*. "I would never claim to you that I knew all the compartments....I could not possibly claim that I knew everything that was going on....Is that a good thing? Probably not. Can we avoid it? Probably not. Can we make it less of a burdensome problem than it is today? Probably. And we need to work on that. But this is just a reflection of complexity, not any vice."

The multiple layers of secrecy aren't simply an impediment to good government; they affected the wars themselves. There wasn't a senior officer who didn't have stories about the negative effect of compartmentalization and secrecy in the real world. One air force officer who had served in Afghanistan recalled that only after

Operation Mountain Storm, the largest coordinated military counterterrorism operation of 2004, did he learn of a compartmented
technology to detect campfires from satellites which, he said,
would have been useful to him. But it had been hidden from him
and, even though lives were at stake, no one had thought to include
him on the BIGOT list.

Vines had his own stories from the battlefield. When he was
ground commander in Iraq, and then in Afghanistan, his troops
would unknowingly capture CIA informants. "This happened to
me maybe forty, fifty times," he recalled. "We caused the agency
major problems." He proposed a solution: place a CIA liaison in his
targeting cell to warn them away from certain people. "I told them,
'I don't need to know anything about the source, you just tell me
no, not him.'" But the agency, afraid of compromising sources by
letting even military officers with the highest security clearances
know who they were, would not go for it. Better to risk having an
informant be caught or even killed than to let an army officer
know of his existence.

According to several senior leaders, only about half of the 150
most highly classified technological programs within the Defense
Department are allowed to be shared with the staff in charge of
developing war plans for individual adversarial countries. The other
half are visible only to senior officials at the Office of the Secretary of
Defense level. A few of the programs are only known by the team
that developed the technology, the security officer in charge of keeping it secret, and the secretary of defense himself. This means that a
decade after 9/11, some war plans are developed without the ability
to incorporate the most exquisite, life-saving technologies available.

Compartmented secrecy can also undermine the normal chain
of command when senior officials use it to cut out rivals or when
subordinates are ordered to keep secrets from their commanders.
One military communications officer recalled how he was forced
to sign a document prohibiting him from disclosing the existence of
a Special Access Program he was assigned to by the civilian office
of the secretary of defense. The officer was even prohibited from

telling his four-star commander, with whom he worked closely every day. The four-star was not part of the operation; therefore, he had no need to know about it, the rules said. In this case, the communications officer was now also reporting to a second, parallel chain of command that was invisible to his regular boss. The arrangement was extremely uncomfortable for the subordinate, as he worked closely with his commander, and the two were supposed to trust each other's judgment.

Defenders of this knotty system of compartmentalization believe such maximum secrecy is essential to maintaining America's edge against its enemies. At the CIA, which works mainly overseas, many of these sensitive activities involve working closely with foreign intelligence services. This collaboration has been responsible for capturing, or helping U.S. teams capture, the majority of senior terrorists. The CIA argues that foreign agencies will not agree to help the agency unless the partnerships are kept secret, and that they will even be denied if made public by the media. But it is also reasonable to assume that these relationships would repair themselves with time, as they often do, according to many intelligence officials, because foreign countries understand that the CIA has by far the best technical means of spying on terrorist groups and has the most extensive understanding of how they are webbed together internationally.

The relationship between the CIA and its partners is actually much firmer than the headlines would have readers believe. And for a handful of countries, such as Britain, Australia, Canada, Germany, Jordan, Poland, France, and Saudi Arabia, the relationship with the CIA is steadfast. Even when relations go haywire in public, deep in the sock drawer, business remains brisk. This is a function of common interests.

Poland, for example, believes it needs an alliance with the United States to guard against Russian influence. The CIA's close, post–cold war tie with Warsaw was cemented in the early 1990s after Polish special forces helped rescue a group of stranded CIA operatives in western Iraq during the first Gulf War. The agency showed its gratitude by funding and training a new Polish special forces unit called GROM. The unit was allowed to do things the Americans could not, as General Sławomir Petelicki, the blond, swashbuckling father of GROM, said as we careened around the streets of Warsaw one afternoon while I held onto the car door for dear life. Someone else told me what he might have been referring to: during the surge in Iraq, GROM commandos were permitted to kill people that U.S. forces could not. At the time, American snipers had to see a weapon in a target's hand before they could shoot. But the elite Polish snipers had more permissive rules of engagement; they could shoot anyone on the streets of Fallujah with a cell phone in hand after curfew, several U.S. military sources said. GROM commandos were considered to be so useful, yet another source explained, that they were assigned to various CIA units in Afghanistan and worked both under the command of the agency's chief of station and the U.S. Navy SEALs.

GROM had also been among the first on the ground in Iraq, along with the CIA, even before the war began. To prove it, one former senior intelligence official in Warsaw brought to our interview the citation he had received, along with the American Legion of Merit medal. It was signed by Defense Secretary Donald Rumsfeld and had been awarded for "highly sensitive and successful operations in support of Operation Iraqi Freedom, from July 2002 to Dec. 3, 2003." The war did not begin until March 2003.

The U.S.-Jordanian intelligence relationship goes back even further. One U.S. officer spent much of his career at the side of King Hussein's son, Abdullah, teaching him about bilateral co-dependence between the United States and Jordan and preparing him for a time when he would be the country's leader and the United States would be asking him for covert favors, just as it had asked his father. When it was obvious that sending American case officers to get close to al-Qaeda followers would not work, the Jordanians volunteered to help out. Five years after 9/11, I found myself in the lobby of the Georgetown Ritz-Carlton listening to a senior Jordanian intelligence officer brag about how his undercover agents had participated in snatching terrorists from around the world. I confirmed his story with several U.S. sources. Such cooperative ventures are the tendrils of Top Secret America.

The relationship with the British is closest of all. A variety of foreign websites showing jihadists beheading Westerners and training recruits in bomb making had been traced back to the United States via IP addresses. American officials were paralyzed by an ongoing debate over whether U.S. law barred the National Security Agency and the CIA from disrupting sites like this that resided, electronically, in the United States, even though their webmasters lived overseas. Lacking clear guidance, it was quicker and easier to suggest to a close ally like Britain that it do it instead. More than once, the British intelligence service had done the favor, covertly destroying the offending sites.

Covert CIA prisons, the so-called black sites,[3] also resided deep down in a compartment of Greystone, designed never to be found. But, as I learned in the process of discovering their locations, there are always going to be limits to protecting anything so highly controversial, no matter what kind of classification label is attached to it. In the end, this is what makes the obsession with secrecy so harmful to the nation's security. Secrets cannot be totally secured by locks or code names or encrypted email or even vaults underground, and acting as if they can be is dangerous, even to national security. The security of secrets ultimately depends upon human beings. Even though many intelligence officers live and work among their own kind, they still have all sorts of reasons for talking about what they know: pride, angst, guilt, a need for praise, a desire to correct the record or to explain away something that sounds evil, or to save the agency from itself, or to stop wrongdoing. As

---

[3] "Black" is a slang expression for a program or unit that is clandestine or covert in nature, meaning its operations are always secret.

Ben Franklin once noted, "Three may keep a secret, if two of them are dead."

Sources expressed every reason imaginable for helping me try to figure out where the CIA was holding its prisoners. Some thought the program was a terrible idea because, although the White House encouraged and signed off on the matter, the CIA would be left holding a very stinky bag once it became public. A secret involving human beings, prisons, companies with false names, employees with false addresses—such a massive exercise in clandestine duplicity could not hold forever, and, in one source's opinion, senior agency officials should have realized that from the start.

"They won't face up to the problem," said one source who spoke with me years ago. "They have no long-term plan" for where to keep the captives. Some CIA old-timers believed that revealing the covert prisons' existence could ruin the agency's reputation, which was why they wanted to make sure I had the whole picture, not just the cartoon version. The president's lawyers, after all, had signed legal opinions declaring that the prisons and the way prisoners were interrogated were legal. The president had even approved of the program. Other people said they despised what they believed the CIA had become: "We've become bounty hunters," one said in disgust. Too much time and energy was spent running the program's stealth infrastructure. "Just let us do our mission and let other people run the fucking penal system."

One morning as I was preparing to leave my hotel room during a trip I made to one Eastern European capital in my effort to locate the prisons, the telephone rang. A CIA officer from headquarters in Langley was on the line. The agency had learned of my visit from some of the people I had interviewed the day before, who had apparently called headquarters in a panic. "My phone has been ringing off the hook," the CIA officer on the line said. "Countries are freaking out about the questions you are asking. Can you close that line of questioning, please…it could affect ongoing operations as we speak. It's having real implications. We could have to stop doing things."

I listened politely but promised nothing.

I was summoned to CIA headquarters upon my return. A senior operations officer in the Counterterrorism Center was waiting for me. He explained that the center had tripled in size since 9/11 and was more dependent than ever on foreign intelligence services to find suspected terrorists. Writing about the secret prisons would embarrass the partners who had agreed to host them in their countries, he said. They might stop cooperating with the United States on other programs. "In many cases they are violating their own laws by helping us," he said. "In many cases we get the approval of the president but not anyone else." Those words were supposed to reassure me but had the opposite effect. Should the *Post* be complicit in something illegal under the laws of the countries in which the prisons were located?

Many of the citizens in those Eastern European democracies had made great sacrifices and taken huge risks to get out from under the corrupting influence of their Soviet-era intelligence services. It seemed hypocritical, even contrary to U.S. long-term interests, for an administration that said its goal was to create democracies out of Iraq and Afghanistan now to be effectively undermining the legal system in Eastern Europe by cutting private deals with intelligence officials there in exchange for U.S. money and equipment that would make them more powerful.

Why do you need prisons in the first place, I asked, trying to elicit a more detailed explanation. Why not bring the detainees to trial?

"Because they would get lawyered-up, and our job, first and foremost, is to obtain information from them," he said.

Why didn't the agency just give the captives access to the International Committee of the Red Cross? By treaty, the ICRC has access to detained military combatants.

White House lawyers had declared al-Qaeda operatives to be unlawful combatants not worthy of such protections, he said. Besides, "countries do this secretly. There are other legal issues involved.... There are a number of things in a democracy"—he stumbled over his explanation—"like how to balance individual rights with national security concerns."[4]

A year later President Bush publicly acknowledged the program's existence, announced he was closing the prisons, and said that the remaining detainees had been transferred into the military justice system at the Guantánamo Bay prison in Cuba. Although there were some hard feelings against Washington among European leaders, the countries involved[5] and other allies in Europe did not bolt from cooperating, and there is no indication that the national security of the United States was gravely harmed by the disclosure.

As we would discover over the course of our investigation into Top Secret America, many things would remain unknown, but the existence of covert prisons was no longer one of them. And, now, neither is this: that not all of the disappeared have been accounted for. At least a dozen people once held by the CIA remain nowhere to be found.

---

[4] President Bush and various members of his national security team asked the *Washington Post* not to publish the secret prison story because, they argued, it would gravely damage relations between the United States and the countries involved. The executive editor of the *Post*, Leonard Downie, decided not to publish the exact locations of the secret prisons but to go ahead with the rest of the story. A barrage of criticism followed from the predictable places, mainly the administration's political supporters. The American public reacted largely with disinterest, although the issue entered the presidential primaries two years later. In Europe, however, publication caused a political firestorm, and each country began an internal inquiry into whether its leaders had hosted a secret prison or had allowed the CIA's aircraft to land or even fly over its airspace with its covert human cargo.

[5] As of publication, none of the leaders or former leaders in the several Eastern European countries that hosted the black sites has admitted to doing so. Human rights groups and various European commissions have identified countries they believe hosted them. The *Post* and the author continue to abide by the initial decision not to name the countries.

CHAPTER THREE

So Help Me God

The thirty-three secure phones ringing all morning in the FBI's tactical command center went silent just seconds after ten o'clock as Barack Obama spoke the last words of that famous promise to the nation, "so help me God." John G. Perren, the special agent in charge, felt like someone had shut off the power in the windowless room of frenzied agents and blinking monitors. The whole city fell quiet. He exhaled one long breath. The United States of America had a new president.

It was an historic day for obvious reasons. The first black man to be elected president was being sworn in, and the largest number of people ever to assemble for a presidential inauguration had come to witness it. They drove, were bused in, took the subway, and walked—marched, really—on streets and over bridges that were supposed to be closed to foot traffic. If ever there was a people's inaugural, this was it, and nothing was going to stop the celebrating, not police barricades, not the numbing cold and wind, not warnings about terrorists. Despite the weight of two long wars, the building economic recession, and a particularly bitter and growing divide between political party leaders, here was an act that transcended these realities: the peaceful transition of power in the most powerful country on earth.

Even for Perren, who, at the age of fifty-five, had been dealing with hardened criminals and terrorists for three decades, it was an emotional moment. It didn't matter whom he had voted for, or that he was empowered to carry a gun and to know secrets most Americans would never know. At this moment, his allegiance passed instantly to the new chief executive. He was proud of this fact as he watched Obama address an audience that was likewise full of emotion. As he so often did, he thought about people who wanted to do America wrong, about terrorists who sought to undermine its openness and force it to become a fortress, to become something other than what it was. This is an open society, eat your heart out, Perren thought to himself. This is how it happens here.

In his pride, Perren ignored what he was certainly in a better position than most people to understand: al-Qaeda's terrorist attacks almost a decade earlier, and the response to them by the United States, had in fact changed his country profoundly, and even now was continuing to skew it in directions that few could assess or even track with any accuracy.

The American government's view seemed to be that no action, no program, no buildup of forces abroad or at home was sufficient, nothing we had devised thus far was ever enough to protect us from another 9/11 attack. Nor was any expense too great to prevent smaller attacks. Perren's FBI, which had witnessed thousands of innocent bystanders die in ugly gangland slayings, Mafia turf wars, and battles between drug lords over the decades, was now also responsible for stopping every person in the United States — citizen or foreign — who was crazy enough to bomb a building, blow up a bridge, or shoot another human being in the name of what was now universally labeled terrorism. As a result, the FBI's counterterrorism structure had grown three times larger than it had been before 9/11. Straitlaced criminal investigators whose goal in life had been to send bank robbers to prison — the sooner, the better—were now trying to turn themselves into spies and the FBI into a domestic intelligence agency that monitored more and more people—with all the appropriate legal authority, of course.

In the refashioned FBI, agents were no longer supposed to be concerned only with gathering evidence to produce court cases and send criminals to jail. With little or no training, they had been forced to become intelligence collectors, too: to watch patiently, not jump too soon, to follow possible terrorists as they developed plots, recruited comrades, and unknowingly revealed the source of their financial support. They were supposed to keep track of people even *thinking* about hatching terrorist plots, and often they helped them turn their fantasies into near-realities with sting operations that included phony al-Qaeda followers and fake bombs. Counterterrorism units took advantage of new technologies to investigate suspects—and people who were not yet suspects—in a dozen new ways. The agency's computers constantly churned, looking for anomalous blips in a sea of data that might represent something nefarious. And although the FBI had the lead on terrorist investigations within the United States, every federal and state agency—including the largest by far, the U.S. military—was trying to get a piece of the action, not only to save the country from terrorism but also so each could grow bigger and more powerful in the process.

By the time of Barack Obama's inauguration, the entire U.S. counterterrorism apparatus had become gigantic, which left a lot less money for other things, like education or health care for indigent kids or badly needed repair of the American civil infrastructure. The national debt soared, and with it America's indebtedness to potentially hostile foreign nations. But Americans seemed willing again and again to make this trade-off, since they kept electing people who said they would spend whatever it took to stop terrorism in this frightening post-9/11 decade. As a result, the massive tangle of counterterrorism agencies, programs, bureaus, bunkers, sensors, and security cameras would expand during the Obama years too. Americans couldn't tell what they were getting for their money, but they could be assured that whatever it was, there was a lot of it—at least $81 billion a year's worth just for national intelligence, according to the government's own, if incomplete, count.

As Obama stood at the podium at the base of the U.S. Capitol, he faced a sea of hopeful citizens stretching well beyond the towering figure of President Abraham Lincoln, watching from his giant marble memorial at the end of the National Mall. But between the new young leader and his supporters were five tons of bulletproof glass, and beyond that 20,000 uniformed guards and 25,000 law enforcement officers enveloping him in a security blanket that spanned from New York to West Virginia. Beyond that, an invisible classified universe of top secret agencies and programs and weapons systems and surveillance capabilities and legal authorities and strike forces and pursuit teams assembled to keep him safe, all part of an intelligence-military-corporate apparatus created to keep the nation's citizens safe, too.

Perren, who resembled the television detective Kojak, was among the most experienced of these top secret guardians in government service. As such, he was part of a cadre of one hundred or so veteran law enforcement, intelligence, and military officers who were still on the job, planning and executing the takedown of Middle Eastern terrorists since their first attempt to destroy the World Trade Center in 1993. Eight years later, as head of the FBI's counterterrorism office in the nation's capital, he had supervised the recovery of bodies and evidence from the smoldering Pentagon, and then had deployed to Iraq to oversee FBI law enforcement assistance to the massive counterterrorism operations in that combat zone.

After his quick pause to reflect on the historical moment, Perren went back to his task of keeping the new president and his supporters safe. His job that day was to track everything trackable within the FBI's authority: incoming foreign intelligence reports transmitted through CIA headquarters in Langley, Virginia, intercepts and wiretaps, undercover intelligence squads mingling in the crowds, chemical weapons teams collecting air samples, sharp-shooters with high-powered telescopes stationed miles away along I-95 North and I-95 South to spot anything unusual heading into the nation's capital.

He, and the FBI, were not, of course, alone: with the U.S. Secret Service in the lead for the inauguration, fifty-six federal, state, and local agencies drew on their most sophisticated technology and skilled personnel. Bomb squads and HAZMAT units from a dozen organizations were ready to deploy, as were SWAT teams, crisis negotiators, and even behavioral analysts to scour intelligence and news reports for hints of trouble. Automatic license plate readers recorded and checked the license plate numbers of virtually every vehicle nearing Washington, DC, from incoming routes through Virginia and Maryland. Even particles of dust floating throughout the city were captured and analyzed at split-second intervals by navy plume assessment teams and the Department of Homeland Security's pathogen detectors, mounted onto standard air-quality monitors to sniff out anthrax, tularemia, and other deadly substances. The local Washington government had squirreled away nearly a million respirators and over 2.5 million surgical masks for medical personnel in case of an outbreak.

To facilitate the massive surge in cell phone calls to and from the nearly two million people on the Mall, private telecommunications companies had placed mobile cellular towers throughout downtown. Government disaster experts also positioned and readied their own mobile command centers and special equipment needed to erect an alternative government-only cell phone system should the civil networks go down or electrical power go dark. Emergency relocation facilities outside Washington were readied, as planes, helicopters, SUVs, and quick reaction military forces stood by to evacuate key government leaders, if the need arose.

As all this was going on, dive teams and Coast Guard boats patrolled the Potomac and Anacostia rivers while, overhead, layers of aircraft capped the largest protective bubble in the world: Air Force F-22 Raptor fighters and Air National Guard RC-26 surveillance aircraft flew above Customs and Border Patrol Blackhawk helicopters, while even higher, surveillance drones relayed real-time, full-motion video back to the dozens of stationary and mobile command centers that were lashed up with the military's many geospatial Google Earth–like data feeds.

Every single one of these military and law enforcement units had multiple backups, even the Colorado-based Northern Command,[1] which had been established to defend the United States within its own borders after the 2001 terrorist attacks. And just in case its own headquarters were attacked, Northern Command kept the famous Cheyenne Mountain underground bunker on standby. In Room 3102 in the underground warren, an electronic map of the United States indicated the locations of the military's most secretive and lethal units, just in case they needed to deploy in a domestic emergency.

By the time the Obama family prepared to move into the White House, it was nearly impossible to find an American unfamiliar with Osama bin Laden. That had been far from the case less than a decade earlier. Indeed, by the time of George W. Bush's election, the circle of people informed of the activities of Osama bin Laden was getting smaller and smaller, while the threat from his organization was getting larger and larger. This was an odd, counterintuitive phenomenon that had been occurring throughout the national security establishment for at least two years.

The reason was simple: secrecy. Too many government agencies kept too many secrets from one another, and the U.S. government kept too many secrets from the American public.

In fact, the more intelligence that was acquired about bin Laden

---

[1] NorthCom, established on October 1, 2002, is supposed to be in charge of the Defense Department's homeland defense efforts and the coordination of defense support to civil authorities when requested. Its area of operation includes the United States, Canada, Mexico, and the surrounding water out to approximately five hundred nautical miles. But many of its missions are already performed by other entities (see chapter 6).

and his terrorist network, the more closely agencies kept that information to themselves. They often didn't share it with other agencies, and they almost always put it out of reach of ordinary citizens by classifying it. As a result, the threat of al-Qaeda terrorism was barely on the public radar, and there was little information available that might have convinced most Americans that their government needed to be pressured to work harder to stop the growing menace. The authoritative National Intelligence Estimates, which offer policy makers the best assessments and predictions of the future from various intelligence agencies on a given subject, briefly mentioned Osama bin Laden in 1997. In subsequent years, as the CIA, the FBI, and other agencies were acquiring piles of damning evidence against him, none of it was ever again published in an NIE until after it was too late. As *The 9/11 Commission Report* summarized so succinctly, referring to Osama bin Laden and al-Qaeda: "It is hardest to mount a major effort while a problem still seems minor."

Michael Rolince, an FBI agent who had investigated the Irish Republican Army, Hamas, and Hezbollah terrorist connections in Boston, should have known just about everything there was to know about al-Qaeda by 1998. But he didn't. "It was an almost entirely classified area in terms of casework," he recalled. "I'd say 'terrorism' [to other agents] and that was the end of the conversation." When Rolince was transferred to Washington that year, he attended a briefing by John O'Neill, the New York City FBI supervisor who made al-Qaeda his life's work (and who died in the 9/11 attack on the World Trade Center towers). "He started talking about being in a food fight with another office over a UBL (for Usama bin Laden, the common abbreviation) investigation, and I didn't have a clue who he was talking about." The problem, Rolince discovered, was that the bureau didn't educate its field agents about terrorism unless they were working a case specifically related to it.

Or consider Russel Honoré's red bag.

Every few days a locked red canvas bag would be hand-carried by a squared-away navy captain to an office next to the National Military Command Center in the Pentagon. The captain would open the lock for Lt. Gen. Honoré, watch him carefully pull out the papers inside, wait until he had finished reading and had returned them to the bag, and then quickly lock them up again. Honoré told me he couldn't take notes on what he read about bin Laden's whereabouts and any plans to stop him. He couldn't seek the advice of other senior officers on the staff of the Joint Chiefs of Staff (JCS),[2] or even mention to them what he had read. Like him, they all had the highest security clearances in the building because, like him, their job was to provide advice to the nation's top military commander, the chairman of the Joint Chiefs, whose job was to provide advice to the president of the United States. As the 9/11 Commission later learned, "at no point before 9/11 was the Department of Defense fully engaged in the mission of countering al-Qaeda, though this was perhaps the most dangerous foreign enemy then threatening the United States."

Al-Qaeda's attack on a navy destroyer, the USS *Cole*, in October 2000, had provided another opportunity to educate the American people on the capabilities and aspirations of bin Laden's network. But soon after the bombing, the 9/11 Commission discovered later, CIA "analysts stopped distributing written reports about who was responsible." They "presumed that the government did not want reports circulating around the agencies that might become public, impeding law enforcement actions or backing the President into a corner."

Inside the White House, the Counterterrorism Security Group (CSG), which included the principal national security officials, shrank to an informal subset that called themselves the "Small

---

[2] The Joint Chiefs of Staff is the senior staff of military officers who advise the president, the defense secretary, and the National Security Council on military matters. It is made up of the chairman of the Joint Chiefs of Staff (CJCS), the vice chairman of the Joint Chiefs of Staff (VCJCS), and the chiefs of the army, navy, air force, and Marine Corps, all appointed by the president following Senate confirmation. Headquartered in the Pentagon, the JCS has no operational authority but has become increasingly important in planning the strategy and tactics of the military's counterterrorism efforts.

Group" and aimed to keep sensitive information even more tightly controlled. The consequence, however, was that fewer minds and eyes focused on the difficult question of how to work against a fluid network about which the United States had so little actionable intelligence. The Small Group, which included only those "cleared to know about the most sensitive issues," according to the 9/11 Commission, reported directly to the president and cabinet members, rather than follow the normal procedure of reporting to more people with greater expertise and more time to deal with the topic.

Typical bureaucratic rivalries also got in the way of organizing a government-wide approach to terrorism in a rational manner, even though such a grave national security threat should have trumped such pettiness. Richard Clarke, the counterterrorism coordinator under President Clinton, told the 9/11 Commission that despite constant pushing from the White House, his position "was limited at the request of the departments and agencies. The coordinator had no budget, only a dozen staff, and no ability to direct actions by the departments or agencies."

The same dynamic existed at the CIA. In 1998, when director George Tenet had issued his now-famous "We are at war" memo—"I want no resources or people spared in this effort, either inside CIA or the Community"—it sounded grand, but little actually happened. As the commission learned, no more resources were added, and apparently few people outside the agency received his declaration—certainly not the American people, because that memo was classified, too.

If so many people with the highest levels of clearance were unaware of the gravity of the threat, regular citizens without security clearances certainly had no idea. It was true that every time an overseas terrorist attack killed enough Americans, the government would disclose a bit more information, as it had after the 1993 World Trade Center bombing, after the East African embassy bombings in August 1998, after the failed 1999 Ahmed Ressam millennium plot, and after the USS *Cole* was attacked.

But it was also true that the contents of the locked red bag delivered to Honoré remained off-limits, even to dozens of senior officers on the Joint Chiefs of Staff who were sworn to secrecy, who could be sent to jail if they broke that promise, and whose jobs were also to come up with ways to keep the country safe.

A Secret Service protective detail had joined Obama on the campaign trail in May 2007, the earliest protection for any candidate in history. It was one of a half-dozen organizations in place that day with its own special operations units, its own snipers, even its own Most Wanted list.

By the morning of the inauguration, FBI and National Security Agency specialists had met with Obama to take a digital print of his voice. His retinas had been scanned, his blood drawn, his DNA officially cataloged. From the lowliest U.S. Capitol Police officer to the most elite "in extremis" commando teams, a special set of watch officers, analysts, special agents, eavesdroppers, collectors, bomb disposal experts, chemical and biological warfare officers, hostage rescuers, bodyguards, communicators, and drivers formed an army dedicated to him alone.

There had been protective shields around Obama's predecessors, but they had been small compared to this. Since 9/11, presidential protection had gone into hyperdrive, doubling in size like every other hidden agency of the post-9/11 intelligence-military-corporate complex, as had planning for keeping government leaders in touch and in charge during and after a terrorist attack. New arrangements for continuing government operations requiring the participation of every agency, from the Department of Defense to the Indian Health Service, had been developed, as had new secure communications systems and backups. Alternative government sites were renovated and new ones built. After 9/11, Vice President Cheney had spent days in a cold war–era bunker on the Maryland-Pennsylvania border; now other such hideouts around the country were reactivated to operate 24/7.

With so much attention focused on the inauguration of the forty-fourth president, regular crimes in the capital region were viewed by law enforcement and intelligence agencies as suspicious activities with possible links to terrorism. Circulated to every one of these agencies was information that a semiautomatic police rifle and ninety rounds of ammunition had been stolen from a marked Howard County Police car in Maryland, along with a department baseball cap. The same day a second Howard County Police car had been broken into. A full box of ammunition was missing. Local authorities entered these two incidents into the FBI's massive Guardian database of possible terrorist activity. They also entered and circulated a report from a check cashing business in Wood-lawn, Maryland, that had received four thousand dollars wired to an individual in increments from the United Arab Emirates over a period of two months. Analysis from the FBI's Guardian database of possible terrorist-connected suspicious activities showed that from January to September 2008, there had been an increase in police uniform thefts in the United States. Of the thirty-seven reported incidents, five occurred in the Baltimore area alone. The FBI was investigating each of these, just in case.

Then, just one week before the inauguration, law enforcement received the most specific threat so far. Al-Shabaab was a Somali terrorist organization that had made clear it had the will and capability to strike overseas, and law enforcement officials believed it had adherents within the refugee communities scattered throughout the United States. Now the allegations of a single source set off a frantic race to find a member of the organization who may have slipped into the country from Somalia with a desire to change history.

The fear was not without cause: just a month earlier, a dozen young men from the Somali community in Minneapolis had left home unannounced to return to the Horn of Africa, and a month before that, a nineteen-year-old who had disappeared from the same Minnesota neighborhood had blown himself up in Somalia in a suicide bombing.

The inauguration tip sent dozens of FBI agents dashing across the country and overseas to interview Somalis and other people the bureau hoped had useful information. It met with the Royal Canadian Mounted Police while the CIA checked its databases and worked its sources in Africa. The National Security Agency trained its listening devices on dozens of locations around the world known as al-Shabaab strongholds. U.S. Immigration and Customs Enforcement (ICE) culled its vast databases for Somali visitors and immigration violators looking for leads. The National Counterterrorism Center (NCTC) doubled up on analysts whose job was to bring all the threads of intelligence together and make sense of it all.

By the eve of the inauguration, investigators had discovered several inconsistencies in the original source's story, chief among them that the supposed suspect turned out to be in prison in Sudan. But because the FBI, which has the lead on terrorism cases within the United States, didn't have time to run every lead to ground, no one relaxed—on the contrary: the Department of Homeland Security's Office of Intelligence and Analysis issued a warning that members of al-Shabaab "may attempt to travel to the United States with the intention to conduct an attack during the Presidential Inauguration." Only two days after the inauguration did they learn that the original tip was actually a "poison pen," a lead from a source that was meant to falsely discredit someone, usually a rival or an enemy. In this case, the source's motive was an unresolved family feud.

The other huge, but unspecific, concern was that a lone gunman or bomber, someone who could be impossible to detect because he would have launched his plot alone and might even be American, would try to kill Obama or lots of his supporters. Lacking any hard leads, the Washington Regional Threat and Analysis Center, a place where the governments of Maryland, Virginia, and the District of Columbia shared and analyzed threat information, had issued a daily summary that warned against just about everything imaginable. The warnings included a log of completely legal demonstrations; authorities believed such activities could provide cover for terrorist or other criminal action. Events to keep an eye on, the center noted, were a protest against Israeli settlements in Gaza, a demonstration in support of immigration reform, another sponsored by Veterans for Peace, an antiwar "Shoe Throwing at the White House," and an anti-abortion March for Life rally. No one was particularly concerned that these were lawful—keeping track of such groups had become a habit of law enforcement agencies across the country.

Several other reports of out-of-town crimes were also in circulation, including a machine gun heist in rural Pennsylvania and the discovery in Maine of radioactive materials and components for a radiological dispersal device in the house of a suspected member of a white supremacist group.

Nuclear terrorism, even more than biological weapons, was the government's collective nightmare. Five years earlier, the FBI had been directed to take over the mission of defending against the threat of domestic nuclear attack because military special operations forces, which had previously had the mission, were overburdened with wars overseas. It remained one of the few triggers for a presidential declaration of emergency rule, the so-called martial law that often appears in Hollywood movies. Perren had helped set up the bureau's domestic Weapons of Mass Destruction Directorate.[3] Obama's inauguration would be the first in which the FBI would be in full charge of stopping a WMD attack before it occurred. Perren believed the bureau was ready.

But ready for what? That was always the problem. In the months leading up to the January 20, 2009, inauguration, Perren

---

[3] In July 2006, the FBI consolidated its WMD-related activities into a single WMD Directorate within the newly formed National Security Branch. Composed primarily of special agents, intelligence analysts, program managers, and policy specialists, the directorate provides national-level WMD crisis management and intelligence support to the U.S. government in matters involving domestic threats associated with biological, chemical, nuclear, and radiological weapons and materials. The directorate also designs training for federal agencies; state and local law enforcement organizations; and public health, industry, and academia partners. At the local level, the FBI has a designated WMD coordinator in each of its fifty-six domestic field divisions.

was kept apprised as the new directorate scoured the inventories of Home Depot–type building supply stores for large purchases of fertilizer and other so-called precursor chemicals that could be used to create massive bombs. Proving their ability to gather data from sources most Americans would have thought private and secure, directorate staff had analyzed pharmacy sales, too, looking for patterns of illnesses that might indicate the leading edge of a biological attack, timed to create a full-blown public health disaster on the day of the swearing-in.

Preparations to detect, disarm, or respond to a release of radioactive material were not new. Daily, ever since 9/11, national mission forces—part air force, part army, part Special Operations Forces, part Department of Energy—had maintained units on standby in case of a nuclear emergency. In doing so, they operated under a broader top secret umbrella program code-named Power Geyser in which the Coast Guard and clandestine Navy SEAL units were responsible for interdicting a nuclear device carried by watercraft or, alternatively, evacuating the president by water, if it came to that.

Nimble Elder, another part of the Power Geyser program, trained and equipped the military and FBI forces to search for, locate, and identify nuclear weapons. Most of its subprograms were managed by the White House National Science and Technology Council (NSTC). The Council's counter-WMD cadre, composed of more than one thousand scientists, included the Attribution Working Group, whose job was to determine which country or terrorist network had detonated the weapon in order to know where to direct an American retaliation. If the nuclear device were found before detonation, it would be disabled and either transported to a navy facility in Maryland for analysis or flown to the Nevada Test Site and disassembled, or intentionally detonated, in G-Tunnel, a 5,000-foot-deep shaft.

Weeks before the inauguration, the president-elect had made sure the people he had chosen for his national security team knew exactly what they were getting into. He asked his team to meet in the presidential transition office, a spacious three floors at 451 Sixth Street, NW, not far from the Capitol, which included a SCIF (pronounced "skiff," for Sensitive Compartmented Information Facility) secure room that could not be penetrated by the best eavesdropping equipment. Run by the Central Intelligence Agency, the transition office SCIF included the intelligence community's top secret communications network, the Joint Worldwide Intelligence Communications System, or JWICS, as well as secure video capabilities.

On January 5, the room was turned into a command center for a mock national security crisis. Present were the people Obama intended to nominate as his national security team: Hillary Clinton as secretary of state, Defense Secretary Robert Gates (who would remain in his role in the new administration), retired Marine Corps general James Jones as national security adviser, Chairman of the Joint Chiefs of Staff Adm. Mike Mullen, Eric Holder as attorney general designee, director of national intelligence nominee retired Admiral Dennis Blair, Department of Homeland Security secretary nominee Janet Napolitano, treasury secretary designate Timothy Geithner, and incoming UN ambassador Susan Rice.

As they all sat around a large conference table, Obama's national security advisers during the campaign, Richard Clarke and Rand Beers, laid out the scenario: Israel was about to bomb Iran. Discuss.

While they debated next steps, Clarke announced some more bad news: al-Qaeda was carrying a nuclear bomb on a freighter headed for Manhattan. Discuss.

The team forgot about Israel and Iran, and called upon a clandestine U.S. rapid-response team to interdict the ship. But the scenario shifted again: the terrorists had slipped off the freighter and onto a boat. Al-Qaeda was now headed to Boston. Discuss.

Before the team could identify which boat carried the deadly device, they were informed it had been offloaded and detonated. Cities along the eastern seaboard were evacuating. Discuss.

They initiated recovery efforts—called "consequence management" in the language of government—but before any resolution could be reached, the harrowing three-hour exercise came to an end. Clarke told them the exercise's code name was Kobayashi Maru. Only Gates chuckled, alone in understanding the reference to the *Star Trek* no-good-options training exercise designed to test the character of cadets on the command track at the fictional Starfleet Academy by putting them in a lose-lose scenario. Welcome to the nightmare of an asymmetric world, Clarke was saying, where even small groups of tattered fanatics or deranged individuals could pose existential threats to the country.

At 9:30 a.m. on inauguration day, as Barack and Michelle Obama made last-minute preparations for their trip to the Capitol, President Bush's national security team met in the White House Situation Room with their incoming counterparts. The subject was what to do about the late-breaking Somali threat. The possibility of canceling the inauguration came up briefly and was quickly batted down. Even though there was great doubt by then about the credibility of the single initial source, because national security officials could not eliminate all possibilities, they had feared they might have missed something big. In the America after the attacks, that was a perpetual fear: that the grains of information would slip through the government's hands again.

Such dread was a large part of the post-9/11 decade. A culture of fear had created a culture of spending to control it, which, in turn, had led to a belief that the government had to be able to stop every single plot before it took place, regardless of whether it involved one network of twenty terrorists or one single deranged person. This expectation propelled more spending and even more zero-defect expectations. There were tens of thousands of unsolved murders in the United States by 2010, but few newspapers ever blared this across their front pages or even tried to investigate how their police departments had failed to solve them all over the years.

But when it came to terrorism, newspaper and other media outlets amplified each mistake, which amplified the threat, which amplified the fear, which prompted more spending, and on and on and on. Europe had broken this cycle with time. There, terrorist acts were treated more like other violent crimes, as part of the modern world that must be confronted, dealt with, but put in a different context. You got to leave your shoes on in the airports of Europe.

As a result of his predecessor's response to 9/11, the government Barack Obama was about to inherit had really become two governments: the one its citizens were familiar with, operated more or less in the open; the other a parallel top secret government whose parts had mushroomed in less than a decade into a gigantic, sprawling universe of its own, visible to only a carefully vetted cadre—and its entirety, as Pentagon intelligence chief James Clapper admitted, visible only to God.

That off-limits America was the one working to protect the president at that very moment. This was a mission everyone could agree was necessary, especially as the new president and his wife thrilled the crowds, and terrified their protectors, by leaping out of the most secure limousine in the world—a GMC Cadillac with five-inch-thick military-grade armor and its own oxygen and fire-fighting systems—to walk a few blocks down the massively blocked-off and controlled Pennsylvania Avenue. The moment would be frozen in time by a thousand cameras capturing the confident, handsome couple. But nothing stood still within the military-intelligence-information complex. It raced as quickly and steadily as it had for the last six or seven years.

All the while, the FBI and the Department of Homeland Security continued to collect and store the names of thousands upon thousands of Americans who had committed no crime but may have done something that looked suspicious in the eyes of a local cop. The database created by these two agencies would be so secret that there would be no sure way for the individuals to even know they were suspected of something.

The FBI and the military were also building huge biometric databases—with fingerprints and iris scans—of nearly 100 million people, people with top secret clearances, Americans in uniform and their families, government retirees, first responders, contractors. Meanwhile, the National Security Agency, the nation's surveillance agency, had made great strides giving military leaders and soldiers information they could use to identify and find terrorists and insurgents on the battlefield, but it was still refusing to clarify the extent to which Americans' emails and cell phone calls were being collected amid the millions of communications the agency vacuumed up each day looking for foreign members of terrorist organizations living in the United States. Everything the NSA did remained so completely classified that it was impossible to guess whether it or its four-hundred-plus top secret contracting companies were following the law, let alone properly spending taxpayer money.

Immigration and Customs Enforcement—the federal government's second-largest law enforcement agency after 9/11—had started operations against suspected terrorists in the United States, too. To that end, it was getting help from the most elite military Special Operations Forces to target and arrest, if need be, suspected terrorists and illegal immigrants.

And even as the Obamas headed toward the bulletproof parade reviewing stand, overseas the CIA was starting a new day targeting individuals from afar using its armed Predator drones, a practice criticized by some as assassination, which had been banned decades before. Many people in Pakistan, where most of the hits took place, saw it as an undeclared war, and their resentment against the United States only grew bigger with each new strike. The CIA and the most elite Special Operations Forces, known as Joint Special Operations Command (JSOC)[4] troops, had taken to killing suspected

---

[4] JSOC was created in 1980 as a hostage rescue force. It began to be revamped after 9/11 as a secret offensive military force engaged largely in intelligence gathering and analysis, killing and capturing top terrorist leaders, and training foreign antiterrorism units in Iraq, Afghanistan, the Philippines, Yemen, and elsewhere (see chapter 12).

terrorists rather than capturing them because there was no convenient place to put such prisoners in the United States, or anywhere else, for that matter. JSOC had grown to ten times larger than the CIA's paramilitary unit and could execute missions without any scrutiny from Congress if the president wanted it that way.

Taking office eight years after the 9/11 attacks, President Obama would discover that the two largest bureaucracies created in response to the attacks—the Office of the Director of National Intelligence[5] and the Department of Homeland Security[6]—still had not found their role among the national security agencies. Many people were particularly disappointed in DHS, which they believed was mostly populated by national security amateurs, relying on former federal employees now working as contractors for twice their old salaries. The problem of government intelligence agencies losing experience to private companies was so severe that CIA director Michael Hayden had prohibited any agency employee who left to join the private sector from returning to the agency as a contractor for twelve months. "I did not want us to become a farm system," he said, but the problem had continued.

Within forty-eight hours of the inauguration, the new presi-

---

[5] The director of national intelligence, a cabinet-level position, is a sort of spy czar whose role is to coordinate all sixteen agencies and departments that make up the intelligence community (IC). The DNI is the principal adviser to the president and the National Security Council for intelligence matters related to national security. The DNI also oversees and directs the implementation of the National Intelligence Program; oversees the coordination of relationships with foreign intelligence services; and establishes requirements and priorities for collection, analysis, production, and dissemination of national intelligence. In reality, the power of the DNI has depended less on the definition given in the legislation than on the titleholder's relationship to the president and to the heads of the various intelligence agencies.

[6] Created in 2003 from the Office of Homeland Security within the White House, which was set up after 9/11. The new cabinet-level Department of Homeland Security is supposed to integrate governmental efforts and agencies involved in airport, transportation and border security, and immigration and customs-related law enforcement. The intelligence component of DHS is one of sixteen members of the intelligence community, although it does not collect intelligence itself. With 88,000 employees, more than half of them private contractors, DHS includes the Coast Guard, Customs and Border Protection, the Federal Emergency Management Agency, Immigration and Customs Enforcement, and the U.S. Secret Service. Some of these subordinate elements are engaged in intelligence collection.

dent issued his first executive orders: the Guantánamo Bay prison in Cuba, supposedly reserved for the most dangerous terrorists, would close within a year. The CIA's secret prisons would be shut down and interrogations not in compliance with army regulations and international law stopped. The whole handling of detainees would be thoroughly reviewed.

After eight years of secret decisions, classified memos, and covert operations by the Bush administration, Obama declared a new day. He signed off on instructions to all agencies and departments to "adopt a presumption in favor" of the Freedom of Information Act. He issued a Presidential Memorandum on Transparency and Open Government.

"Openness will strengthen our democracy and promote efficiency and effectiveness in Government," the memorandum read. "Transparency promotes accountability and provides information for citizens about what their Government is doing."

But the new leader's idealism quickly faded once he took office. Few of Obama's transparency initiatives would come to pass. Guantánamo remained open. Some suspected terrorists were sent to prisons run by foreign governments for interrogation rather than trial. Covert operations stayed the centerpiece of the new president's plan of attack. As the glow of the inauguration faded, Obama embraced the intelligence-military-corporate apparatus, too, and the enduring hidden universe continued to grow larger and more secret every day.

CHAPTER FOUR

An Alternative Geography

The most hidden part of the world the new president would inherit had a nickname all its own: "Special." But after 9/11, so many things were labeled "special"—special mission, special activities, special access—that the people who worked on highly classified programs began coming up with alternatives. Sensitive Activities, Extraordinary Activities, Strategic Activities signaled an even more special status. The designations had proliferated so promiscuously that the official in charge of keeping track of them for the director of national intelligence admitted one day that nobody any longer knew what all of them meant.

"You may be talking about one thing, but the person you are talking to is hearing or understanding a completely different category. So it can get very confusing," he said. "We have explained this to several DNIs now who have all kinda gone, 'Did you guys do this on purpose?'"

The new cornucopia of acronyms and adjectives confused the very people who were supposed to be directly involved with protecting the United States, and threw sleuths like Arkin off the track, too—for a while. He was particularly fond of "special" discoveries because they were such a challenge. It was never a straightforward revelation. For instance, in the fall of 2003, he found a "technical correction" on page 6 of the 62-page House of Representatives' Emergency Supplemental Appropriations. In the long "operations and maintenance" section devoted to the Defense Logistics Agency (DLA), which buys everything from toilet paper to uniforms for the military, he noticed $15 million was restored for something called DPAO, which would turn out to be one of those "special" discoveries, but for the time being there was not even an explanation for it, nor even a spelling out of the acronym.

Digging further, in a U.S. House of Representatives budget document he found more details on that $15 million. In fiscal year 2003, the report said, the office of the secretary of defense assigned the Defense Logistics Agency (DLA) something called the Defense Policy Analysis Office—DPAO—which was intended to "address the development of DoD support policies, plans, concepts, procedures, and operations as requested by supported organizations." The mission description seemed too intentionally bland, Arkin thought, and a logistics agency was an odd place for a new policy office to be. The paper trail indicated that the $15 million had initially been deleted because the DPAO's duties were seen as redundant with the work of other agencies, but then had been mysteriously restored.

Arkin wrote "Defense Policy Analysis Office" at the top of an index card and put it in his Secret Units box, where it remained for nearly a year, until one day a source sent him two CD-ROMs' worth of unclassified and "For Official Use Only"[1] documents for a different project he was working on. There, in the thousands of documents from the newly created Northern Command, was a single page mentioning a civilian liaison officer from DPAO who had been assigned to another bit of alphabet soup—"N/NC-J39."

---

[1] This designation protects unclassified information from being distributed publicly. It allows limiting its circulation to official circles, such as law enforcement, which can also carry the label Unclassified Law-Enforcement Sensitive, or LES. Examples are Department of Homeland Security threat assessments.

It gave Arkin the chills because J39 was one of the oldest entries in his Secret Units file. In the mid-1990s, when he was writing about the emergence of a new kind of warfare — information warfare[2] — J39 kept popping up. J39 was a staff office assigned to the Joint Chiefs of Staff, and run out of a warren of offices in the bowels of the Pentagon. The office managed the most highly classified cyberwarfare programs and weapons intended not to blow things up but to screw things up, things such as electronics or computer controls, using high-powered microwaves and blackout-inducing carbon fibers that could short-circuit enemy electrical power grids.

J39 programs were called Special Technical Operations, or STOs,[3] a mysterious range of activities that includes cybersabotage and that, back then, had begun to pop up in every military command in charge of fighting wars in a particular region. N/NC-J39, the acronym after the liaison officer's name, stood for the NORAD[4] and Northern Command's own J39 office, which connected DPAO and the new domestic military command to some type of highly classified information warfare.

Another year went by before Arkin came up with anything else on DPAO. This time it was from the fiscal year (FY) 2006 defense

---

[2] Information operations (IO) are those operations primarily engaged in influencing foreign perceptions and decision making. During armed conflict, they also include efforts made to achieve physical and psychological results in support of military operations. Military IO capabilities include psychological operations (PSYOP), military deception (MILDEC), and operations security (OPSEC), which are measures to protect the security of U.S. operations and information and further their goals.

[3] Special Technical Operations (STO) involve "nonkinetic" (for example, nonexplosive) modes of warfare, from classic electronic warfare to the latest cyberwarfare and directed energy techniques. Though STO is often used in military documents to refer to space-related activities, the emergence of a wide variety of nonkinetic weapons has expanded beyond that domain.

[4] NORAD, the North American Aerospace Defense Command, is a U.S.-Canadian military organization charged with warning of attacks against the United States from missiles, aircraft, or spacecraft, and with control of airspace over North America. The commander is responsible to both the U.S. president and the Canadian prime minister. The NORAD and Northern Command Center is the central collection and coordination facility for a worldwide system of sensors designed to provide the commander and the leadership of Canada and the United States with an accurate picture of any aerospace or maritime threat.

budget, which said the organization had been transferred to the air force but gave no reason why. A couple of months later, after a routine request, Arkin received a set of documents from the Defense Information Technology Contracting Organization (DITCO), an obscure agency in charge of finding contractors to physically wire one related defense and intelligence office to another, a necessary task given the overlap of secure, encrypted government lines that supplemented the regular phone systems. Buried in its list of the latest available jobs was a request for a secure high-capacity circuit to be installed between J39's Special Activity Division in the Pentagon and the fifteenth floor of a building in Crystal City, Virginia, leased by DPAO. A second requirement was listed for the same circuit to go between those two buildings and an air force organization only identified as XOIWS in a building in Rosslyn, Virginia.

In the dialect of the air force, "XO" stood for the director of operations of the air force; "I" for the information operations chief one step down; "W" for the Information Warfare branch one more step down; and "S" for the Information Operations (IO) office at the bottom. Influence operations, as the name suggests, are aimed at secretly influencing or manipulating the opinions of foreign audiences, either on an actual battlefield—such as during a feint in a tactical battle—or within the civilian population, such as in undermining support for an existing government or terrorist group. They are also deeply involved with broader efforts to sway international opinion in line with American interests.

Sometimes this involves ploys such as planted newspaper stories and political advertising campaigns for foreign leaders supported by the United States. Other operations have involved intentionally passing disinformation to foreign leaders or spies in highly classified deception operations. In most cases, American involvement is hidden.

Using the address Arkin gave me for DPAO, and armed with a map that the building's property managers had put online for prospective lessees, I worked my way through the confusing underground shopping complex and tunnels that link buildings leased to the federal government in Crystal City.

Subterranean Crystal City had an *Alice's Adventures in Wonderland* feel. In its passageways, the wallpaper was printed with giant photographs of tulips and fields of daisies, as if a visitor were Alice after sampling the DRINK ME bottle. Parts of the complex looked like any other mall, with food courts and clothing stores. In other areas, it resembled an indoor city of dry cleaners and shoe repair shops and even doctors' offices, all to service the thousands of people working in the offices just above. At the food court you might find families dipping fries into ketchup, but down certain corridors connecting different office buildings, nearly everyone was in uniform or wore a government or corporate lanyard with ID and security cards. At these empty dead ends, where the foot traffic was reduced to almost nothing, the only place to get coffee or food was a 1950s-style deli that sold Necco wafers and saltwater taffy. Big gray security locks replaced doorknobs, office numbers replaced office names. One flight up, at street level, trucks with "communications intelligence" painted on their sides idled next to a big black GMC Yukon XL SUV with tinted windows.

The street-level lobby of DPAO's building contained an automated office directory. Every few seconds the name of the thirty or more organizations in the building scrolled down a monitor mounted on the wall. The names were familiar: names of contractors intimately associated with American intelligence and military agencies: L-1 Identity Solutions, Applied Research Associates, SAIC. A few government offices were named. Although the contracts Arkin had discovered had indicated that the special wiring was to be installed on the fifteenth floor, the last floor listed on the monitor was the fourteenth. According to the lobby directory, DPAO did not exist.

The elevator told another story, though: when I stepped into it, I saw a button for the fifteenth floor, and pressed it.

A cardboard sign reading Defense Policy Analysis Office was tacked up on the door of suite 1501. On the door was a gray electromagnetic lock, the kind whose combination can be changed often to prevent unauthorized entry. Below the lock was a small gray box with a camera inside, shielded by a clear Plexiglas dome. A warning sign said that behind the door was a secure facility. Anyone without the proper clearance should leave.

I wrote down the names of the offices on the other side of the hallway—"Combating Terrorism Technology Support Office" and "Office of the Secretary of Defense, Homeland Security"—and left.

The second office in the DPAO circuit triangle sat just across from the Key Bridge, which connects Washington, DC, to Rosslyn, an austere section of Arlington over the Potomac River. Like Crystal City, Rosslyn houses the government's overflow and the hundreds of contractors who service the Defense Department and the intelligence community. The air force XOIWS office here overlooked a rundown brick apartment building but was otherwise surrounded by sleek glass office high-rises sporting the logos of the corporate defense-intelligence giants: BAE, Northrop Grumman, and Sparta, all well-known companies but, here in northern Virginia, mere soldiers in the army of government consultants.

Arkin's documents had indicated that the special circuits were to be installed in Suite 300, to which the lobby directory had no reference. On the surface, it didn't exist. Over the course of our investigation, we would find this pattern repeated again and again: buildings without addresses, offices without floors, acronyms without explanation.

The building directory had both corporate and government entities. One was named the Policy Support and Special Programs Division, not XOIWS but a suspicious-sounding entity to add to our growing stockpile of secret organizations. The phrase "Special Programs" was a dead giveaway to anyone who even dabbled in intelligence or defense literature. It was a term that had originated at the dawn of the nuclear age when, in order to discuss topics surrounding the highly classified subject of atomic weapons—say, how to transport them—the army had come up with what became a not-so-secret nickname: Special Weapons. The word *nuclear* was never uttered. When President John F. Kennedy fell in love with the army's Green

Berets, they similarly became army Special Forces, an acknowledgment of their often secret role in warfare. Special this and special that followed, all the way up to Defense Secretary Donald Rumsfeld organizing an Office of Special Plans in the aftermath of 9/11. It was the office that had incorrectly determined that there was a link between al-Qaeda and Iraq, and had incorrectly determined that Iraq possessed biological, chemical, and nuclear weapons.

Exiting the Rosslyn elevator on the third floor, I was greeted, improbably, by a Welcome sign and a big black arrow pointing down the hall to the XOIWS office. The hardware and camera on the door were nearly identical to the equipment protecting the people inside the Defense Policy Analysis Office in Crystal City. Next to the door was a printed warning often seen outside defense offices. Slipped into a plastic sleeve, it read: "Force Protection Condition Bravo."[5] This was Defense Department dialect for "an increased or more predictable threat of terrorist threat." In reality, since the initial frenzy of September 11 had died out, the threat level had remained at bravo, much like Homeland Security's permanent shade of yellow. But this particular Arlington neighborhood, which was around the corner from a church, a gas station, and popular restaurants, was a safe place to work, in a safe part of the country.

I had driven by these areas hundreds of times, never questioning what was going on in the generic buildings that were set back from the street. Now secret doors seemed to be everywhere. I returned to Crystal City with new eyes. This time, I noticed the armed guards for the first time, and more corridors I couldn't go down without a badge. I found more office directories with missing floors. Indeed, some of the directories for twenty-story buildings were completely blank except for the name of one convenience store in the lobby. There were surveillance cameras everywhere — always rolling, hidden in corners or draped by shadows.

---

[5] "Force Protection Condition" is the Defense Department's terrorist threat warning system. Condition bravo is a "somewhat predictable terrorist threat level; security measures by agency personnel may affect the activities of local law enforcement and the general public."

DPAO turned out to be just one single strand of investigation among the hundreds we pursued on the way to mapping the DNA of the secret post-9/11 world. Not all the strands were as small as DPAO seemed to be. Some were housed in massive structures, strategically hidden behind cover names, banks of trees, or tall mountain ridges. Some were underground, like the bunker in Olney, Maryland, to which some congressional leaders had been whisked after the 9/11 attacks. That bunker, since refurbished, was located along a country road. Its guardhouse is barely visible, but by looking carefully at the Federal Emergency Management Agency's contracts for guard and facility maintenance services, Arkin had learned that the facility was quite large—90,000 square feet and under 75 acres, with a newly built helicopter pad, communications towers, and vent stacks.

Olney, though, was far from the largest secret site. One source had told me that there was a lot of CIA activity in one particular rural northern Virginia community. On Google Earth, Arkin and I went through the secret locations in northern Virginia that were listed in his database. Within minutes we'd found what we were searching for: a massive complex on the top of a tree-covered mountain. It looked like it was undergoing construction, just as my source had claimed. I decided to take a look a few days later.

Such expansion had become the unquestioned norm in the post-9/11 world. Each new organization spawned its own microclimate and geography. Each birthed a cadre of specialized contractors. Some companies were founded just to service a particular niche in the counterterrorism world, like those providing remote fingerprint readers or suppliers of regulation fencing for top secret buildings. Each large organization started its own training centers, supply depots, and transportation infrastructure. Each agency and subagency manned its own unit for hiding the identities of undercover employees and for creating cover names and addresses for them and for their most sensitive projects. Each ecosystem developed a set of regional and local offices. And yet there was little that was Darwinian about this jungle, because there was no necessity for positive adaptation: the food supply—in this case, federal dollars—was assured, and the lack of in-depth oversight meant that reproduction was easy and certain.

It had taken me an hour and a half to find the CIA site; I'd started out from my home in Washington. Once at the facility, I cruised around the fenced and barbed wire perimeter at the foot of the mountain. Small, discreet U.S. Property signs warned hunters and horseback riders to stay away. Around one bend in the road, a huge parking lot filled with black Escalade security vans was visible through the trees. Around another bend a sign cautioned drivers: Range in Use.

At the entrance, a quaint historic marker announced the origins of the U.S. Army Training Center. I couldn't see a thing up the steep road so I turned in and headed up, slowly. A series of unfriendly signs cautioned me to stop: WARNING: Unauthorized persons not permitted; WARNING: Turn around if you do not have official business.

I decelerated to a crawl. At the top I found a spiffy new security center off to the right, and a guard station with reflective mirrored walls to the left. More warning signs made it clear that no one without the proper identification should have come this close and that the guards were well armed, so I stepped slowly from the car. A young man in what were supposed to look like army battle fatigues came out of the guard post. His head was shaved; his eyes, covered with Ray-Ban shades. His military uniform said POLICE above the pocket patch, which immediately announced that he was not in the army at all. Military police don't wear such outfits, and he was also missing the MP armband or any other military rank or patch identifiers, including the usual last name stitched above the breast pocket.

"Can I ask you a question?" I asked politely.

"Okay," he responded, nicely enough.

"I just drove past the sign that said Range in Use. Do they use it both in the day and at night? I'm just wondering."

"It's very busy," he replied, shaking his head yes.

"What is this place, anyway?" I asked.

"It's a training center for the army and other agencies...and for law enforcement agencies, too, and others."

He was telling the truth, or a small corner of it. I learned later from people who frequented the facility that the mountaintop range was a training center for the CIA's rapidly expanding contract workforce of security specialists—people like Raymond Davis, who would later be briefly jailed in Pakistan in 2011 after shooting two would-be assailants. The job of these specialists was to hide in foreign countries and discreetly manage security for agency operatives meeting with sources and traveling through risky neighborhoods. The Global Response Staff had become a necessary addition in the expanding secret wars. The CIA's longtime training site at Camp Peary, near Williamsburg, Virginia, and its contract firing range at a Blackwater facility in Moyock, North Carolina, were either too crowded or too far away to be convenient for officers and contractors needing to prepare for overseas assignments and brush up on their tradecraft and weapons skills before deploying. (Blackwater was the private security firm that had gotten in so much trouble in Iraq and then changed its name to Xe Services LLC.) This place, on the other hand, was convenient.

Like many installations in this secret world, the CIA facility sat in the middle of a completely normal community. Near the entrance, in fact, was a lovely cottage with an English garden. Such proximity was both intentional and, in many cases, inevitable: the post-9/11 secret world has become so vast that it is impossible to keep it within isolated boundaries. Besides, it was much easier to keep government employees happy and to hire all the private contractors the government needed if people only had to drive to work from their comfortable homes in suburbia.

The gigantic training center was not the only place the expanding CIA had moved into when its ranks began to swell after 9/11. Despite its public reputation, bolstered by spy novels and action films, the CIA is among the smallest of all the intelligence agencies. After the attacks, however, it had increased its office space by one-third. It took over two newly built large office buildings near the Smithsonian Air and Space Museum Center abutting Dulles International Airport, built two other complexes in the nearby Virginia cities of Fairfax and McLean, and moved into another in Herndon, Virginia.

Every one of those buildings had to have a Sensitive Compartmented Information Facility. Indeed, in the post-9/11 world, you couldn't even get in the sandbox without one of these rooms-within-a-room certified by U.S. security officers as impenetrable by electronic eavesdropping or other sophisticated surveillance technology.

As important to a man's self-image as the power of his car's engine or his motorcycle's rumble, SCIF size had become a symbol of status. "In DC, everyone talks SCIF, SCIF, SCIF," said Bruce Paquin, owner of a construction company that builds SCIFs for the government and private corporations. "They've got the penis envy thing going. You can't be a big boy unless you're a three-letter agency and you have a big SCIF." Some are as small as a closet; others are four times the size of a football field. The army manages over five hundred SCIFs in the DC area alone; SCIFs are present even in civil departments like Agriculture and Labor.

Over six months, I visited dozens of addresses with SCIFs in Washington, DC, and its surrounding counties. Often I found myself confirming the information we had in our database, and just as often I added to it. Just as the missing fifteenth floor had been evident as soon as I had entered the elevator, it didn't always take a huge amount of sleuthing to discover new, concrete information. Each address became another dot on the map. As the dots gathered and clumped, a sort of alternative geography of the greater Washington region began to show itself. This was not quite an invisible geography, but it was a deceptive one. Much of the area looked essentially as it had before 9/11, even with all the new developments and construction. For a significant chunk of the post-9/11 buildup, the part that preceded the housing market collapse and economic downturn, it was not strange to see some sort of construction around every turn. What was different now was that these offices housed thousands of people who worked and lived in a world dedicated to secrecy; who were connected to each other via secure, encrypted telephone and email cables. These constellations, not surprisingly, usually fell within a small radius from particular government agencies. Using his expanding database of top secret government organizations, agencies, companies, and jobs, Arkin gradually determined various links between government efforts and the private companies within each apparent cluster.

One day I drove west along Route 66 with an address Arkin had given me after we had decided to try to find a Defense Intelligence Agency office that analyzed underground bunkers. It turned out to be particularly hard to find. It wasn't on Google Maps or the other mapping software that we typically examined first to check out whether there was the telltale perimeter fencing of a secure building, or to count the parking spaces to get a sense of how many people worked in a particularly secretive location. As a Michaels craft store and a Books-A-Million gave way to the regional offices of corporate giant Lockheed Martin, I turned left off the exit ramp. There, two shimmering-blue five-story ice cubes stood out among the other concrete block structures. Like most of the drivers streaming by these buildings, I ordinarily would never have given them a second thought. Yet a small sign hidden near some boxwoods indicated that the structures belonged to the National Geospatial-Intelligence Agency (NGA),[6] one of the sixteen major

---

[6] The National Geospatial-Intelligence Agency, renamed from the National Imagery and Mapping Agency (NIMA) in 2003, supports the Defense Department with mapping and geospatial imagery, intelligence and analysis. It is one of the sixteen members of the intelligence community and is headquartered in Bethesda, Maryland (but moving to a new headquarters in Springfield, Virginia). Geospatial intelligence (GEOINT) consists of imagery, imagery intelligence, and geospatial (mapping, charting, and geodesy) information of the physical features of Earth and underground. Prior to 9/11, the U.S. Geologic Survey was responsible for producing imagery and geospatial data for the United States.

intelligence agencies, and one that had changed its name and expanded its mission after 9/11. Its job was to analyze satellite and other intelligence images, to map Earth's geography, and, most important, to provide an up-to-the-minute visual picture for war planners and military commanders on the ground. Once named the Defense Mapping Agency, it had expanded as the geospatial intelligence service for the entire government, from the intelligence community to the EPA. It was the government's own Google Earth.

Across the street, in an understated chocolate-brown business complex, I scribbled down all the corporate names I found on little signs on the office doors. One of them was named Carahsoft, a firm we hadn't yet run across. Subsequent digging revealed it to be a leading intelligence agency contractor specializing in mapping, speech analysis, and data harvesting. A giant in its field, its sign was so small I would have missed it if I had blinked at the wrong time.

Nearby was the government building we were looking for: the Underground Facility Analysis Center. There was no visible sign, and its actual address is nowhere publicly listed. But we knew from talking to officials in the military and by reading job descriptions for potential employees how important the center had become in evaluating weapons that could be used in caves in Afghanistan like the ones Osama bin Laden was believed to be hiding in at one time or another after the United States invaded the country to find him. Center technicians were also helping to develop a new generation of weapons designed to disrupt enemy command center communications when bombing them was not possible.

The NGA was a perfect example of post-9/11 expansion. It had outgrown its half-dozen Washington-area facilities and was busily building a new $1.8 billion headquarters in nearby Springfield, Virginia, south of the Pentagon. When completed, it will be the fourth-largest federal building in the Washington area and home to 8,500 employees. (The construction site is surrounded by view-obstructing trees, and all entrances are blocked and heavily guarded against unauthorized entry.)

The new NGA campus was only one of dozens of new government buildings springing up around Washington—so many that we'd quickly determined that trying to look into all of them was an impossible task. Even just focusing on the largest, Arkin determined that the Washington area had thirty-three large complexes for top secret intelligence work under construction or already finished since 9/11. Together these buildings occupied the equivalent, in square footage, of nearly three Pentagons or twenty-two U.S. Capitols. The cost of construction: unknown. Our counting challenge was shared by the federal government, which, as we would discover, had no idea how many agencies and subagencies were spending taxpayer money.

I first stumbled into what would turn out to be the densest concentration of government offices and private companies doing top secret work in the country after the Defense Department agreed to let me sit in on a class on cipher locks and other ways to protect classified material. The Defense Security Service (DSS) classroom in Elkridge, Maryland, a place you would never ordinarily happen upon, was located near the parking garage behind Baltimore-Washington International Thurgood Marshall Airport and, unbeknownst to me at the time, an annex of the National Security Agency.

The first indication of its otherworldliness was a lawn sign advertising not the newest tract of homes but a job fair at Joe's Café for "Cleared" personnel. "Cleared" meant people with security clearances. Joe's Café turned out to be a rather ordinary coffee and sandwich place, except for the giveaway pens and cardboard hot cup holders imprinted with the names of intelligence contractors. Ordinary except for the posters on the windows that weren't advertising turkey sandwiches but intelligence analyst and IT jobs at the National Business Park across the way, hidden behind a bank of thick, tall trees.

From the DSS classroom building, I looked out over a four-square-block area of office buildings—all painted the same dark brown, all with the same reflective copper-colored glass windows, and none with anything but a three-digit number on top to distinguish it from the next. No company logos, no names and addresses on the mailboxes. I called Arkin, gave him the addresses, and he looked at his database and came up with a company or organization name to match each one.

As I drove around, I found other clues to the area's strange nature, like a museum of defense electronics. Instead of a welcome sign, a red warning notice was posted in the lobby: Authorized Personnel Only, it read. For a museum?

The entrance of many of the buildings in the area had small signs out front: COPT, Corporate Office Properties Trust. I phoned Arkin again, with a half-dozen COPT addresses. He dug around the company's website and I dove into their public financial statements. It turned out to be one of the largest providers of leased government office space for secure buildings, meaning SCIFs, in the nation.

I found a commercial real-estate agent, Dennis Lane, to give me a tour of the region. He took me to more secure office parks the government leased. We drove the perimeters of a dozen other buildings that he or some other real-estate agent he knew had leased to the government for secret business. Some had names out front too dull to mean anything: Foreign Systems Integration Center and DCMA Special Programs East. I passed those addresses to Arkin, who looked them up and then would find other interesting addresses in the same office park, only to discover more government organizations and more corporations doing top secret work nearby. I rigged my computer to the armrest so he and I could Google-Earth these complexes together and discuss the next block to explore. Each drive yielded more clues, more addresses that could be put in the database or into an Internet search engine to produce another obscure company or a government office that we had never heard of before but which often sounded exactly like the half-dozen we had found earlier.

★   ★   ★

We were not the only ones to notice the vast scale of this concrete expansion of the terrorism-industrial complex. People who worked inside it did, too. Many of the newest buildings appeared, from the outside at least, to house utilitarian, unattractive offices. Maj. Gen. John M. Custer III, head of the army's intelligence school, who had spent most of his time after 9/11 in war zones but had been inside more than his share of new intelligence buildings, described these edifices to me as being "on the order of the pyramids."

This was not the half of it.

In 2010, five miles southeast of the White House, the young Department of Homeland Security broke ground for its new headquarters. The largest of the post-9/11 cabinet-level departments, DHS already had a massive 230,000-person workforce, the third largest after the departments of Defense and Veterans Affairs. Now a $3.4 billion testament to its efforts was rising from the crumbling brick wards of the former St. Elizabeths psychiatric hospital in the Anacostia section of southeast Washington. It will be the largest government complex built since the Pentagon and a major landmark in the permanent alternative geography of Top Secret America.

The alternative geography projects also crisscross the country, to Denver-Aurora, Colorado, where the largest federal neighborhood outside Washington is still growing; to Tampa–St. Petersburg, Florida, where the military's Central Command and Special Operations Command overflow into the rundown business parks of St. Petersburg; to San Antonio, headquarters of military information warfare and air force intelligence; and Arnold, Missouri, where the National Geospatial-Intelligence Agency's mapping facility shares the street with Target and Home Depot. A $1.7 billion NSA data storage warehouse is planned near Salt Lake City. In Tampa, the Central Command's new 270,000-square-foot intelligence center will be matched by an equally large new headquarters building, and then, after that, by a 51,000-square-foot building just for its Special Operations section. In Miami, the Southern Command responsible for Latin America and the counternarcoterrorism war there constructed a 600,000-square-foot headquarters building for $400 million. Just north of Charlottesville, Virginia, a new intelligence analysis center, the Joint Use Intelligence Analysis Facility, will consolidate 1,000 defense intelligence analysts on a secure rural campus to manage the overflow of army intelligence and the Washington-based Defense Intelligence Agency.

As impressive as all that may be, it pales beside the clandestine metropolis rising around the nation's capital. Ask anyone who knows Washington, DC, and they will say the federal city is defined by the White House, the Capitol, the Mall, and the Lincoln, Jefferson, and Washington monuments. Passengers on flights into and out of Ronald Reagan Washington National Airport can pick out the other points of political and cultural power: the five-sided Pentagon, the majestic National Cathedral, the towering office buildings and shopping malls of Tysons Corner near where the revolution in information technology was launched in the 1980s, beginning the permanent transformation of the region.

The alternative geography, on the other hand, would be defined by the CIA's aging white Langley headquarters and its new annexes near Dulles Airport, the National Reconnaissance Office's[7] aqua blue steel buildings in Chantilly, Virginia, and the Defense Intelligence Agency's gigantic, sailboat-shaped headquarters on Bolling Air Force Base just across the Potomac River from National Airport.

But the capital of this alternative United States of America is found some twenty-four miles to the north, close to Interstate 95, and closer to Baltimore than Washington, in the neighborhood where I first visited the cipher lock training class. The many business parks there were larger and mostly unadorned. The extended-stay hotels for contractors and traveling government employees were paler than others elsewhere. Even the Starbucks Coffee shop looked off. It was located in a stark white office building, and at 11:00 a.m., when many Starbucks are brimming with break-time con-

---

[7] Established in 1961 but only declassified in 1992, the NRO is one of the sixteen intelligence agencies of the federal government. It is in charge of designing, building, launching, and maintaining the nation's intelligence satellites.

versations, this one was empty. Finally, at lunchtime, a stream of customers with corporate lanyards and security badges came in, half of them in uniform. We called it The Loneliest Starbucks in America.

Little else around this community was what it appeared to be, either. The brick warehouse was not just a warehouse—drive through the gate and around back, and there, hidden away, was the government's future personal security detail: a fleet of black SUVs that had been armored up to withstand explosions and gunfire. On closer glance, the new gunmetal-colored office building was a kind of hotel where businesses could rent eavesdrop-proof rooms for meetings and training sessions. Even the manhole cover in between the two low-slung buildings was not just a manhole cover. Surrounded by cement cylinders, it was an access point to reach a secret government cable. "TS/SCI," one of my escorts whispered one afternoon as I was visiting the building next door— the abbreviations for Top Secret/Sensitive Compartmented Information, and what that means is that only those with the highest clearances are allowed to know what information the cable transmits. And no surprise, because this was near the National Security Agency, which is also the nation's premier offensive cyberforce.

The Baltimore-area Top Secret America cluster turns out to be the largest of a dozen such clusters across the United States. This fact is unknown to most people, and that is the way the government wants it. When the GPS on a car's dashboard suddenly gets stuck in a frustrating loop, trapping the driver in a series of U-turns near the National Security Agency, it's because the NSA takes countermeasures against infiltration that don't distinguish between spy equipment and personal travel aids.

Not surprisingly, from almost any direction near its headquarters, the NSA is difficult to see. Trees, walls, and sloping landscape obscure its presence from the highway, and concrete barriers, fortified guard posts, and warning signs stop drivers without authorization from entering the grounds of the largest intelligence agency in the United States. Its budget, much of it for technology, has doubled since 9/11, the exact amount classified but estimated at over $25 billion annually.

Beyond all those concrete barriers loom huge buildings with row after row of opaque, blast-resistant, and eavesdrop-proof windows, behind which an estimated thirty thousand people are reading, listening to, and analyzing an endless flood of intercepted conversations and communications twenty-four hours a day, seven days a week.

From the road, it's impossible to tell how large the NSA has become; military construction documents submitted to Howard County, however, reveal that its buildings occupy 6.3 million square feet—the size of the Pentagon—and are surrounded by 112 acres of parking spaces. As massive as that might seem, the documents indicate the NSA is only going to get bigger: ten thousand workers will be added over the next fifteen years. It will cost $2 billion to pay for just the first phase of expansion. An overall increase in size will boost its building space to nearly ten million square feet.

The NSA sits within the larger Fort Meade army base, which hosts eighty government tenants in all, including several large intelligence organizations. Just beyond the perimeter is where the companies that thrive off the NSA and other intelligence organizations begin and fan out ten miles from the NSA headquarters, covering some 254 square miles. Together they inject $10 billion from paychecks, contracts, and service businesses like hotels and restaurant into the region's economy every year. In some parts of this cluster, they occupy entire neighborhoods. In others, they make up mile-long business parks connected to the government agency's large campus through hidden bridges studded with forbidding yellow warning signs.

The largest is the National Business Park—285 tucked-away acres of wide, angular glass towers that go on for blocks. The occupants of these buildings are contractors who in their other, more publicly noticeable locations purposely understate their presence.

But in the National Business Park, a place where only other intelligence contractors would have reason to go, their office signs are a full story tall and at night glow in bright red, yellow, and blue: L-3 Communications, CSC, Northrop Grumman, General Dynamics, SAIC.

Even at 9:00 p.m. in the confines of the National Business Park, office lights remain on here and there. The 140 rooms of the Marriott Courtyard are completely occupied, as usual, with guests, such as the one checking in who says only that he's "with the military."

More than 250 companies—fully 13 percent of all the firms working for the government on programs at the top secret classification level—have a presence in the Fort Meade cluster. Some have multiple offices, such as Northrop Grumman (nineteen) and SAIC (eleven). In all, there are 681 locations in the Fort Meade cluster at which businesses conduct work at the top secret level for the National Security Agency and the rest of the intelligence community.

Some of those locations are in parklike settings with eco-friendly buildings of shimmering glass and award-winning modern art sculptures, all hidden behind banks of lush trees. Others are in areas that are mostly asphalt, cement, parking lots, extended-stay hotels and large, pillbox offices in every shade of brown and displaying only an address number. In another part of the cluster, yellow buses that carry children to school park outside highly secured buildings where intelligence is shared with Britain, Canada, Australia, and New Zealand and the grade of the fencing is inspected by the NSA security staff.

In still another neighborhood, the juxtaposition of old and new was jarring; a gigantic warehouse with sensitive equipment inside sat next to two modest homes, one with a vegetable garden out back. "It used to be all farmland, then they just started digging one day," said Jerome Jones as he tended his garden, a cement wall looming beyond the tomato plants. "I don't know what they do up there but it doesn't bother me. I don't worry about it."

The building is sealed off behind fencing and Jersey barriers and is larger than a football field. It has no identifying sign. It does have an address, except that Google doesn't recognize it. Type it in and what Google displays is another address, every time.

"6700," the sign says outside the gate.

No street name. Just 6700.

Soon, there will be one more feature in the Fort Meade cluster mix: a new four-story building near a quiet gated community of upscale town houses that the builder boasts can withstand a car bomb.

Commercial real-estate agent Lane, the building's owner, had his engineers reinforce the steel beams to meet government specifications for security. The senior vice president of a local real estate firm has become something of a snoop himself when it comes to his NSA neighborhood. At fifty-five, he has lived and worked in its shadow all his life and has schooled himself on its growing presence in his community. He collects business intelligence. He has his own network of informants, executives like himself hoping to make a killing off an organization many of his neighbors don't know a thing about. Lane takes note when the NSA or another secretive government organization leases another building, hires more contractors, and expands its outreach to the local business community. He's been following construction projects, job migrations, corporate moves. He knows local planners are estimating that another 10,000 jobs will come with an expanded NSA and another 52,000 from other intelligence and information technology organizations moving to the Fort Meade post.

Lane was up on all the gossip months before it was announced that the next giant new military command, Cyber Command,[8] would be run by the same four-star general who heads the National

---

[8] Established in 2009 and located in Fort Meade, Maryland, Cyber Command is headed by the director of the National Security Agency, but as a four-star command, it is an independent entity, with independent roles and responsibilities. It centralizes command of U.S. government cyberspace operations (offensive and defensive), organizes existing cyber resources of the U.S. government and intelligence community, and synchronizes the defense of U.S. military networks.

Security Agency. "This whole cyber thing is going to be big," Lane says, a twinkle of excitement in his eyes. "A cybercommand could eat up all the building inventory out there."

Lane knows this because he has witnessed the post-9/11 growth of the NSA, which now ingests 1.7 billion pieces of intercepted communications every twenty-four hours: telephone calls, radio signals, cell phone conversations, emails, text and Twitter messages, bulletin board postings, instant messages, website changes, computer network pings, and IP addresses. And that was what lurked behind some of those doors, those along the secure corridors in Crystal City, those in dull-looking office buildings in dull-looking business parks in cities around the country: computers delivering images and reports from the U.S. government's own internal search engines, banks of television monitors showing a satellite-fed stream of briefings, intelligence reports, news, and video-teleconferences on a closed-circuit television network that connected commanders, intelligence officers, and analysts on six continents. And beyond that the information technology (IT) companies that developed and staffed the government's computer systems, and beyond that the intelligence and military offices that were supposed to help protect all of this. And beyond that still, the separate multi-billion-dollar computer networks for each agency and its many subagencies; the 24-hour command centers; the 365-day-a-year watch floors and fusion centers—31 of them in the Washington area alone—where intelligence from many different agencies was linked together and analyzed. And this is why the NSA is never empty. Its mathematicians, linguists, techies, and cryptologists—the cryppies—flow in and out around the clock. The ones leaving descend the elevators to the first floor. Each is carrying a plastic, bar-coded box. Inside is a door key that rattles against the side of the box as he walks. To those who work here, it's the sound of a shift change.

As employees just starting their shifts push the turnstiles forward, those who are leaving push their identity badges into the mouth of the key machine. A door opens. They drop their key box in, then push out through the turnstiles. They go to the parking lot, and drive slowly through the barriers and gates protecting the NSA, passing a steady stream of cars headed in. It's almost midnight in the Fort Meade cluster, a sleepless place, the capital of Top Secret America, growing larger, even ten years after September 2011.

Our map of this hidden world had its dots and lines, but that had only really told us what was on the surface. Half of the alternative geography of the United States is anchored in an arch that includes the National Security Agency, stretching from Leesburg, Virginia, forty-five miles west of the Capitol, to Quantico, forty miles to the south, then back north through Washington and curving northeast to Linthicum, just north of the Baltimore-Washington International Thurgood Marshall Airport. But, as spies and their governments throughout history have learned the hard way, information means little unless connections can be made. To understand Top Secret America, we would have to go deeper.

CHAPTER FIVE

Supersize.gov

Following the instructions of a trusted source, late one night I pulled my car up next to the pedestrian tunnel near the Pentagon parking lot and waited. Soon another car rolled next to mine and I got inside. We drove a short way and parked close to one of the building's more obscure entrances. My companion, well known to the guards, was able to usher me in without my having to hand over my Pentagon press pass or sign in.

Once inside, we walked through the wide halls that, this late at night, were so empty our footsteps echoed. Although I had been to the Pentagon hundreds of times, I'd never seen the building in this way.

Up stairways, down corridors, and through a series of vaulted rooms we nearly trotted until a final door was unlocked. It opened onto a suite of offices where a general was waiting.

His duffel bag and armored vest lay in the corner. He was on his way to another tour in a war zone and had something on his mind that he wanted to share before he left. We went into a closet-like room and sat in front of his computer. He turned it on and looked into the tennis ball–sized camera mounted on top of the monitor. The camera recorded his face and scanned his iris, transmitting an image to the central database, verifying his identity, and granting him access to predetermined levels of classification. Not a second later, he was in.

What he wanted to show me was something I was not supposed to see: a volume of intelligence reports so large it made him mad just thinking about having to look through them all, which he was supposed to do, every day. As he scrolled down page after electronic page, dozens of icons raced by, each representing a different analytical website produced by a different government agency, many of them military intelligence, a few CIA, and the others a collection from an alphabet soup of names, all of which not even he was familiar with. Post-9/11, government agencies annually published some 50,000 separate serialized intelligence reports under 1,500 titles, the classified equivalent of newspapers, magazines, and journals. Some were distributed daily; others came out once a week, monthly, or annually.[1] The senior intelligence officer grew visibly angry as he showed me a listing of just a few of these digital reports: CIA World Intelligence Review, CIA WIRe, Spot Intelligence Report, Daily Intelligence Summary, Weekly Intelligence Forecast, Weekly Warning Forecast, IC Terrorist Threat Assessments, NCTC Terrorism Dispatch, NCTC Spotlight. He turned to the in-box on his desk, focusing on the printed intelligence reports he received rather than those transmitted electronically. The in-box was full to the point of overflowing. He waved the thickest report around—it was fifty pages and glossy-covered—and slammed it down. "Why does it have to be so bulky? Jesus! Why does it take so long to produce?" The data, he scoffed, was outdated by the time it had arrived. A good deal of once valuable,

---

[1] Serialized intelligence reports are distinguished from both raw intelligence reports and special intelligence reports. Raw intelligence is immediately reported by the collector and serves as the basis for serialized reporting (daily, weekly, monthly, etc.) by subject or geographic location. Special intelligence reports are those reports—like National Intelligence Estimates or individual subject reports—that are produced on request or as needed. Both serialized and special reports are considered finished intelligence (and are often referred to as FINTEL).

expensively obtained information had been leeched of its value by virtue of the delay in getting it to the relevant people—if, that is, the relevant people even found it among mountains of pages and millions of kilobytes.

Indeed, the print overload was particularly counterproductive, the officer said, because too many long, redundant reports caused decision makers to avoid the electronic pile altogether. Frustrated, senior officials would rely on their personal briefers to tell them what they needed to know; those briefers, also overwhelmed, usually relied on their own particular agency's analysis, ignoring those from other sources. Thus a post–9/11 goal of breaking down walls to give decision makers a broader analysis, all easily accessible online, was completely defeated.

One of the government's solutions to this indiscriminate overproduction had been to create, in 2010, yet another publication, an online newspaper named *Intelligence Today*. Every day, a staff of twenty-two culled twenty-nine agencies' reports and sixty-three analytic websites on the classified networks, selected the best information, and packaged it by originality, topic, and region, producing a daily publication that was dozens of screens long. The director of national intelligence pointed out that, with *Intelligence Today*, intelligence from every agency was being consolidated and distributed throughout government for the first time. Such an effort had been nine years in coming, he said. But instead of welcoming the innovation, many officials inside the military and intelligence community had rolled their eyes. It was, they complained, another new product, just more to read.

Overproduction may be inevitable in the digital era, when the ability to collect and store raw information has exploded exponentially. "I'm going to be honest, I don't know how many products we produce," another senior official responsible for analysis across the entire intelligence community said. Surveying all of the intelligence websites feeding the national security system, he had determined that sixty of them should have been closed down for lack of usefulness. Some agencies had turned their sites into little more than cherished personal projects, the classified equivalent of an unread blog. In any case, "like a zombie, it keeps on living," the official chuckled darkly.

So who produced all of these pages? Analysts never got the glory that operatives received; no one proposed 007 movies or action-packed spy novels about them. Yet they are at the heart of the work done in Top Secret America. All the billions of bytes of data intelligence agencies collected were useless without people to review and assess their significance. They synthesize the transcripts of interviews with informants, spies, and detainees, the translations of the National Security Agency's overseas signals intercepts, and the FBI's telephone wiretaps. Analysts make sense of documents that are stolen and captured or taken from the pockets of terrorists or the trash bins of foreign government buildings. For much of the cold war, analysts specialized in understanding foreign institutions — armies, governments, bureaucracies — but in the age of 9/11, their focus turned to individual terrorists, cells, families, and villages. Imagery analysts scrutinize satellite and aircraft photography and the full-motion video from drones. Technical analysts process even more complex data: heat signatures, noise, or the metadata associated with our ever-moving electronic world. Analysis was greatly enhanced by computers that sorted through the huge volume of captured overseas conversations, names, and topics of discussion and cross-referenced them by geographic location. But in the end, analysis required human judgment, and the usefulness of those judgments depended on the quality of the analyst. Good analysis should drive everything in the intelligence arena, including what kind of information CIA operatives need to steal or ask detainees about, and what kinds of operations should be undertaken to achieve that goal. Good analysis helps commanders devise new, more effective tactics or tweak old ones. It helps policy makers come up with new strategies to achieve, for the United States, a more secure position in the world.

Unfortunately, the quality of analysis in the age of al-Qaeda terrorism took a hit after 9/11 with the exodus several years later of experienced veterans in midcareer into the lucrative private sector. As a result, half of government analysts throughout the intelligence world had been hired in just the past several years. In fact, two-thirds of the analysts at the CIA have less than five years of experience. Two-thirds of FBI analyst positions didn't even exist before 9/11. The shortage of analysts has led to a greater reliance on outside contractors, and this has led to two additional problems. Corporations poached senior talent from government by offering larger salaries. They also offered to train prospective analysts straight out of college, which meant, in reality, on-the-job training at taxpayer expense. Analysts are among the intelligence community's lowest-paid employees, the ones who carry their lunches to work to save money, twenty- and thirty-year-olds making $40,000 to $60,000 a year. "There's only so much we can do to increase the expertise of a new kid we hire out of Georgetown" or out of the government's intelligence analysis academies, said the head of analysis for the Office of the Director of National Intelligence. "There's only so much you can do to make that person a real expert, because that requires time on the target." And while it was evident that these new hires lack experience, the sheer quantity of hires added to the mess. Furthermore, in contrast to the cold war era, when there was one primary target and analysts were hired out of specialized Soviet studies programs and spoke fluent Russian, a typical analyst hired these days knows very little about the priority countries—Iraq, Iran, Afghanistan, Pakistan, and Yemen—when he or she first comes on board. Most are not fluent in the relevant languages, either. And while the CIA and other agencies have made an effort to recruit native speakers, the number needed far exceeds the number available, particularly in jobs requiring the highest security clearances.

Thus, although there are probably twice as many analysts throughout government today as there were on September 10, 2001, too many of them can do little but move the same intelligence around; they lack the expertise and ability to go beyond what has already been packaged and presented. The analysts simply flood their commanders and policy makers with marginally informative and redundant conclusions.

"It's the soccer ball syndrome. Something happens, and they want to rush to cover it," said Richard H. Immerman, who, until 2009, was the assistant deputy director of national intelligence for Analytic Integrity, the office that oversees analysis for all the agencies but has little power over how individual agencies conduct their work. "I saw tremendous overlap" in what analysts worked on. "There's no systematic and rigorous division of labor." Even the analysts at the gigantic National Counterterrorism Center (NCTC)[2]—established in 2003 as the pinnacle of intelligence, the repository of the most sensitive, most difficult-to-obtain nuggets of information—got low marks from intelligence officials for not producing reports that were original, or even just better than those already written by the CIA, the FBI, the National Security Agency, or the Defense Intelligence Agency.[3]

It's not an academic insufficiency. When John M. Custer III was the director of intelligence at U.S. Central Command, he grew angry at how little helpful information came out of the NCTC. In 2007, he visited its director at the time, retired vice admiral John Scott Redd, to say so, loudly. "I told him," Custer explained to me, "that after four and a half years, this organization had never pro-

---

[2] Established by the Intelligence Reform and Terrorism Prevention Act of 2004, the NCTC's mission is to integrate and analyze all intelligence on terrorism and counterterrorism and to design strategic counterterrorism plans. Located in McLean, Virginia, the NCTC is a subordinate organization of the Office of the Director of National Intelligence. It maintains the Terrorist Screening Database (TSDB), an authoritative list fed by two primary sources: international terrorist information from NCTC and domestic terrorist information from the FBI.

[3] The Defense Intelligence Agency (DIA), a combat support agency of the Department of Defense, is the leading provider of foreign military intelligence and one of the largest components of the intelligence community. Established in 1961, and headquartered at Bolling AFB in southeast Washington, DIA primarily conducts intelligence analysis through a network of air, ground, naval, missile, and space-related intelligence centers. It has a small human intelligence (HUMINT) section as well.

duced one shred of information that helped me prosecute three wars!" Redd was not apologetic. He believed the system worked well, saying it wasn't designed to serve commanders in the field but policy makers in Washington. That explanation sounded like a poor excuse to Custer. Mediocre information was mediocre information, no matter on whose desk it landed.

Two years later, as head of the army's intelligence school at Fort Huachuca, Arizona, Custer still got red-faced when he recalled that day and his general frustration with Washington's bureaucracy. "Who has the mission of reducing redundancy and ensuring everybody doesn't gravitate to the lowest-hanging fruit?" he asked. "Who orchestrates what is produced so that everybody doesn't produce the same thing?" The answer in Top Secret America was, dangerously, nobody.

This sort of wasteful redundancy is endemic in Top Secret America, not just in analysis but everywhere. Born of the blank check that Congress first gave national security agencies in the wake of the 9/11 attacks, Top Secret America's wasteful duplication was cultivated by the bureaucratic instinct that bigger is always better, and by the speed at which big departments like defense allowed their subagencies to grow. This included the National Security Agency.

Retired air force general Michael Hayden was in charge of NSA on 9/11. A personable, articulate intelligence officer whom many people easily call "Mike" despite his four stars, he oversaw its subsequent expansion. Under him, NSA had grown larger and more powerful than any other single intelligence-collecting organization. "Doubling down"—doubling the number of employees—"was the rule of thumb," Hayden recalled, and he'd doubled down like no other previous NSA director. Under Hayden, NSA expanded its work into new parts of the world against new targets, requiring new language skills and technologies. It was the NSA's responsibility to probe certain parts of the Internet too. But quality did not necessarily follow quantity, Hayden admitted. "Effective we were. Efficient we were not," he said.

"The redundancy," he added, "is a truth."

Arkin and I wanted to see if we could calculate the growth in agencies after 9/11 and then count how many were doing the same work as each other and/or preexisting agencies. The results were stunning.

Looking at only government organizations working at the top secret level on counterterrorism and intelligence, Arkin counted twenty-one new organizations created in just the last three months of 2001, among them the Office of Homeland Security and the FBI's Foreign Terrorist Tracking Task Force. In 2002, thirty-four more organizations were created. Some tracked weapons of mass destruction, others joined the cyberwar and collected threat tips. Still others coordinated counterterrorism among different agencies, attempting to tame the growing information load. Those were followed the next year by thirty-nine new organizations, from the formidable Department of Homeland Security to Deep Red, a small naval intelligence cell working on the most difficult terrorism problems.

In 2004, yet another thirty organizations were created or redirected toward the terrorism mission. That was followed by thirty-four more the next year and twenty-seven more the year after that; twenty-four or more each were added in 2007, 2008, and 2009. After two years of investigating, Arkin had come up with a jaw-dropping 1,074 federal government organizations and nearly two thousand private companies involved with programs related to counterterrorism, homeland security, and intelligence in at least 17,000 locations across the United States—all of them working at the top secret classification level.

With more work, he discovered that 263 of these organizations had been established or refashioned in the wake of 9/11.[4] But the

---

[4] None of this included new organizations created in Afghanistan and Iraq, or organizations at the state and local level, or the numerous local federal offices that Top Secret America added to small-town America.

biggest growth had come within the many agencies and large corporations that had existed before the attacks and had since inflated to historic proportions. For example, the Pentagon's large Defense Intelligence Agency, which collects and analyzes defense-related intelligence from countries around the world, had grown from 7,500 employees in 2002 to 16,500 at the end of 2010, DIA officials told me. Thirty-five FBI Joint Terrorism Task Forces[5]—"joint" because they included representatives from law enforcement, the military, intelligence, and the private sector—ballooned to 106 total, with over 5,000 agents and analysts involved daily.

As we learned more about Top Secret America, we sometimes thought Osama bin Laden must have been gloating. There was so much for him to take satisfaction from: the chronic elevation of Homeland Security's color-coded threat warning, the anxious mood and culture of fear that had taken hold of public discussions about al-Qaeda, the complete contortions the government and media went through every time there was a terrorist bombing overseas or a near-miss at home. We imagined bin Laden and his sidekick, Ayman Zawahiri, pleased most by this uncontrollable American spending spree in the midst of an economic downturn. It was evident from the audiotapes secretly released after 9/11 that they both followed the news and would have known that thousands of people had lost their homes, that many more had lost their jobs, that states were cutting back on health care for poor children and on education just to stay afloat and to allow state fusion centers and mini-homeland security offices everywhere to stay open. They would have known, too, that the major American political parties were tearing themselves apart over how to stop deficit spending and reverse the economic free fall, and that they still feared

---

[5] Under the direction of the FBI, a Joint Terrorism Task Force (JTTF) brings together federal, military, state, and local law enforcement entities to investigate, analyze, and develop sources on terrorism within the United States. From 35 on 9/11—the first was established in New York City in 1980—the number of JTTFs grew to 106 by 2011. The largest, in New York, Washington, DC, and Los Angeles, include hundreds of employees and liaison officers from intelligence, law enforcement, military, and civilian agencies; the smallest are no larger than a dozen or so people.

al-Qaeda as a threat more frightening than the Soviet superpower of the cold war.

And this is exactly what a terrorist organization would want. With no hope of defeating a much better equipped and professional nation-state army, terrorists hoped to get their adversary to over-react, to bleed itself dry, and to trample the very values it tried to protect. In this sense, al-Qaeda—though increasingly short on leaders and influence (a fact no one in Top Secret America would ever say publicly, just in case there was another attack)—was doing much more damage to its enemy than it had on 9/11.

Budget figures told just part of the story. As Arkin categorized the functions of the top secret–level organizations, what Hayden referred to as inefficiencies and redundancies came to life. For example, at least thirty-four major federal agencies and military commands, operating in sixteen U.S. cities, tracked the money flow to and from terrorist networks (what the government calls "counterthreat finance").

Some of the most intense infighting revolved around all things digital. Dueling organizations have fought over who will lead in securing U.S. computer networks, who should supervise and launch offensive cyberwarfare—which includes disrupting enemy websites, attacking enemy financial and electrical systems, and planting deceptive information on networks—and who should be responsible for tracking spies, hackers, and other intruders.

Although a new military Cyber Command was inaugurated in 2010 to coordinate and manage cybersecurity, warfare, and espio-nage, the Department of Homeland Security created its own cyber-security apparatus, while the FBI, CIA, NSA, and at least three other major military commands each had large cyberdivisions of their own. In all, twenty-one federal organizations dealing with this same issue had been established after 9/11. And not only did much of their efforts directly overlap, but a good portion of their energy was spent not in improving efficiency but battling for insti-tutional supremacy.

Part of the reason agencies were still haggling over which one would lead the others was the financial windfall to be gained from coming out on top. Such a windfall would be counted in billions of dollars, to be spent internally or—in a pattern increasingly common in Top Secret America—on contracts to private corporations.

"Sometimes there was an unfortunate attitude of bring your knives, your guns, your fists and be fully prepared to defend your turf," recalled Benjamin A. Powell, who served as general counsel for three directors of national intelligence until he left the government in 2009. Why? "Because," Powell explained, "it's funded, it's hot, and it's sexy." For Washington-based agencies, the Global War on Terrorism was a far-off one, in someone else's country; the War over Money was tangible, immediate, and waged with every bureaucratic weapon available. Watching the squabbles firsthand, it was often difficult to tell which was the priority, fighting terror or fighting for funds.

Another area bogged down with redundancy was influence operations, called IO. Some of the overlap was due to the disturbing fact that few in government could even agree on what the term IO meant. The White House National Security Council created a new committee to lead the effort to reach out to Muslims in the United States and abroad. Meanwhile, the Strategic Command, where the discipline of influence operations was born, began a Partnership to Defeat Terrorism unit to come up with pro-democracy messages it would broadcast overseas in Muslim countries in which support for U.S. counterterrorist actions was not very strong. And the military Special Operations Command spent tens of millions of dollars to help U.S. embassies throughout the world create pro-America media campaigns, for use by host governments, some of them clandestine in order to obscure the role of the United States.

But that was hardly the end of it. Some of the money devoted to influence operations ended up in the Defense Policy Analysis Office because part of IO involves military deception, DPAO's job, according to several sources. Elena Mastors, who worked in DPAO for several years trying to come up with a way to influence the thinking of terrorists, concluded that there were simply too many people in the office, and far too many of them didn't know anything about terrorists associated with Islamic fundamentalism, which is who they were trying to deceive.

"We are too big," said Mastors, who left DPAO in 2007, disgusted by how many people without any expertise were assigned to the office. "We don't need all these people doing all this stuff. You just need a group of really smart people.... But it just keeps growing. Someone says, let's do another study, and because no one shares information, everyone does their own study.... It's about how many studies can you orchestrate" and "how many people can you fly all over the place" to conferences and seminars.

Nobody was arguing that all influence operations programs needed to be under one roof. But at the same time, it seemed impossible to defend the fact that in Top Secret America even those qualified to do something ended up being squeezed and squashed and distracted by internal rivals. "Everybody's just on a spending spree," Mastors said ruefully. "It wouldn't be so bad if it wasn't duplication."

Over time, we discovered that one of DPAO's missions was to create fissures within terrorist groups and deceive them about U.S. operations. It was supposed to create false online personas who would enter certain chat rooms to gain more information about potential terrorists and to spread false rumors about them. It also disrupted website communications and dreamed up other operations that several senior Pentagon officials described as not very useful.

DPAO was just one small part of the duplicative U.S. government image machine. When the Pentagon decided it needed a better way to communicate its message to the people of Iraq and Afghanistan, it created at least ten classified programs that cost $9 million in fiscal year 2005. Within five years, those programs had grown to "a staggering $988 million request" for fiscal year 2010. A 2011 House Appropriations Committee report noted that many items in the Pentagon's request appeared "alarmingly non-military," careening into areas where the armed forces had little or no expertise, including "propaganda, public relations, and behavior modification messaging." This was another characteristic of Top Secret America, that every department and agency believed it needed control over its own influence operations, its own cyberoperations, its own counterterrorism analysts, its own everything. Congress did try to do something to rein in the IO spending by paring down the Pentagon programs in the appropriations budget. At the same time, Defense Secretary Robert Gates, responding to those congressional concerns, put a hold on the new programs until his office could determine if the projects were wastefully redundant or helpful. That pause didn't last long: General David Petraeus, then commander of the U.S. Central Command in charge of U.S. forces in Afghanistan, Iraq, and the larger Middle East, lobbied the armed services committees, saying his programs in this area were critical to the mission's success. Because Congress was dependent on Petraeus for success in those two war zones, and trusted he knew best, most of the money was restored.

Not only was redundancy resistant to reduction, it had a way of multiplying. When roadside bombs (called IEDs, for improvised explosive devices) became the greatest cause of casualties in Iraq, the army set up an IED task force to investigate ways to stop these crude weapons. The Marine Corps, too, set up a working group. Finally, the Pentagon established a Washington-based joint organization—the Joint Improvised Explosive Device Defeat Organization, or JIEDDO, to undertake a militarywide effort to counter this deadly, low-tech terrorist weapon.

JIEDDO is a perfect example of how an ad hoc crisis task force can become a permanent multi-billion-dollar agency. Working from undisclosed office buildings in Crystal City, Reston, and Charlottesville, Virginia, JIEDDO has grown to about four hundred military, civilian, and contractor personnel. In fiscal year 2010, to deal with the surge of U.S. troops into Afghanistan, the JIEDDO budget increased from an initial $1.88 billion to $2.98

billion, and then to $3.465 billion. JIEDDO had so much money that it hired 1,200 contractors, according to the Government Accountability Office.[6] It also oversees more than three hundred research projects aimed at stopping IED attacks. It has developed its own intelligence agency (which will compete and overlap with other, existing intelligence services—themselves overlapping with each other), its own training facilities, and its own top secret "special activities." It even has its own air force.

That the army and marines each had their own expensive, non-collaborating IED-related projects going was not the end of the military's budget-related interest in the subject. The availability of funds for counter-IED projects prompted each of the services to create its own IED Center of Excellence, a common military slogan for a research center. One senior official at the contracting giant SAIC admitted that each of these centers is replicating the same work, even cross-hiring the exact same contractors. If one defense of the overlap was that having multiple, independent efforts might more quickly lead to a solution, the fact that nearly everyone was using the same contractors to provide expertise meant the fresh ideas were limited.

One of the most duplicated tasks of all was that of "fusion," the collection of information from myriad sources to be organized and analyzed for a fuller picture of terrorist or other threats. Arkin called government agencies for a complete list of all fusion centers in the area, and I visited half a dozen of them to see what they each produced. It was obvious these had proliferated by the dozens after 9/11. Arkin made another one of his charts to show them all. In the Washington region alone there were thirty-one national fusion, or watch, centers. They monitored everything from CNN to the latest top secret satellite images. With the exception of a few places that meshed incoming intelligence reports in order to come up

---

[6] The U.S. Government Accountability Office (GAO), established in 1921, is an independent budget and accounting agency that works for Congress. GAO investigates how the federal government spends taxpayer dollars, and the head of GAO is the comptroller general of the United States.

with terrorist targets for soldiers in the field, most fusion centers were simply a kind of super-briefing machine for senior leaders, one that replaced the PowerPoint presentations of the 1990s with flat-screen interactive, geo-located presentations.

For example, at the National Maritime Intelligence Center in Suitland, Maryland, an enormous fusion center collected information for its leaders on the real-time location and ownership of commercial vessels around the world; but there was nothing in particular that the center's senior people did with the information. Instead, it was the responsibility of a completely different set of four-star commanders with their own separate fusion centers to make operational or military policy decisions regarding those vessels—and they obviously didn't need another fusion center near Washington advising them when they had their own.

The same was true for the new whiz-bang fusion center at the Special Operations Command in Tampa. Its two-story video wall, and the real-time images from overseas that could be fed into it, allowed commanders standing in the room to monitor the location of Special Operations Forces around the world on a minute-by-minute basis. But those leaders weren't the ones who made decisions about those troops. They didn't oversee or conduct operations, nor did they direct intelligence gathering. Those who did make the relevant decisions got their information from elsewhere, so the value of having a center that cost tens of millions of dollars to set up and maintain a real-time view of operations was not at all clear, although it made the commanders feel in the loop.

Most fusion centers look similar, with the same rows or clusters of computer stations facing two or three wall-sized television screens and maps. More elaborate centers have a VIP balcony where senior policy makers, members of Congress, admirals, and generals can watch the inaction from above. The experience is not that different from sitting in a movie balcony watching six very slow-moving films at once.

The issue of wasteful duplication, represented by the many fusion centers, the many agencies doing the same work, the many contracts and research projects on information operations, was not just a question of money down the drain. Sometimes redundancy actually impeded an agency's mission. Lack of disciplined focus, not lack of resources, was one of the reasons why no one in the army's gigantic counterintelligence apparatus ever gave proper weight to flashing warning signs of budding extremists within its own organization. A good example of this was army major Nidal Malik Hasan's alleged murder of thirteen colleagues and wounding of another thirty-two at Fort Hood, Texas, in November 2009.

In the days after the shootings, one of my good sources sent me a PowerPoint slide Hasan had presented to medical school colleagues the year before. It showed how Muslims in the army could become alienated from the military if they were asked to kill other Muslims. The army, Hasan recommended, should offer these soldiers a way to leave the service, or it would risk "adverse events."

Some of Hasan's medical colleagues thought the presentation was bizarre, but some of his instructors thought the study gave them a good opportunity to understand a different mind-set—not Hasan's, but that of other Muslims in the army he was presumably describing. They did not see him as a threat, just a little odd.

As the doctors and psychiatrists at Walter Reed Hospital pondered the insights Hasan laid out, the one organization charged with identifying actual threats within the army had no idea anything was amiss. Just twenty-five miles up the road from Walter Reed, the Army's 902nd Military Intelligence Group—the largest counterintelligence organization in Top Secret America—had been doing little to train army personnel on indicators of radicalization. They hadn't even been searching army ranks for violent Islamic extremists, although this was, in fact, the 902nd's main mandate. Nor did the 902nd have a good working relationship with the FBI counterterrorism units that had begun—and then dropped—an investigation of Hasan after they'd found emails between him and a well-known English-speaking radical cleric in Yemen, Anwar Awlaki, whom U.S. intelligence had identified as a terrorism facilitator and was monitoring.

In fact, instead of figuring out how to find radicalized soldiers, the 902nd, which was directly responsible for finding spies and terrorists within army ranks, was busy creating a program to do what the FBI and the Department of Homeland Security were already mandated to do: the much sexier job of assessing the general terrorist threat in the United States. Working under a program its commander named RITA, for Radical Islamic Threat to the Army, the 902nd special agents and intelligence analysts had quietly been gathering information on Hezbollah, Iranian Republican Guard Corps, and al-Qaeda student organizations in the United States. Despite the fact that RITA had consumed the attention of the 902nd for a year, the assessment "didn't tell us anything we didn't know already," the army's senior counterintelligence officer told me later, in the aftermath of Hasan's rampage. It was another case of wasteful duplication, and of another real job—radicalization within army ranks—left unattended.

Lack of coordination had plagued the counterterrorism effort before 9/11 but became a huge problem in the years that followed—and remains so today. Better coordination was supposed to have been addressed in 2004, when the Bush administration and Congress set up yet another organization to take charge of the whole mess. In the middle of that year's election season, the 9/11 Commission proposed the creation of the Office of the Director of National Intelligence to direct and manage every agency and coordinate them all. Democratic presidential hopeful Senator John Kerry immediately endorsed the commission's recommendations. Bush followed soon afterward.

But the leaders of the intelligence agencies were horrified. Restructuring the entire intelligence universe, in the midst of two wars—a deteriorating battle of attrition in Iraq and a festering insurgency in Afghanistan—and with al-Qaeda leader Osama bin Laden still at large, Somalia crashing toward failed statehood, and the safety of the 2004 Summer Olympics in Greece in question, seemed extremely reckless. The window for concern stretched forward, too: the newly created National Counterterrorism Center and its FBI counterpart, the Joint Terrorism Task Force, had already been hastily moving into their new secret building in northern Virginia to be in place for the election, an event analysts worried might be an occasion for a terrorist attack.

The NSA's Hayden said the timing for such a massive reorganization was all wrong: "If you'd have asked me and the other leaders of the community...we would have said, 'Oh, we don't think this is a real good idea. We're kind of busy right now. Restructuring is not at the top of our agenda." Many of those in charge believed that the Central Intelligence Agency, which was supposed to coordinate and help manage the work of all U.S. intelligence agencies in addition to performing its espionage and analysis role, should simply be given more authority and more resources to do a better job as chief manager. But that was not the plan of those on Pennsylvania Avenue, and mainly for political reasons—to soothe the grieving 9/11 families and make it appear to the American people that the president was taking decisive action.

Hayden and his colleagues believed that for the new position to work as intended, its leader would have to be given clear authority to overrule the various agency heads and to manage the overall budget. But the law that Congress was about to pass (the Intelligence Reform and Terrorism Prevention Act) gave the DNI *responsibility* over all intelligence matters, not *authority* over all intelligence matters. It was a crippling distinction. Hayden had been right: for the position to work, the DNI had to be the supreme authority. But the Intelligence Reform and Terrorism Prevention Act had been cast poorly; in reality, none of the agencies wanted to give up the power they had over their budgets, personnel, and mission, and neither did the many congressional committees that supervised them and funded them. These committees were the source of real power in Washington. President Bush wanted to satisfy the 9/11 families, who blamed the structure of the intelligence community for the failure to prevent the terrorist attacks. He was not willing, however, to take on entrenched interests. Many senior officials in his administration did not think the reorganization was even necessary.

Still, the week before Christmas 2004, Bush signed into law the most sweeping changes in the intelligence world since the National Security Act of 1947. The law was so obviously problematic that the president of Texas A&M University, Robert Gates, turned down the position of director, in part because the job description didn't even include the power to hire and fire. Ambassador John D. Negroponte, a respected diplomat but not an expert in the more contentious field of intelligence, was the backup choice.

Even before Negroponte reported for work, turf battles began. The Defense Department shifted billions of dollars out of one budget (the national intelligence budget) and into another (the military intelligence program) so that the Office of the Director of National Intelligence would have only advisory status, according to two senior officials who watched the process. The CIA promptly reclassified some of its most sensitive information at a higher level so that the multiagency National Counterterrorism Center staff, now part of the Office of the Director of National Intelligence, would not be allowed to see it, said former intelligence officers involved.

They got away with it because the new organization had no power to compel them to share anything. Without authority by law, the success of any DNI has come to depend on personal relationships, most important among them those he is able to establish with the chiefs of the separate intelligence agencies. "The original concept of a DNI was that an empowered DNI . . . could have overview of the entire thing," Gates later told me. "My view is that the compromises that were made in passing the Intelligence Reform Act really inhibited the ability of the DNI to carry out what most people thought the DNI should do."

The DNI, Gates said, was more like the chairman of a powerful committee than the CEO of a company. "He has authorities and he has power, but, at the end of the day, he's got to sort of lead and persuade people to follow in all these disparate organizations." That "sort of" hedge was indicative of the fuzziness that accompanied any assessment of the office's actual leverage. Perhaps not surprisingly, those who accepted the job found it tremendously frustrating. In the time-honored way of Washington, the older institutions, with their congressional backers and special-interest associations, worked to undermine the new kid on the block, and by 2010, there had been five DNIs in less than six years, and many intelligence officials remained unclear about just what the DNI was actually in charge of. Retired admiral Dennis Blair, who served as the director of national intelligence from the beginning of the Obama administration until May 2010, told me that things were improving; that he didn't really believe there was overlap and redundancy in the intelligence world. "Much of what appears to be redundancy is, in fact, providing tailored intelligence for many different customers." But, in his own case, the fact that the DNI had such little authority was a big reason he no longer had the job.

Blair insisted progress was being made on many issues that have dogged the intelligence community for years. The FBI and CIA were getting along better, he said. The NSA had sped up the time it took to get relevant intercepts and other data to fighters on the ground so they could use it to find targets to strike. The Defense Department and the DNI were trying to coordinate better on budget matters, information sharing, and lines of authority.

When Blair was director, his model for change had been the historic 1986 Goldwater-Nichols[7] legislation that had reorganized the Defense Department, forcing the separate military services to work together more effectively. Blair hosted interagency meetings every day to promote collaboration. He addressed banal problems no one else wanted to take on but which he considered crucial to making progress—changing the way new technology was pur-

---

[7] The Goldwater-Nichols Defense Department Reorganization Act, passed in 1986, was meant to eliminate the destructive rivalries between the military services and to force them to work better together. It elevated the chairman of the Joint Chiefs of Staff to the role of principal military adviser to the president, with the chiefs of all services acting as advisers to the chairman. To force better cooperation in wartime, it put one four-star commander in charge of all military forces and operations within a specific geographic region—the Central Command, for example. All the service chiefs opposed the act at the time of its creation. Many experts have repeatedly called for a Goldwater-Nichols II to reorganize, and force better cooperation between, all national security agencies. The DNI is a pale version of the chairman's role under the act.

chased, setting up compatible computer networks and standard security classifications, establishing a common set of tradecraft standards so people from one agency could better understand what people from another agency actually did. If analysts used different terms for the same thing, how could an analyst from one agency ever understand an analyst from another? If spies used different vetting procedures for their confidential sources, how could anyone judge the credibility of a source's information? Blair also established a common type of job evaluation and pushed hard at getting people from different agencies to work together collegially.

But the sheer size of the post-9/11 expansion seemed to overtake the positive changes. "There has been so much growth since 9/11," said Gates, "that getting your arms around that—not just for the DNI, but for any individual, for the director of CIA, for the secretary of defense—is a challenge."

Size was a problem for the Office of the Director of National Intelligence, too. The agency that was established to manage the growth quickly became a symbol itself of the ever-expanding universe of top secret activities.

When it opened in the spring of 2005, the Office of the Director of National Intelligence's eleven employees were stuffed into a secure vault in the New Executive Office Building one block from the White House. They taped butcher paper to the walls to draw up their first ideas about restructuring. A year later, the office took over two floors of the gigantic new Defense Intelligence Agency headquarters at Bolling Air Force Base.

But in April 2008, the DNI moved again, this time to a permanent home, a 500,000-square-foot superstructure in pricey McLean, Virginia, with two parking garages and a suspended glass-enclosed cafeteria. Now, every weekday morning outside a subdivision of mansions, a line of cars wait patiently to turn left, then crawl up a hill and around a bend to a destination that is not on any public map and not announced by any street sign.

Liberty Crossing, as the place is nicknamed, tries hard to hide from view. But in the winter, leafless trees can't conceal a mountain of cement and windows the size of five Walmart stores stacked on top of one another rising behind a grassy berm. One step too close without the right badge, and men in black jump out of nowhere, guns at the ready.

Past the armed guards and the hydraulic steel barriers, at least 1,700 federal employees and 1,200 private contractors work at the Office of the Director of National Intelligence and the adjoining National Counterterrorism Center. The NCTC is supposed to be the agency leading all analysis of terrorism and advising the president and other agency heads on operations. The two organizations share a police force, a canine unit, and thousands of parking spaces.

The practical effect of the Office of the Director of National Intelligence's unwieldy expansion was visible, on a much smaller scale, in the office of Michael Leiter, the director of the National Counterterrorism Center until 2011. Leiter spent much of his day flipping among four computer monitors lined up on his desk. Six hard drives sat at his feet. The data flow was enormous, with dozens of databases feeding separate computer networks that cannot interact with one another.

There was a long explanation for why these databases were still not connected, and it amounted to this: It's complicated to do, and some agency heads don't really want to give up the systems they have. But there was some progress: "All my e-mail is on one computer now," Leiter explained one day in his office. "That's a big deal."

Because so much is classified, illustrations of what goes on every day in Top Secret America can be hard to ferret out. But every so often, examples emerge. One, from the fall of 2010, showed the post–9/11 system simultaneously at its best and at its worst.

After eight years of effort and growth, counterterrorism operations to locate and kill leaders of an al-Qaeda affiliate in Yemen were at full throttle. Terrorists in Yemen were thought to be actively plotting to strike the American homeland, and, in response, President Obama had signed an order sending dozens of secret commandos there. The commandos had set up a joint operations center in Yemen and packed it with consoles, hard drives, forensic

kits, and communications gear. They exchanged thousands of intercepts, agent reports, photographic evidence, and real-time video surveillance with dozens of top-secret organizations serving their needs
from the United States.

That was the system as it was intended.

But when that dreaded but awaited intelligence about threats
originating in Yemen reached the National Counterterrorism Center for analysis, it arrived buried within the daily load of thousands
of snippets of general terrorist-related data from around the world
that Leiter said all needed to be given equal attention.

Instead of searching one network of computerized intelligence
reports, NCTC analysts had to switch from database to database,
from hard drive to hard drive, from screen to screen, merely to
locate the Yemen material that might be interesting to study further. If they wanted raw material—transcripts of voice intercepts
or email exchanges that had not been analyzed and condensed by
the CIA or NSA—they had to use liaison officers assigned to those
agencies to try to find it, or call people they happened to know
there and try to persuade them to locate it. As secret U.S. military
operations in Yemen intensified and the chatter about a possible
terrorist strike in the United States increased, the intelligence
agencies further ramped up their effort. That meant that the flood
of information coming into the NCTC became a torrent, a fire
hose instead of an eyedropper.

Somewhere in that deluge was Umar Farouk Abdulmutallab.
He showed up in bits and pieces. In August, NSA intercepted
al-Qaeda conversations about an unidentified "Nigerian." They
had only a partial name. In September, the NSA intercepted a
communication about Awlaki—the very same person Major Hasan
had contacted—facilitating transportation for someone through
Yemen. There was also a report from the CIA station in Nigeria of
a father who was worried about his son because he had become
interested in radical teachings and had gone to Yemen.

But even at a time of intense secret military operations going
on in the country, the many clues to what was about to happen

went missing in the immensity and complexity of the counterterrorism system. Abdulmutallab left Yemen, returned to Nigeria, and on December 16 purchased a one-way ticket to the United States. Once again, connections hiding in plain sight went unnoticed.

"There are so many people involved here," Leiter later told Congress.

"Everyone had the dots to connect," DNI Blair explained to lawmakers. "But I hadn't made it clear exactly who had primary responsibility."

Waltzing through the gaping holes in the security net, Abdulmutallab was able to step aboard Northwest Airlines Flight 253 without any difficulty. As the plane descended toward Detroit, he returned from the bathroom with a pillow over his stomach and tried to ignite explosives hidden in his underwear. And just as the billions of dollars and tens of thousands of security-cleared personnel of the massive 9/11 apparatus hadn't prevented Abdulmutallab from getting to this moment, it did nothing now to prevent disaster. Instead, a Dutch video producer, Jasper Schuringa, dove across four airplane seats to tackle the twenty-three-year-old when he saw him trying to light something on fire.

The secretary of Homeland Security, Janet Napolitano, was the first to address the public afterward. She was happy to announce that "once the incident occurred, the system worked." The next day, however, she admitted the system that had allowed him onto the plane with an explosive had "failed miserably."

"We didn't follow up and prioritize the stream of intelligence," White House counterterrorism adviser John O. Brennan explained later, "because no one intelligence entity, or team, or task force, was assigned responsibility for doing that follow-up investigation."

Incredible as it was, after all this time, after all these reorganizations, after all the money spent to get things right, no one person was actually responsible for counterterrorism.

And no one is responsible today, either.

Blair, acknowledging the problem, created yet another new team to run down every important lead. He also told congressional leaders he needed something from them: more money and more analysts. Leiter, the director of the NCTC, also pleaded for more analysts to join the roughly three hundred he already had working on terrorism. For its part, the Department of Homeland Security asked for more air marshals, for more and better body scanners and more analysts, too, even though it can't find nearly enough qualified people to fill its intelligence unit, and instead must resort to hiring more contractors.

In Top Secret America, more is often the solution.

By 2010, in the middle of the longest recession ever, the budget for intelligence had become 250 percent larger than it was on September 10, 2001, without anyone in government seriously trying to figure out where the overlaps and waste were. No one was trying to figure out where all the ineffective programs were, either. The budget had been estimated to be $75 billion a year, which did not include all the military's spending on counterterrorism and intelligence. Then, out of the blue, the newly appointed director of national intelligence, James Clapper, announced in October that the total was $80.1 billion. That did not even include $58 billion for the Department of Homeland Security. Nor did it include all the billions of dollars spent by the Defense Department on counterterrorism and homeland security through its gigantic Northern Command in Colorado.

Clapper had become DNI after Blair resigned when it became evident that, without a close relationship with Obama, his power had greatly diminished. His departure left a revealing void: even the person who was supposed to be in charge wasn't in charge at all. Without anyone in charge, there was even less of a chance that Top Secret America could right itself.

CHAPTER SIX

One Nation, One Map

In the basement of a newly renovated building in Colorado, an army of people in uniform and shirtsleeves is working on a map of North America unlike any ever created. It is a multidimensional, multimedia, top secret compendium of very specific data accumulating at a dizzying rate. The ultimate dream of those behind it is to be able to point to any block in any city in the United States and gain instant access to the expanding universe of digitized information for that location, from speed cameras to wireless network signals, street level photography and video, property records, electricity consumption, floor plans and security layouts, even traffic light sequences. Also incoming would be ultra-high-resolution imagery that can peer into backyards, and other advanced technologies available to pinpoint activity inside the walls of an office building, power station, or, with proper approval, a private home, from the living room to the bathroom to the children's bedrooms.

Some of the users of this unprecedented surveillance tool are based inside Northern Command, America's newest military command, and the first in modern times to be focused not on some distant outpost of the world but on America itself. Evidence of their focus can be seen in the poster mounted on one office wall, stark letters declaring their mission: One Nation, One Map.

Until the attacks on New York and Washington in 2001, the military on home soil planned overseas wars and watched for incoming missiles and bombers but was only otherwise barely focused on the American interior. But then a handful of men in sports attire, armed only with airline tickets and razor blades, demonstrated the nation's vulnerability not to another army but to a small organization using unconventional methods of warfare. Overnight, airports, bridges and power grids, reservoirs and food supplies—all became potential targets in the eyes of the people charged with protecting against another 9/11-style attack. The October 2001 anthrax incidents, which were immediately (and wrongfully) assumed to be the work of international terrorists, added to the belief that another multiple-target and even a multiple-mode attack, including one involving weapons of mass destruction, was in the cards.

Members of a terrorist force otherwise indistinguishable from legal residents and even American citizens, willing to die for their cause, could strike anywhere. Suddenly the familiar grid of city streets and ribbons of interstate highways and electricity distribution had become a potential battlefield. Defense of the homeland meant building a deep knowledge of the facilities in cities and towns across the country.

For the past century, protecting American territory has been the responsibility of civil authorities and state governments. In the post-9/11 war against al-Qaeda, though, internal security has increasingly become a federal matter, and one in which the Department of Defense is at the center. Through Northern Command, no fewer than eighteen generals and admirals—men who once commanded combat troops in Iraq and Afghanistan, or prepared for missions against the Soviet Union and China—have as their sole focus defending the North American continent.

That defense is coordinated from a cluster of gleaming white buildings at Peterson Air Force Base, on the edge of Colorado Springs. By gargantuan national security standards, Northern Command, or NorthCom, as military people call it, is tiny, both in cost and in its call on resources. (It is indicative of the titanic sums spent in the post-9/11 era that NorthCom's costs are considered minuscule even though its refurbishment required $100 million.) But its place in Top Secret America's complex geography is significant; those eighteen generals and admirals are supplemented by eleven generals from the reserves and National Guard[1] also in residence at NorthCom headquarters, all of them officers who have been activated and federalized to tend to the day-to-day duties of national homeland defense. Another five National Guard officers are stationed in Washington, DC, with specific domestic contingency planning responsibilities at the Pentagon. In turn, they are backed up by more than 250 additional generals belonging to the National Guard, the old militia force born of the colonial-era minutemen and drawing on a tradition that treated local security and enforcement of laws as a local matter.

At multiple facilities stretching from Florida to the nation's capital, from Texas to Alaska and Hawaii, Northern Command's leaders work with a staff of three thousand people—including hundreds of contractors, lawyers, and intelligence officers in subordinate air, army, and navy commands.

---

[1] The National Guard, the oldest component of the armed forces, traces its history back to the earliest English colonies. Responsible for their own defense from Indian attack and foreign invaders, the colonists organized their able-bodied male citizens into militias. These militias later helped to win the Revolutionary War, and the Constitution recognized them as a separate entity from the federal armed forces, giving the states the power to appoint officers and raise and train their own forces. In World War I, the Guard was called into federal service to fight overseas for the first time, and since then its ranks have been outnumbered by permanent standing federal forces. Since 9/11, multiple headquarters in each state have been consolidated into a Joint Force Headquarters (JFHQ), streamlining command and control more in line with federal forces. States have also signed various compacts allowing militias to be used across state lines, and the federal government has gained more control over the Guard, which has developed a larger Washington headquarters and greater political influence.

Northern Command has additionally spawned a series of new organizations with the intention of making the National Guard more than just a state militia, allowing it to mobilize across state borders and handle duties of both martial law, should it ever be declared, and domestic intelligence, which focuses on Washington's counterterrorism and homeland security priorities. Hidden beyond talk of cooperation and modernization and the post-9/11 patter of a singular national security effort, the effect is to have quietly transformed the Guard from fifty-four local entities into a single force shorn of the federal-state distinctions at the core of American governance since its inception.

In order to coordinate this massive new federal undertaking, Northern Command officials needed to know a colossal and unprecedented amount of information. For example, to fulfill their immediate task of supporting civil authorities in crisis, Northern Command planners needed to know runway length in each of 5,000 public airports in America, the weight limits of tens of thousands of highway bridges, and locations and capacity of fuel storage facilities that might supply military operations. Disease watchers, on alert for a biological or chemical attack, needed access to near-real-time reports on water quality in 1,800 federal reservoirs and 1,600 municipal wastewater facilities. WMD specialists wanted to know the location and potential vulnerability of each of America's 66,000 industrial chemical plants and every source of radiological material, be it a nuclear power plant or hospital, a university research lab or a nuclear bunker.

As with most projects begun in the aftermath of 9/11, the Pentagon and the federal government marched forward with the assumption that they needed to start from scratch. But the real detail of fire and police stations, hospitals and schools — all of which would turn into national security outposts or could become rallying points and shelters after a natural disaster or terrorist action — resided at the state and local levels, where emergency managers and first responders were already collecting this information.

The mapping of the homeland fell principally to the National

Geospatial-Intelligence Agency (NGA), one of the largest three-letter Washington-based members of the intelligence community.

Now responding to the needs of two new organizations—NorthCom on the military side and the Department of Homeland Security on the civilian side—NGA, with the assistance of the U.S. Geological Survey, began to apply to the United States the mapping matrix it used for battles overseas. The Homeland Security Infrastructure Program, the formal name for the NGA's mapping effort, began in 2005 with over three hundred layers of data, including everything from political boundaries to chemical facilities, hotels, Internet service provider locations, school buildings, and water bottling stations. The objective was to identify critical infrastructure out of a database of some eleven million facilities—bridges, dams, power lines, factories, communications towers—essential to public safety and the continued functioning of the economy. The focus was on the 120 most important urban areas, encompassing more than 80 percent of the population, but the number was soon increased to 133 when planners were embarrassed by the realization that thirteen state capitals had been left off the priority list. For some areas, such as the southern border, even more detailed mapping was ordered up: illegal infiltration routes, the locations of border security cameras and motion sensors, and security gaps, including the improvised tunnels under the border. Much, but not all, of this information was already available on the Internet or from commercial vendors, but the government had a particular need for consistency, detail, and pinpoint accuracy so that it could be assured that there would be identical displays of relevant information across federal, state, and local jurisdictions.

By necessity, the map, which has primarily focused on those 133 cities and on border security and drug enforcement in the Southwest since 9/11, will always be a work in progress. Construction, revamped traffic patterns, additional cell phone towers, campus expansion projects—all of these and more needed to be accounted for, while new requirements and uses may be identified. Some locations, like the southern border and the nation's capital, are nearly fully mapped and wired for detailed surveillance. Less high-profile places remain very much works in progress.

Nevertheless, the displays that can already be pulled together in the NorthCom command center are awe-inspiring. Everything that can be portrayed in an automated way is brought together into what is called the "common operating picture": real-time tracking of thousands of commercial and military aircraft, naval and commercial shipping activity; alerts of computer viruses; imagery of satellite orbits; pinpoint tracking data on the whereabouts of the president and other top officials; and the immediate status of all active and reserve military forces, including troop strength, battle readiness, and alert condition. Some threat intelligence has also been included—missile launches and other "hot" events detected by infrared warning satellites; radar emissions automatically logged by ground, marine, air, and satellite interceptors; video feeds from drones and reconnaissance aircraft.

In the main operations room of the basement command center, rows of watch-officer desks face a video wall of twelve screens, six feet by six feet, which is being fed cable television channels and situational awareness data—maps and reconnaissance images that spell out the location of assets and threats and show who is where and what is moving. The latest and "hottest" images are capped by "box scores" that grade the up-to-the-minute status of North American defense: air, land, maritime, space, and cyber. Box scores is an apt term: to the uninitiated, the columns and figures are meaningless, but like expert baseball junkies, watch officers and planners see the whole game in an instant, from a Federal Aviation Administration (FAA) alert of an airliner incoming to Los Angeles that's squawking on a wrong frequency, to a hit on a radiation detector in the Port of Baltimore, to a winter storm closing in on the Midwest that has put the Federal Emergency Management Agency (FEMA) on alert.

Around the room's walls are more monitors with additional box scores showing the current level of command center security classification, which depends on who is present and what type of information is being presented; local times around the world; the status of the restricted airspace around the National Capital Region; the DEFCON (defense readiness condition) of the U.S. military worldwide; and other alert levels. The command duty officer, who sits in the middle of the rows of desks, can put the contents of any computer monitor up on the large video wall, including the dozens of chat windows that are constantly occupied and monitored by groups of analysts and specialists. The list goes on and on: at any one time, the command's staff is typically monitoring and providing assistance in as many as half a dozen declarations of presidential emergency for floods or storms; keeping an eye on more than one hundred active duty units operating outside military bases; logging counterdrug and border missions being conducted in support of the Department of Homeland Security or the Drug Enforcement Agency; keeping tabs on reconnaissance and unmanned drone flights over America—all the while following the news media as they would an enemy's maneuvers, all the way down to perusing a daily document prepared by Northern Command's press office listing which military and local reporters are working on what stories, and what, even before the stories are published, the "talking points" should be in response.

The main entrance of NorthCom headquarters, with its austere banks of narrow strip windows and the central rocket-shaped glass-to-the-sky atrium, suggests a space motif fitting for the previous tenant, Space Command,[2] before it was moved to Omaha and merged with yet another major military organization, Strategic Command. The existing 140,000-square-foot structure, just a thou-

---

[2] U.S. Space Command (SPACECOM), established in 1984 and shut down in 1992, was previously one of the unified joint commands with functional rather than geographic responsibilities—military operations, weapons, exercises, plans, and strategy related to space. Headquartered at Peterson AFB, its commander was "triple-hatted," serving also as commander in chief, North American Air Defense Command, and commander, Air Force Space Command.

sand feet from Highway 24 on the northern edge of the Colorado Springs Municipal Airport, was expanded by 20 percent in that $100 million renovation. A second glass atrium was built along the length of what used to be the building's rear, creating a long glass-topped promenade between the old structure and a new two-story annex. In contrast to this soaring grandeur, outside is a remarkably modest 9/11 memorial—a Pentagon-shaped planter filled with Pennsylvania soil and a protruding steel beam from one of the twin towers.

NorthCom's headquarters is pointedly not hidden away in an impregnable or secret location. Though the command began out of a temporary headquarters in the iconic Cheyenne Mountain bunker of the joint U.S.-Canadian North American Aerospace Defense Command operations center, Pentagon brass resisted that cold war trope of survivability underground and moved the group into its renovated quarters to allow it to remain accessible to its nonmilitary partners. The rationale is symbolic of a new kind of command for a new kind of war, a war in which information and coordination are at least as important as old-fashioned defenses thought to be secure—and one in which private companies are so intimately involved that proximity to them has become a tactical necessity.

But there is an underground contingency plan. Just in case the new command headquarters is attacked, NorthCom and its sister command—NORAD, which detects and scrutinizes every Russian, Chinese, North Korean, or Iranian missile launch, day and night—both maintain subterranean backups at the mountain. And just in case everything goes down—command headquarters, the mountain, the nation's telephone system, and the electrical grid—NorthCom also operates a fleet of six giant eighty-foot-long eighteen-wheel trucks sitting ready on twenty-four-hour alert in a barricaded compound at F. E. Warren Air Force Base, outside Cheyenne, Wyoming. The trucks, officially called the Mobile Consolidated Command Center, could take to the highways at a moment's notice in a fifty-vehicle security convoy. A super-secret unit created to survive a full-scale nuclear war, they contain everything required— their own generators, SCIFs, a top secret local area network, satellite dishes, codes, and emergency decision handbooks—to direct a response to multiple terrorist attacks, launch American nuclear weapons, or even take over command of the United States government, if necessary.

NorthCom and NORAD's combined basement command center is about the size of a large department store. The sprawling rooms with their laminated desks and cookie-cutter cubicle appointments are the epitome of government drab and information age wired. Discreet cameras and ceiling-mounted projectors with dual screens fuel the ubiquitous PowerPoint briefings and video-teleconferencing (VTC) that connect the staff here with the far-flung bureaucracy. In the small conference room—called, creatively, "the Small Conference Room"—a dozen computer monitors clutter the table. Each monitor has a green and a red sticker affixed at the top, reminding users they can connect to both the unclassified and the secret-level networks. For security purposes, each monitor also has a cover, a leatherette protector that mostly dangles behind on two Velcro-attached tabs but can be flipped over the screen when someone who doesn't have a security clearance is present.

Next door is the even more closed-off intelligence "egg" (each of the separate sections in the basement command center is called an egg by NorthComers), which mirrors the other area's functions but operates at classified levels beyond the access of most of the NorthCom staff and most of the Canadians who work here. Monitors include feeds from the three-letter intelligence agencies—CIA, NGA, NSA, NRO,[3] DIA—via several sources: the Modernized Integrated Database, which tracks foreign military forces and infrastructure; the National Threat and Incident Data-

---

[3] The National Reconnaissance Office (NRO), established in September 1961, was originally a classified joint agency of the DoD and the CIA. Its existence and its mission—satellite reconnaissance—were officially declassified in September 1992. Headquartered in Chantilly, Virginia, the NRO designs, builds, and, with the air force, operates the nation's reconnaissance satellites, which collect imagery, geospatial intelligence, source data, and signals intelligence data for the intelligence community, of which it is a member. Most of its satellites are built and maintained by private corporations.

base, which tracks up-to-the-minute intelligence on terrorist activity; customized military and intelligence maps that receive feeds from other, automated databases that monitor the physical and cybersecurity of the industrial and utilities sectors; the CIPFIN[4] portal, which keeps an eye on the same in the commercial finance sector; and the Medical Situational Awareness Tool, which tracks disease outbreaks and potential pandemics.

At top secret classification levels that narrow access even further, analysts use even more databases: terrorist watchlists; the National Counterterrorism Center Online terrorism "datamart," a repository of more than seven million terrorism documents and the only interagency forum that exchanges counterterrorism information derived from spies; and GIANT, the tool that monitors the health and security of the ubiquitous U.S. global positioning system of satellites.

Room 111, a section separate from the closed intelligence egg, is home to the Special Technical Operations (STO) cell, an even more compartmented facility populated by cyberwarriors from the CIA, the NSA, the FBI, and military Special Operations whose work is so highly classified that it is impossible to know whether they are there to defend against digital attack or to aggressively engage in it.

NorthCom's bewildering array of internal websites, portals, databases, and search engines owes its very existence to the problems encountered on 9/11 and punctuated during Hurricane Katrina: first responders—police, fire, and emergency medical personnel—found it nearly impossible to communicate with each other or with the National Guard or federal agencies. That inability wasn't merely technical but perceptual: every agency had a different view of the situation on the ground, and no one had a complete or accurate

---

[4] The CIP for Finance (CIPFIN) database is an element of the Defense Critical Infrastructure Program (CIP), which identifies and assesses the security of physical assets and cyberassets and infrastructures in the public and private sectors that are essential to national security. Using this database, the Defense Finance and Accounting Service (DFAS) monitors the security and health of the financial services sector and infrastructure required to sustain the military.

picture of the status of the response force, the civilian population, or the threat, and certainly not in real time. Although Katrina happened four years after the terrorist attacks (and after a security spending spree that exceeded $2 trillion), emergency response agencies still weren't even using the same maps—thus the emphasis now on One Nation, One Map.

Because of the United States' 250-year-old legal and cultural tradition of keeping the military out of domestic civilian affairs, North-Com has had to be particularly sensitive to any appearance of domestic spying or other encroachments on civil liberties. (That was one of the big reasons for so much coordination when it came to press coverage and talking points.) In order to maintain the separation, NorthCom has cooperative and cordial relationships not only with Homeland Security, the FBI, and the other civilian agencies but also with each of the states, with many major city governments, and with the National Guard's distinct locally oriented factions, each of which has a contentious relationship with the active military.

Such interagency diplomacy comes into play every two weeks when representatives from five dozen federal departments and agencies convene in NorthCom's basement conference room. A typical meeting begins promptly at 1300 hours (1:00 p.m.), the PowerPoint agenda for the next hour and a half visible on the projection screen. A Northern Command liaison office in Washington is present over video-teleconference, and each of the headquarters directorates (operations, logistics, communications) and subordinate commands are either there in person or represented by liaison officers also visible and audible through VTC. Shirtsleeves outnumber uniforms three-to-one. (Contractors, though embedded on various staffs, are identifiable by the color of their badges or, if there is any confusion as to who is really who, by the letters CTR that appear next to their names.)

Some meetings can be dominated by discussions of subjects not related to the war on terror—a volcano eruption in Iceland, for example. Or take a meeting in which no hurricane or presidential emergency hogs the spotlight: each staff directorate and major agency is allotted time to update the assembled with announcements and news. Despite the opportunity, some participants just pass—the CIA and NSA representatives to NorthCom do so stone-faced, clearly not predisposed to share.

Workdays at NorthCom headquarters are punctuated by an endless series of these videoconferences. By the time the interagency group meets—and it is just one of many similar gatherings at more than a dozen commands and agencies worldwide—the tenor is somewhere between dreaded high school reunion and a weekly family meeting reviewing nothing more significant than the grocery list. As at most open government meetings, it was extremely rare that anything particularly controversial was said, and no dirty laundry was intentionally aired. Between the lines of each routine acronym-laden, unemotional briefing, attendees kept an ear out for any hints of bureaucratic weakness or change. Indeed, the intelligence of most interest was often that which concerned Washington's ups and downs.

At a briefing on national airspace, an FAA representative's flat, pilotlike intonation telegraphed *routine exercise in bureaucratic chair shuffling*, but to a more attentive ear, something astounding was revealed: a dramatic increase in unmanned aerial drones flying over the United States. The FAA representative described new procedures for managing access to American airspace, which is split into two categories—that owned by the military and that owned by the FAA for civilian aviation. Each entity needs permission to put anything in the other's airspace. An elaborate set of rules and procedures for managing this potential conflict has evolved over time. As the use of drones has dramatically expanded overseas—for surveillance, targeted killings, and, recently, to transport supplies to isolated outposts—the number of drones in U.S. airspace has escalated, too.

Domestic use of military drones is mostly for training drone operators and pilots, but the numbers are surprising: a printed map of the United States pasted on a cubicle wall in the operations egg anticipated thirteen different kinds of military unmanned aerial vehicles flying from ninety-four U.S. locations by 2016. The U.S. Customs and Border Patrol has its own Predator drones, used for border surveillance; the Coast Guard has some to keep a video eye on coastal waters; and NASA, together with other research and development agencies, fly drones for imagery collection and for trying out new advanced sensors, such as those that detect people and equipment under heavy tree cover.

In May 2006, the FAA issued its first certificate of authorization for the military to fly Predator-type drones in U.S. civilian airspace in support of disaster response, an authorization that came after the agency had been denied their use, for safety reasons, in the aftermath of Katrina. That certificate was followed by comparable drone authorizations for Customs and Border Patrol and even limited authorizations for Arizona law enforcement authorities; the Maricopa County sheriff's office even purchased its own drones after becoming convinced that using them would ultimately be cheaper than flying manned helicopters to assess accidents and hostage situations.

None of the domestic drones are armed, and in December 2010, the Pentagon took the step of formally banning the use of armed drones in American airspace. The stated reason was that the potential for accidents was too great, but the fear of a political outcry figured into the calculus as well, particularly since many of those drones operate on and around the Mexican and Canadian borders.

Drones may keep pilots safe, but there are still risks. On August 2, 2010, a navy drone lost communication with its ground station seventy-five minutes into a test flight in southern Maryland, and then failed a second time to follow its preprogrammed fail-safe, an automatic prompt for a return-to-base flight path. As it headed into Washington's restricted airspace, Admiral James "Sandy" Winnefeld Jr., then NorthCom commander, coordinated with the FAA and the navy and was about to scramble fighters to shoot down the rogue drone when ground technicians finally reestablished control.

It won't be the last time an out-of-control domestic drone poses a threat to people on the ground. And in the air, should a drone collide with a passenger jet, the results could be catastrophic.

Calling U.S. air traffic control "a mess," one NorthCom watch officer worried that thousands of additional drone flights (together with less expensive commercially available ultralights and advanced toy planes) could create a nightmare scenario. And the worry wasn't just that our own drones might malfunction and crash. "The next 9/11 with an unmanned drone," the NorthCom officer said. "Just think about it."

Another seemingly routine agenda item during the interagency meeting was really anything but routine. An air force lieutenant colonel bullet-pointed his way through a brief discussion of a money-saving proposal to consolidate the NorthCom air operations center, now at Tyndall Air Force Base in Florida, with that of the Southern Command, a more senior command that oversees U.S. military operations in South America and has an air operations center in Arizona. NorthCom is scheduled to lose almost one hundred headquarters staffers in upcoming budget cuts, but the briefing slides indicated that no personnel would be cut with the air operations consolidation. One of the nonmilitary people in the room sensed something incongruous.

"What does it mean?" he asked. "What's the practical effect?"

Greater efficiency, the colonel answered tersely. No operational impact.

"The consolidation means *nothing?*" the befuddled civilian asked, his question trailing away in the rush of the quickly moving agenda.

Yet far from meaningless, the consolidation of the flight centers was a barometer for a much larger issue: after 9/11, every major regional command acquired its own air operations center. Most of them are expensive and geographically separate from their own command headquarters. Every command got its own joint intelligence center, with the requirement for hundreds of analysts who in turn required their own common operating pictures and datasets, as well as their own maps that often duplicated the work already being done by the national agencies. The creation of NorthCom had required the creation of its own set of intelligence analysts, its own air operations center, its own everything. As the agenda item suggested, that duplication had become too obvious to ignore.

Every major combatant command has to contend with defining its role and jockeying for resources and authority. But in the case of NorthCom, the conditions were truly unique. It was the responsibility of the intelligence agencies, the FBI, and the Department of Homeland Security, which controls the old border patrol and immigration authorities, to detect terrorists coming to America, whether by airliner, ship, or over the border. Investigating an actual or suspected terrorist was an FBI or local law enforcement matter. If a Mumbai-style attack terrorized Houston, for example, it would be federal and local SWAT teams that responded, possibly augmented by National Guard units called for state active duty—not North-Com, which had no troops directly under its command.

Homeland security in Hawaii and the Pacific territories was a matter for the more senior Pacific Command in Honolulu, not NorthCom. And though the military headquarters responsible for Washington, DC, is officially under NorthCom, the area's significance as the home of the White House, Congress, the Pentagon, and the FBI meant the Washington-based headquarters effectively functioned as an independent entity unto itself. "Sometimes we feel like we report to them," a NorthCom planner griped.

Even in the case of the two hottest threats to domestic security, cyberattacks and weapons of mass destruction, NorthCom was not in charge. National protection of the U.S. electronic lifeline is the responsibility of DHS and the new four-star military Cyber Command at Fort Meade, Maryland, activated in 2009. It—not NorthCom—controls all military electronic defenses and would fight any cyberwar affecting U.S. assets. Inside the United States, the FBI, not NorthCom, is responsible for cybersecurity.

In 2005, the Strategic Command in Omaha, and not North-Com, was given the mission of countering the global WMD threat, with the FBI taking the lead inside the United States. Were military Special Operations Forces called upon to deploy for super-secret operations to prevent a WMD attack at home, they would ultimately fall under Special Operations Command in Tampa or the FBI, not NorthCom.

In fact, the only unit that the NorthCom commander commands is the Joint Task Force Civil Support in Virginia, a small headquarters organization set up in 1999 to deal with the consequences of the use of WMD that itself is dependent upon other military services to supply units in an emergency.

To those familiar with NorthCom's existential dilemma, the interagency group meeting segued from the cryptic and unsatisfying announcement of the plan to consolidate northern and southern command air operations centers to another bureaucratic slight: a new Defense Department regulation regarding protection of the critical infrastructure in the United States. It would be hard to imagine a more obvious role for NorthCom than defending essential infrastructure on U.S. soil. But out of eighteen critical sectors identified in the U.S. government's National Infrastructure Protection Plan, only one, the "defense industrial base"—hundreds of thousands of plants, factories, and offices that produce the hardware and software needed by the American military—was actually under DoD's purview, and that sole military responsibility was assigned not to NorthCom but a variety of other defense agencies and commands: Strategic Command was given responsibility for the space sector of the defense industry, Transportation Command for the transportation sector. The Defense Security Service was made responsible for industrial security inspections. In fact, in the July 2010 directive on infrastructure protection, NorthCom wasn't even mentioned.

With the exception of defending against a direct attack by another military—which essentially boils down to NORAD's pre-9/11 missions plus naval defense of the coast—NorthCom's actual homeland security mission was incredibly limited. The only military support it could offer civilian federal, state, and local agencies was to help clean up following a terrorist attack or a major disaster—and even then only if the president declared a national emergency or if they were invited by state and local authorities.

Even in the civil support role, NorthCom did little that the National Guard or the army wasn't already doing prior to 9/11, and it had to be careful not to step on the toes of the powerful and politically wired National Guard establishment, which itself was bolstered after 9/11 by the appointment of a Washington-based four-star general to lead it.

But there is one area in which NorthCom has unambiguously taken the lead: *preparation* for the civil support role following an attack involving weapons of mass destruction, which the government expansively defines as including a wide range of nightmare possibilities—chemical, biological, radiological, nuclear, or even high-yield explosives (CBRNEs). Not surprisingly, reference to this was on that day's interagency group agenda—specifically, an upcoming exercise named Vibrant Response which simulated the civil support response to a domestic WMD attack.

In fact, there isn't an interagency coordination group meeting that doesn't return again and again to the specter of saboteurs or snipers or suicide bombers cutting loose in a shopping mall. That is grim enough, but the status of those events as acts of war, as opposed to brutal crimes, is ambiguous. There's nothing ambiguous about a suitcase nuke. Arkin obtained and examined more than 120 internal agendas and minutes for the interagency group covering the period 2005 through 2011 and found only eight meetings that did not deal with some aspect of potential terrorists wielding weapons of mass destruction in the United States.

"The gravest danger to the American people is the threat of a terrorist attack with a nuclear weapon"; this was Obama's first White House foreign policy agenda point, announced the day after the inauguration. Six days later, Robert Gates, in his first congressional testimony as the new administration's secretary of defense, told the Senate Armed Services Committee, "One of the greatest dangers we continue to face is the toxic mix of rogue nations; terrorist groups; and nuclear, chemical, or biological weapons."

After 9/11, the Bush administration directed numerous intelligence assessments of the actual domestic threat from terrorists wielding WMD. The results were always the same: lots of evidence existed that al-Qaeda had pursued the development of biological and chemical weapons and had even tried to obtain nuclear materials, and lots of such claims had been made by Osama bin Laden and his cohorts. This was piled on top of vague intelligence that some Russian nuclear weapons had gone missing. And, as in the case of Iraq under Saddam Hussein, since U.S. intelligence couldn't prove that al-Qaeda, domestic militia groups, or lone-wolf terrorists didn't *already* have or couldn't obtain CBRNE, the possibility that they did had to be planned for.

In March 2003, just weeks after President Bush appointed him assistant secretary of defense for Homeland Security, Paul McHale signed a classified memorandum directing that NorthCom build itself up to the point of being able to react to not just one and not just two nearly simultaneous catastrophic WMD events in the United States, but a minimum of three and a maximum of six.

Why three? Why six?

An army officer assigned to NorthCom said it was three because that was the number of locations attacked on 9/11; and six because that would mandate a capability to quickly assist all geographic points in the continental United States even with multiple simultaneous events. A senior intelligence officer who witnessed the development of this requirement said the numbers were just gut guesses, and never based upon any intelligence or even upon some sophisticated simulation or war game. And though funding considerations weren't a factor, once planning started for three to six exercises, the money was needed to implement it.

Whether such a multipronged threat is likely or not, it is North-Com's responsibility to prepare, train for, and, if the time ever comes, execute an effective response. "Effective" in a WMD event is defined as managing mass casualties, maintaining order, and establishing the conditions in which recovery can begin. To this end, in 2003 NorthCom was directed to create three standing units dedicated full time to prepping for a WMD catastrophe.

Ten small National Guard WMD teams existed before 9/11, one assigned to each FEMA region; the Marine Corps also had a chemical and biological incident response force (called CBIRF and established in 1996) for the purpose of search and rescue in a WMD-contaminated environment. The post-9/11 NorthCom units, charged with responding to a WMD catastrophe anywhere in the country within forty-eight hours of an attack, would be given the unlikely nickname Sea Smurf, for the mouthful acronym of their official designation: Chemical, Biological, Radiological, Nuclear, and High-Yield Explosive Consequence Management Response Force (CCMRF).

Because of the demands that the actual wars in Iraq and Afghanistan put on soldiers, the first of the three Sea Smurf units, the 1st Heavy Brigade Combat Team of the 3rd Infantry Division based in Georgia, didn't even begin training until October 1, 2007. That brigade had just returned from a fifteen-month surge-deployment to Iraq. The army did its duty, but it wasn't until the following June, five years after McHale's memo, that the Pentagon assigned "operational control" of the 4,700-person CCMRF to NorthCom, an arrangement that lasted only until October 2009.

One month later, in November 2009, NorthCom mobilized 4,000 people for Vibrant Response 10.1, its largest-ever field training drill. The exercise was taken right out of *National Planning Scenario* No. 1, a set of planning scenarios created for the entire federal government and approved by the Homeland Security Council in the fourth year of the Bush administration and affirmed by its successor: terrorists detonate a ten-kiloton nuclear device in downtown Indianapolis and thousands are dead and dying, the urban landscape a jumble of flattened buildings and irradiated rubble.

The Muscatatuck Center for Complex Operations, near Butlerville, Indiana, served as the stage for the grim drama. Once the home of the Indiana Farm Colony for Feeble-Minded Youth, the 1,000-acre urban warfare site had been refurbished to resemble a small city, with a nine-mile road network, underground tunnel systems, houses and buildings, a hospital, parking garages, a power plant, schools, and a police station. The mock city was replete with upended cars and manufactured piles of debris, smoke pots and burning straw simulating fires, even expert role players contracted to act as injured and irradiated residents.

The response teams, suited up in moon suits (radiological, biological, and chemical protection gear), rappelled, burrowed, directed, and simulated while exercise referees hovered nearby and VIPs watched. Identifier teams roved the wreckage in their all-terrain vehicle (ATVs), taking radiation readings and looking for chemical and biological traces that had been seeded by the umpires. Survivors were gathered together at decontamination stations, where they were washed with miraculously available and abundant water. The "residents" were then directed along neatly marked lanes — based upon levels of exposure and severity of simulated wounds — to immaculately clean tented medical stations. There, mannequins were saved; hysterical actors were reassured. The CBRNE Consequence Management Response Force's first full-scale, full-deployment exercise was declared a success, confirming, NorthCom's briefing slides said, "CCMRF's capability to deploy to and support a catastrophic CBRNE Consequence Management event from a standing alert status." Mission accomplished.

But even in peacetime, even with months of preparation, endless meetings, modeling and pre-exercise exercises, with everything in the country working perfectly, it took this Vibrant Response force more than a week just to *get* to Indiana and set up. What's more, when they got there, everyone worked under brilliantly sunny skies, and because of local restrictions on air traffic and noise, very little to none of the exercise activity took place at night.

Compare these vacationlike conditions to the panic, chaos, and physical disruptions of an actual WMD attack — in which there wouldn't be nice decontamination lanes to triage compliant survivors and calm doctors and nurses—and the mission of responding effectively within forty-eight hours could be considered unlikely to come close to success. In fact, NorthCom officials have faced a hurricane of criticism from auditors and observers for both the readiness and the adequacy of the CCMRF program. A 2009 War College study documented that the command is unprepared, undermanned, unable to mobilize, and suffers from inadequate transport. And if the immediate response unit was able to get to a contaminated area, it could only handle about 120 casualties an hour, a horrifying mismatch with the *National Planning Scenario* for a single ground-level ten-kiloton nuclear detonation by a terrorist in the center of Washington, DC, which estimates 57,000 immediate deaths from the blast and as many as 180,000 radiation deaths in the first twenty-four hours.

The Government Accountability Office has levied similar critiques, and the army not only stiff-armed NorthCom for years in allocating a combat unit but has now managed to shed responsibility for CCMRFs 2 and 3, foisting the mission off on the National Guard. Then came the final bureaucratic indignity for NorthCom: after just one year, the CCMRF was "allocated" to the command rather than assigned. In simpler terms: the supposedly full-fledged homeland defense combatant command would have to ask permission if it wanted to activate its allocated unit or take control of the National Guard.

Now, as the PowerPoint slides ticking off in the interagency group meeting were making clear, NorthCom was facing another mission adjustment: the three dedicated CCMRF units with a force of approximately 15,000 would be transformed into a single unit a third the size—just 5,200—renamed the Defense CBRNE Response Force, which would be "faster, more flexible," according to the upbeat assessment in the presentation. The Defense Department, the slides declared, would now focus on creating five-hundred-person "all-hazards" National Guard "homeland response forces," one in each of ten FEMA regions—a force that would be prepared by as early as 2012 but, tellingly, under the control of state governors. NorthCom is nowhere to be found in the chain of command between the secretary of defense and the National Guard.

The interagency group briefing slide on the status of WMD consequence management again seemed designed to minimize the appearance of any loss on the part of NorthCom, but the truth of the command's diminished status, even in this, the one area in which it had seemed to have unambiguous leadership, showed up in a final bullet: under the new arrangements, all the response units weren't even obligated to come to the aid of NorthCom; rather, the military services could make forces available "to the greatest extent possible."

These developments were heartbreaking to those who had spent years building up Northern Command. But the fact that Northern Command would even continue to exist as a major, four-star-led, geographic military command, with virtually no responsibilities, no competencies, and no unique role to fill, demonstrated the resiliency of institutions created in the wake of 9/11 and just how difficult it would be to ever actually shrink Top Secret America. Northern Command, with its $100 million renovated concrete headquarters, its two dozen generals, its redundant command centers, its gigantic electronic map, and its multitude of contractors, looked as busy as ever, putting together agendas and exercises and PowerPoint briefings in the name of keeping the nation safe.

If it took Northern Command a surprisingly long time to get to Indiana, it wasn't because it lacked directions. Indeed, as NorthCom's status diminishes, the national One Map continues to grow. Over eleven million individual records have now been entered, almost double the number appearing three years earlier. A total of 44,000 government entities have been identified and mapped, 116,000 emergency services, and 182,000 public health facilities. Thirty-two new datasets were included for military recruiting stations, quite a few of which had been the target of protests and even attacks. Seventeen thousand "national symbols" were also included, as were 315,000 "public venues," and a hodgepodge "other" category that included "places of worship."

The Pentagon has gone out of its way to soften the official jargon to make the mission less offensive-sounding. After 9/11, military planners replaced the phrase "Military Support to Civil Authorities" with "Defense Support of Civil Authorities" (DSCA), a less martial wording in an ever more militarized America. Similarly, in its voluminous January 2011 *Handbook* laying out planning factors to be used by local military forces operating in the United States, the Pentagon sternly instructs, "***do not use the terms*** 'Intelligence, Surveillance and Reconnaissance (ISR)' or 'Intelligence Preparation of the Battlefield (IPB).' The appropriate terminology in a DSCA environment is *Incident Awareness and Assessment*" (emphasis in original).

But information will always be information, even while the intent can change. And there is already abundant evidence, from what is happening in communities and local police stations throughout the nation, that the intent is sometimes less than purely to offer support and solace to the afflicted. Consider the careful cataloging of places of worship on The Map.

Most states keep track of places of worship as part of their emergency management missions, and many since 9/11 have developed faith-based cooperative initiatives where police work with religious communities to prepare for a hostile event such as an act of violence or vandalism. But not all states had yet shared their data, and the federal government wanted to know more.

In 2008, the National Geospatial-Intelligence Agency decided to purchase its own information on places of worship. It went to a small company, Ionic Enterprise (since bought and gone out of business), that was already tracking the data for commercial vendors and numerous state governments. The government asked for the data to be delivered in four subgroups—Catholic churches, Protestant churches, mosques, and synagogues—with quarterly updates, according to the mapping contract. A young NorthCom intelligence officer acknowledged that some state officials were befuddled by the priority the federal government placed on religious institutions, but, as the officer explained, "It isn't only first response that's important." She added, "Our responsibility is also to look at the threat." The threat *to* religious institutions? Or the threat *from* religious institutions? She didn't say. The details of the contract for the dataset itself reveal an odd emphasis: only churches with congregations greater than 750 people are tracked, while *all* mosques and synagogues are tracked. The divisions are even starker in the June 2010 DHS *Geospatial Concept of Operations*, a 161-page document that contains "the authoritative data matrix" for map users. There, two separate subcategories exist under public venues: "houses of worship" and "mosques." And in the sensitive North-Com intelligence egg and in Room 111, where the Top Secret version of The Map is kept, intelligence officers can consult the Integrated Common Operating Picture, where "Muslims in America" is one of the categories of information collected and mapped, 24/7.

In the top secret version of the nation's geography, the government tracks all threats picked up by U.S. intelligence and law enforcement in the past forty-eight hours. NorthCom analysts and interagency liaison officers from the CIA, the NSA, the FBI, and other intelligence agencies can access the raw intelligence—the actual reports from local authorities, in many cases—and can interact with colleagues across the nation via specialized chat rooms for those following gangs, drugs, human smuggling, or reports and even suspicions about people and places on the map just possibly linked to terrorism. As the young intelligence officer in the top secret egg proudly summed up: "It's all here."

CHAPTER SEVEN

"Report Suspicious Activity"

(road sign on Sixteenth Street NW, in Washington, DC)

On February 9, 2011, Janet Napolitano, the secretary of the Department of Homeland Security, delivered some terrible news to Congress. The terrorism threat against the country, she announced, had not diminished despite the enormous counter-terrorism effort and decade-long war—in fact, it had only gotten worse. In some ways, "the threat facing us is at its most heightened state" since the attacks a decade ago, she said, slowly reading every word of her prepared testimony.

Of particular concern was the inclination of some potential terrorists living in the United States to brew plots and carry them out by themselves, without the help of larger, more easily detectable networks. Traditional counterterrorism methods will not be enough to find the lone wolf, a terrorist operating alone, without a network, Napolitano stated. "State and local police will more often be in the best position to notice the signs of a planned attack."

For all the drama in her words, there was something amiss

about the moment. Napolitano read her statement in a monotone, as if reciting an obscure budget document. No one in the House committee room looked fazed. Neither did members of the audience, who sat expressionless, even bored. Reporters on deadline didn't rush her for details afterward. In fact, they looked a little bored, too. Napolitano's testimony ended up being a one-day story, and, in most newspapers, didn't even make the front pages.

If the people in charge of Top Secret America were really convinced the situation was as dire as Napolitano claimed, they weren't sharing enough information with an impatient public and a press by now numb to the drone of perpetual yellow alerts for their warnings to ring true. The few known attempted bombings seemed to be minor incidents, as there had never been a danger to public safety. Weeks earlier, a construction worker had been arrested during an FBI sting operation in Baltimore; he had attempted to set off a bomb outside a military recruiting center. There was little public or press interest in that, either. When a Somali-born student was arrested in Portland, Oregon, during a similar FBI operation—this time the bomb was supposed to explode at a downtown Christmas tree lighting ceremony—members of Congress barely said a thing.

But it was hard not to notice all of the portable traffic signs cropping up along the eastern seaboard. The signs displayed alarming messages: "Report Suspicious Activity." "Terror Tips?"

"What's that all about?" friends and colleagues would ask. "Is there something going on?"

Yes, something was going on, and it wasn't as easily identifiable as a group of military officers behind closed doors at NorthCom trying to map the nooks and crannies of the United States. It was more obscure and decentralized, harder to touch and feel.

There had been a disturbing trend in the last five years, in settings around the country: Pennsylvania, Virginia, Tennessee, Ohio, South Dakota, and California. No single event was particularly troubling in isolation—but together they began to form a picture. An undercover police officer in Maryland had been sent to spy on nuns protesting the wars. Environmentalists showed up on terrorism bulletins in Pennsylvania. Public park cleanups and gatherings of animal rights activists were monitored by authorities in Virginia. The Ohio, Kentucky, and Indiana regional fusion center declared that terrorist sleeper cells thrived in diverse neighborhoods where there was "an easygoing attitude toward different cultures," as if multiculturalism itself was a threat to the republic.

The increasing frequency of such events coincided with investment by police departments around the country in the kind of technology that overseas had helped elite military units find a single terrorist in a haystack of nobodies. Police departments also bought equipment to identify large numbers of people without their knowledge—the same kind that U.S. soldiers and spies used in foreign wars, hot and covert. These tools were not hard to find or purchase: the same corporations that developed and sold so many of these useful gadgets and software programs to American military antiterrorism squads were now setting their sights on places like Phoenix, Memphis, and Sioux City.

The transition from public to private commerce was easy for the corporate side of Top Secret America. With slick advertising and marketing, a variety of companies, large and small, presented themselves as the nation's protectors, bragging about how their products had helped the U.S. Army identify insurgents, track clandestine activity, and disrupt all things criminal and nefarious. Their campaigns tapped into the patriotism and culture of vigilance inherent in law enforcement agencies, and also the feeling that they could become connected to the center of power, where the action was, by using these technologies.

L-1 Identity Solutions, for example, sells American police departments the same type of handheld, wireless fingerprint scanners used by U.S. troops to register entire Iraqi villages during the insurgency. Other companies sell local law enforcement authorities devices to detect the location of mobile phones, a technology used by troops and intelligence agencies in Iraq and elsewhere.

Thermal infrared cameras made by the FLIR Corporation, like

the night vision devices it makes for the military, were deployed by police in several American cities. Those cameras could see through metal, alerting police to someone hiding, say, in the trunk or on the floor of a car. (They could even tell, by the heat signature underneath its chassis, whether the car had just been turned off.) In Arizona, the Maricopa County sheriff's office purchased the sort of facial recognition equipment prevalent in war zones, using it to record some nine thousand biometric digital mug shots a month, many of them of illegal immigrants. And, just as soldiers in the field did when trying to keep towns free of insurgents, many American police departments purchased equipment allowing them to record images of license plate numbers belonging to every car going through toll booths and tunnels.

Such surveillance was especially intense around larger cities, especially those that had felt the direct impact of the 9/11 attacks. Soon, said authorities in the Washington area, everyone who drives into the nation's capital will have his car tracked and recorded, a high-tech, invisible version of the so-called ring of steel that the British government imposed on London during the Irish Republican Army killings there in the early 1990s and broadened after 9/11. Lower Manhattan was the first U.S. location to set up a web of similar surveillance, a system also used by U.S. troops in Afghan and Iraqi communities.

That many of these advances were initially developed for use in foreign wars was a double bonus for some of the companies that had made them. Often the technology development itself had been partly subsidized by the government. Elite Special Operations units tasked with killing and capturing terrorists drove technological advances in rapid analysis, allowing operators to fuse biometric identification, captured computer records, and cell phone numbers to map the hierarchy of al-Qaeda and insurgent networks, making thousands of connections within minutes so commandos could launch surprise raids within hours. Here at home, the Department of Homeland Security and its state affiliates were increasingly enamored with the idea of using similar technology to collect photos, video images, and other personal information about U.S. residents in the hopes of teasing out terrorists.

As governor of Arizona (2003–9), Napolitano built one of the strongest local intelligence organizations outside of New York City. Now the public face of the administration's aggressive efforts to capture and coordinate domestic information throughout the country, she wanted every state and local law enforcement agency to feed data to the FBI and to DHS. "This represents a shift for our country," she told New York City first responders on the eve of the ninth anniversary of 9/11. "In a sense, this harkens back to when we drew on the tradition of civil defense and preparedness that predated today's concerns."

Her statement was startling because of the clear reference to the cold war, which also became the dark days of McCarthyism, when citizens were encouraged and pressured to turn in people they suspected of being Communist sympathizers. Back then, an obsessed and paranoid FBI had drawn up a black list, vacuuming up not only many Americans whose association with communism was tangential but also the names of countless individuals who had little or no sympathy for the doctrine or its practice. Without enough evidence to prosecute many of these suspects on espionage or sedition charges, the FBI instead ruined their careers and reputations. FBI director J. Edgar Hoover's covert COINTELPRO (Counter Intelligence Program) sent undercover agents to disrupt and discredit political figures and groups it deemed subversive. These included civil rights leaders such as Martin Luther King Jr., organizations like the National Association for the Advancement of Colored People, and Vietnam-era antiwar protesters. As far as Hoover was concerned, the burden to prove innocence rested on the accused, not the accuser, a complete reversal of the system enshrined in the Constitution.

At a congressional hearing in March 2010, California Representative Jane Harman, a liberal advocate of stronger domestic intelligence, reminded colleagues about such past domestic abuses: "Let's not fool ourselves. If homeland security intelligence is done the wrong way, then what we will have is...the thought police and we will be the worst for it." The solution, she added, was clarity and openness, and neither existed as of yet. "We need clear definitions about what we are doing. We need transparency and a process to hold people accountable. We need to shut down what doesn't work and we know can't work. The rule of law must always apply."

Transparency remains embryonic, but the federal-state-corporate partnership has produced a vast domestic intelligence apparatus that collects, stores, and analyzes information about tens of thousands of U.S. citizens and residents, many of whom have not been accused of any wrongdoing. It involves a web of 3,984 federal, state, and local organizations, each with its own counterterrorism responsibilities and jurisdictions, according to Arkin's calculations. At least 934 of these organizations have been created since the 2001 attacks or reorganized since then; or they became involved in counterterrorism for the first time after 9/11.

Just as in other parts of Top Secret America, the effectiveness of these programs, as well as their cost, is difficult to determine. Since most of the money for these programs came from state budgets, information about spending on state security should have been accessible. But it wasn't, or at least the records weren't easy to find. Public accountability is limited to a handful of statistics. There is little disclosure about how things really work—and few people, if any, truly understand how the entire system is woven together. Local reporters were constantly frustrated by state offices that simply refused to explain how the state's new intelligence center and data collection worked. Most of the time, none of it was classified top secret or even secret until it reached the FBI. But much of it was classified "law enforcement sensitive," which meant it could be withheld from the public.

When Harman spoke of the need for transparency, she was also addressing government agencies themselves. For even the institutions at the core of Top Secret America are often in the dark. The Department of Homeland Security, for example, does not know how much it spends each year on state fusion centers, which bring together and analyze information from various agencies within a state. The DHS has given $31 billion in grants since 2003 to state and local governments for all kinds of projects, including fusion centers, a department spokeswoman said, but she said the federal agency doesn't actually track all the programs the money is used for. Nor does it bother to track which programs are effective. At least four other federal departments also contribute to local efforts, but the bulk of the spending every year comes from state and local budgets that are too disparately recorded to figure out an overall total.

In addition to the new Department of Homeland Security and all the other organizations created in the wake of the 9/11 attacks, Napolitano, the FBI, the National Security Agency, and even the CIA, in a more limited way, had inherited a structure pioneered by the Bush administration that allowed for closer coordination not only against foreign terrorist networks but also against American citizens who appeared to authorities to be acting suspiciously.

This new normal, enshrined in the 2001 Patriot Act, was at the core of an all-out effort to prevent terrorism before it happened. To achieve this, the Patriot Act had taken a giant step by abandoning a measure enshrined in American law since 1978 to prevent any more COINTELPRO abuses: it dismantled the separation between criminal cases, which require a high standard of evidence of a crime to initiate, and intelligence investigations, whose goal is to obtain more information, not pursue criminal cases, and which therefore can be launched with much less solid information. The new Patriot Act unleashed the FBI once again, allowing it to spy more, use more informants, listen in on more conversations, infiltrate more groups, collect more email and voicemail, access and store more financial and personal records, and cross-reference more data than it had before. The justification needed for these investigations had to begin with more than a hunch, but could be based on considerably less than the kind of evidence that was required to justify such tactics before 9/11.

This meant the bureau was now cleared to gather information not for criminal prosecution in a court of law but to further its own understanding of how suspected groups and networks inside the United States operated. Formal preliminary investigations could be opened with less actual proof of wrongdoing than in the past. And while on paper racial profiling was banned, in practice it happened all the time. A man who looked Middle Eastern couldn't be stopped for simply walking down the street, but he could be stopped for walking in front of a federal building several times looking curious.

With advances in technology and the right approvals, the government could also now capture a person's digital exhaust, the revealing data a human being gives off in the course of daily life — when buying groceries or gas or beauty supplies, surfing the Internet, using a cell phone or ATM, flying from country to country or driving from state to state. This data could be married with biometric and law enforcement records, such as fingerprints and previous arrests, and stored on law enforcement servers, allowing officials to build and share lengthy profiles of both suspected terrorists and ordinary citizens who someone believed were acting suspiciously.

By allowing information about individuals not subject to a criminal investigation to be collected without their knowledge, the Bush administration had also weakened the safeguards written into the Watergate-era Privacy Act of 1974. The act guaranteed that, with the exception of ongoing criminal investigations, individuals could know what the government had collected on them, and it ensured that the information would not be inappropriately shared. Now all sorts of data and observation about private citizens circulated freely among the FBI, state and local police and fusion centers, and the Department of Homeland Security. The default assumption became to err on the side of the nation's safety. Most citizens were not allowed to find out if their names were among the circulating files. This prohibition was to prevent them from being tipped off and modifying their behavior.

Napolitano was the first to publicly advocate a more aggressive use of these Bush-era revisions. Arguing that the wars in Iraq and Afghanistan hadn't stopped the pipeline of terrorists into the United States, she in essence declared the Bush administration's rationale for going to war in Iraq a failure. "The old view that 'if we fight the terrorists abroad, we won't have to fight them here' is just that—the old view," she told police and firefighters in a speech. The new problem, she explained, was "home-grown terrorists," even though most of them were not homegrown at all but young immigrants from Somalia, Afghanistan, and Pakistan with easy access to inspirational jihadist websites and how-to manuals.

Napolitano and many in the Obama administration believed that the next iteration of terrorism to hit the United States would be attacks by disaffected immigrants. These so-called lone wolves were difficult to detect and stop. Their only hope was to turn ordinary citizens and hometown beat cops into informants for the FBI. The slogan she chose for her campaign was "See Something, Say Something." The implication of Napolitano's strategy was to extend the terrorism battlefield beyond the nation's capital and its largest cities and into the American heartland, and to turn local law enforcement agencies into surrogates for federal counterterrorism teams. Ideally, citizens themselves would become counterterror informants, paying close attention to any anomalies they noticed.

From the beginning, determining an effective and proportionate response to the threat of terrorism was challenging for local and state authorities. In Tennessee in 2001, state officials canceled flights and banned parking within three hundred feet of airport terminals after airplanes were turned into fuel-filled missiles on 9/11. National Guardsmen with rifles appeared. So did canine patrols. Tennessee lawmakers gathered at the governor's mansion for secret

Each day at the National Counterterrorism Center, in McLean, Virginia, workers review at least five thousand pieces of terrorist-related data from intelligence agencies and keep an eye on world events. (Melina Mara/ *Washington Post*)

Liberty Crossing, in McLean, Virginia, houses the headquarters of the Office of the Director of National Intelligence and the National Counterterrorism Center. (Michael S. Williamson/*Washington Post*)

Richard Zahner, then army deputy chief of staff for intelligence, appears in a video presentation at the Defense Intelligence Agency conference for contractors in Phoenix. (Michael S. Williamson/*Washington Post*)

John Rizzo served thirty-four years in the CIA, much of it as the agency's senior deputy legal counsel. After 9/11 he signed off on every covert program, including the Counterterrorism Center's kill list of suspected terrorists. (Central Intelligence Agency)

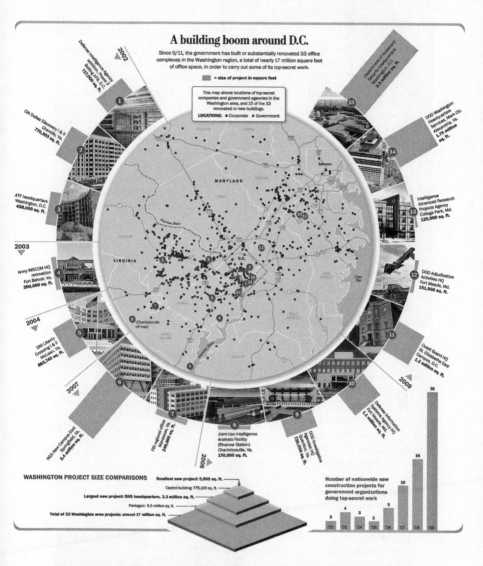

A building boom around D.C.

Since 9/11, the government has built or substantially renovated 33 office complexes in the Washington region, a total of nearly 17 million square feet of office space, in order to carry out some of its top-secret work.

■ = size of project in square feet

This map shows locations of top-secret companies and government agencies in the Washington area, and 15 of the 33 renovated or new buildings.

LOCATIONS: ● Corporate ◆ Government

2002
Defense Intelligence Agency addition #3 Bolling AFB, D.C. 717,000 sq. ft.

1 Department of Homeland Security headquarters Washington, D.C. 3.3 million sq. ft. **15**

DIA Dulles Discovery I & II Chantilly, Va. 770,903 sq. ft.

2 DOD Washington Headquarters Services, Mark Ctr. Alexandria, Va. 1.75 million sq. ft. **14**

ATF headquarters Washington, D.C. 438,000 sq. ft.

3 Intelligence Advanced Research Projects Agency College Park, Md. 120,000 sq. ft. **13**

2003
Army INSCOM HQ renovation Fort Belvoir, Va. 200,000 sq. ft.

4 DOD Adjudication Activities HQ Fort Meade, Md. 151,900 sq. ft. **12**

2004
DNI Liberty Crossing I & II McLean, Va. 863,760 sq. ft.

5 Coast Guard HQ St. Elizabeths East Campus, D.C. 1.2 million sq. ft. **11**

2007
NGA Next Campus East Springfield, Va. 2.4 million sq. ft.

6 Defense Information Systems Agency HQ Fort Meade, Md. 1.4 million sq. ft. **2009** **10**

7 FBI regional office Manassas, Va. 249,000 sq. ft.

8 Joint-Use Intelligence Analysis Facility (Rivanna Station) Charlottesville, Va. 170,000 sq. ft.

9 DOD Investigative Agencies HQ Quantico, Va. 770,000 sq. ft.

MARYLAND

VIRGINIA

WASHINGTON PROJECT SIZE COMPARISONS

Smallest new project: 5,900 sq. ft.
Capitol building: 775,100 sq. ft.
Largest new project: DHS headquarters, 3.3 million sq. ft.
Pentagon: 6.5 million sq. ft.
Total of 33 Washington area projects: almost 17 million sq. ft.

Number of nationwide new construction projects for government organizations doing top-secret work

2   4   3   2   5   10   16   31
'02 '03 '04 '05 '06 '07 '08 '09

Since 9/11 the federal government has built or substantially renovated thirty-three office complexes in the Washington, DC, area, a total of seventeen million square feet of office space, in order to carry out its top secret work. (*Washington Post*)

Law enforcement personnel stand guard during President Barack Obama's 2009 inaugural parade. The new president had the largest entourage in history, with twenty thousand uniformed guards and twenty-five thousand law enforcement officers enveloping him in a blanket of security, much of it invisible, that spanned from New York to West Virginia. (Preston Keres/*Washington Post*)

By President Obama's inauguration, FBI supervisor John Perren was part of a cadre of a hundred or so veteran law enforcement, intelligence, and military officers who were still on the job, planning and executing the takedown of Middle Eastern terrorists since the first attempt to destroy the World Trade Center in 1993. In 2001, as head of the FBI's counterterrorism office in the nation's capital, Perren supervised the recovery of bodies and evidence from the smoldering Pentagon and then deployed to Iraq to oversee FBI law enforcement assistance to the massive counterterrorism operations in that combat zone. (Federal Bureau of Investigation)

The FBI's Inaugural Command Center brought threat information from the sixteen U.S. intelligence agencies together for analysts to review. It also included real-time video feeds from surveillance cameras located on hundreds of buildings and street corners and along the main streets and highways leading into the nation's capital. (Federal Bureau of Investigation)

Director of National Intelligence James Clapper, right, briefs President Obama on intelligence matters. Clapper is the fifth DNI in six years. The DNI is supposed to be the head of all intelligence agencies but isn't actually. (Pete Souza/The White House)

At his command center at CIA headquarters, CIA director Leon E. Panetta monitors the progress of the operation at the compound in Abbottabad, Pakistan, on May 1, 2011. (Central Intelligence Agency)

A constellation of counterterrorism command centers in the Washington area

Sixty-seven centers — from national-level departments to the smallest agency — monitor overlapping bits of intelligence and keep an eye on U.S. government and military activities 24/7.

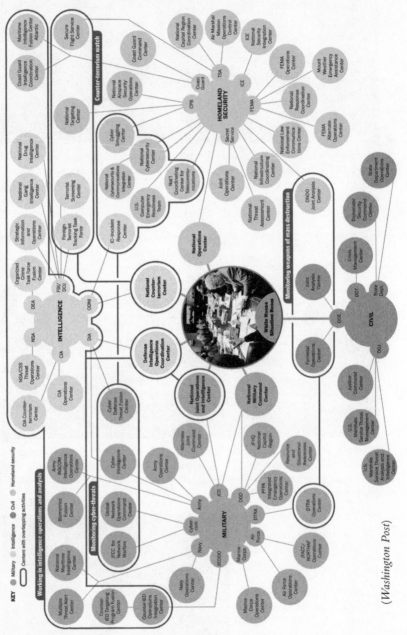

KEY ● Military ● Intelligence ● Civil ● Homeland security ⬭ Centers with overlapping activities

(Washington Post)

The National Security Agency, the nation's eavesdropper, never sleeps. NSA buildings in Maryland total 18.6 million square feet of space, 1.3 times the size of the Pentagon. (Sandra McConnell, NSA)

The National Business Park complex of private corporations is conveniently located just blocks from the National Security Agency, for which most of the corporations work. (Michael S. Williamson/*Washington Post*)

Converging in hubs across the country

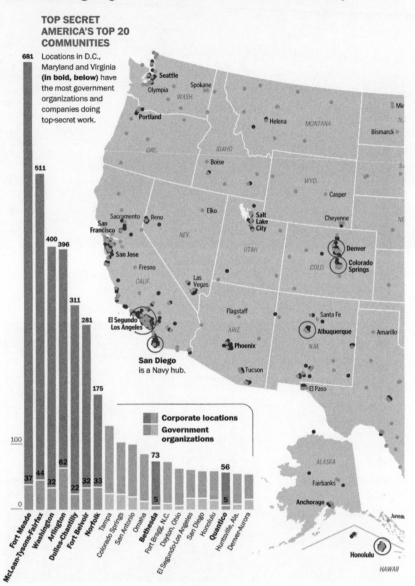

TOP SECRET AMERICA'S TOP 20 COMMUNITIES

681 Locations in D.C., Maryland and Virginia **(in bold, below)** have the most government organizations and companies doing top-secret work.

San Diego is a Navy hub.

Corporate locations
Government organizations

Bar chart values: Fort Meade 681, McLean-Tysons-Fairfax 511, Washington 400, Arlington 396, Dulles-Chantilly 311, Fort Belvoir 281, Norfolk 175, Tampa, Colorado Springs, San Antonio, Omaha, Bethesda 73, Fort Bragg N.C., Dayton Ohio, El Segundo-Los Angeles, San Diego, Honolulu, Quantico 56, Huntsville Ala., Denver-Aurora

37 44 32 62 22 32 33 5 5 100 0

Companies doing top-secret work tend to locate near the government organizations they are doing business with. The Washington area is America's hot spot for such contractors.

LOCATIONS: ● Corporate ● Government

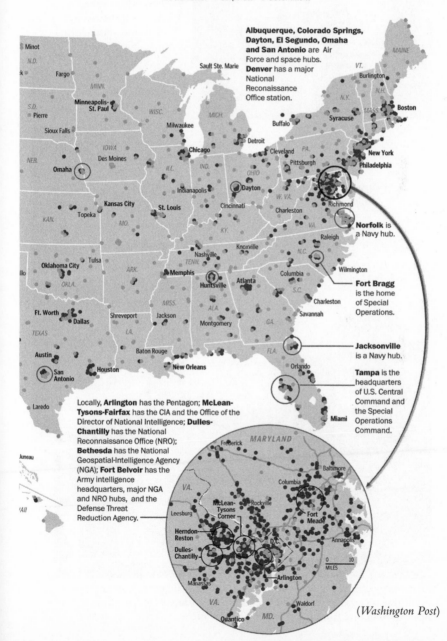

Albuquerque, Colorado Springs, **Dayton, El Segundo, Omaha and San Antonio** are Air Force and space hubs. **Denver** has a major National Reconnaissance Office station.

Norfolk is a Navy hub.

Fort Bragg is the home of Special Operations.

Jacksonville is a Navy hub.

Tampa is the headquarters of U.S. Central Command and the Special Operations Command.

Locally, **Arlington** has the Pentagon; **McLean-Tysons-Fairfax** has the CIA and the Office of the Director of National Intelligence; **Dulles-Chantilly** has the National Reconnaissance Office (NRO); **Bethesda** has the National Geospatial-Intelligence Agency (NGA); **Fort Belvoir** has the Army intelligence headquarters, major NGA and NRO hubs, and the Defense Threat Reduction Agency.

(*Washington Post*)

Stars engraved on the wall of the CIA represent people who have died in the line of duty. Of the twenty-two stars representing people killed since 9/11, eight are for private contractors. (Central Intelligence Agency)

A local café near the National Security Agency advertises a job fair for people with security clearances. (Michael S. Williamson/*Washington Post*)

IT companies doing business with the Defense Intelligence Agency sponsor a nighttime social at a Phoenix convention for contractors and the government officials who buy from them. (Michael S. Williamson/*Washington Post*)

Representatives from various agencies, including local police and fire departments, the National Guard, the Tennessee Bureau of Investigation, and the FBI, attend a threat briefing at the National Guard headquarters in Nashville. (Michael S. Williamson/*Washington Post*)

Retired admiral Dennis Blair was the third director of national intelligence. He resigned when it became clear that the position lacked the authority he was promised when he took the job. (Office of the Director of National Intelligence)

Police in Memphis out on patrol use an automatic license plate scanner enhanced with databases created by the department's high-tech guru, former police detective John Harvey. (Michael S. Williamson/*Washington Post*)

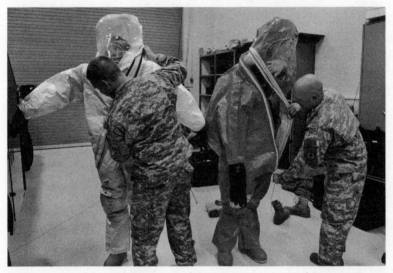

In the garage of the 45th Weapons of Mass Destruction Civil Support Team, members go through biohazard-suit training. From left: Sgt. Jason Barfield (in suit), Sgt. Mike McIntyre, Sgt. David Owen, and Sgt. Tony Dooley (Michael S. Williamson/*Washington Post*)

At the Memphis Police Department's Real Time Crime Center, Officer Brian Shivley watches one of the many video feeds from cameras placed throughout the city. (Michael S. Williamson/*Washington Post*)

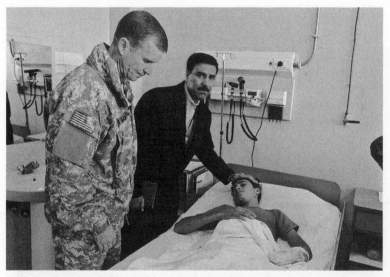

Gen. Stanley A. McChrystal was the commander who reinvented the Joint Special Operations Command before being promoted to commander of NATO's International Security Assistance Force and United States Forces–Afghanistan. Here in a December 23, 2009, photo, he listens to a story of abuses faced by a wounded Afghan soldier recuperating at the Afghan National Army Hospital. (U.S. Army Sgt. David E. Alvarado)

An MQ-1 Predator drone armed with a Hellfire missile flies a training mission. The Predator's main overseas mission is conducting surveillance and armed reconnaissance, but it also is used in targeted killings of suspected al-Qaeda leaders and other so-called high-value targets, individuals whom the U.S. government is trying to kill. (U.S. Air Force)

With JSOC equipment, U.S. forces demonstrate entry tactics for a counter-terrorism force composed of coalition and Iraqi forces in Baghdad. (Chief Mass Communications Specialist Michael B. W. Watkins/U.S. Navy)

An air force combat controller, armed with an M4A1 carbine, pictured in Afghanistan. The controllers help guide special operations AC-130 gunships and other aircraft toward their targets on the ground. They played a pivotal role in ousting the Taliban from power in 2001 and in directing strikes against high-value targets. (Staff Sgt. Jeremy T. Lock/ U.S. Air Force)

A special operations commando in Iraq. (Chief Mass Communications Specialist Michael B. W. Watkins/U.S. Navy)

President Barack Obama studies a document held by James Clapper during the Presidential Daily Brief in the Oval Office, February 3, 2011. (Pete Souza/The White House)

briefings on possible targets. They were advised to switch their own official license plates to ordinary ones so that they could keep a low profile. The Tennessee National Guard and military installations went on alert. Within three weeks, the governor appointed a retired brigadier general to head the state's antiterrorism campaign and a new Homeland Security Council to coordinate the actions of a dozen agencies charged with protecting the state. Tennessee governor Don Sundquist promised the new effort would cost "very little" money. Emblematic of the economizing, the new Office of Homeland Security squeezed its tiny staff into the Veterans Affairs office downtown.

But frugality quickly gave way to fervor. Just eighteen months later, state politicians had coughed up millions for a new bureaucracy, and the federal funding floodgates opened. Today Tennessee's Homeland Security Department alone has a staff of twenty-eight and an annual budget in the millions, and occupies two floors of the looming Tennessee Towers State Office building, as well as three regional offices. Forty-five terrorism liaison officers have been appointed to keep small towns and rural communities up-to-date on threats identified by Washington and elsewhere. The FBI opened three new Joint Terrorism Task Forces in Tennessee (in Nashville, Knoxville, and Memphis). All members of the JTTFs needed security clearances, some at the top secret level; such clearances were highly coveted. To transfer the classified information from FBI headquarters on Pennsylvania Avenue to Tennessee, workmen laid encrypted cable lines and built SCIFs in Memphis. In Tennessee alone, over a thousand law enforcement officers participate in counterterrorism and homeland security training, learning to stop possible terrorists, communicate with each other quickly, and respond to catastrophic attacks. Despite the expensive buildup, however, the reality in Tennessee and most other cities and towns across the country is that there just isn't enough terrorism-related work to keep everyone busy. A sample day in Utah saw one of five intelligence analysts in the state's fusion center writing a report about the rise in teenage overdoses of an over-the-counter drug. Another was making sure the visiting president of Senegal had a safe trip. Another had just helped a small town track down two people who claimed to be selling magazine subscriptions but who were pocketing the money themselves, a far cry from a national security problem.

In nearby Colorado, at the state's Information Analysis Center, a few investigators were following terrorism leads, but others were looking into illegal Craigslist postings and online World of Warcraft gamers. In fact, the vast majority of fusion centers across the country have transformed themselves into analytical hubs for *all* crimes, from school vandalism to petty drug dealing. They use federal grants, handed out in the name of homeland security, to combat everyday offenses.

This overcapacity arose because after 9/11, local law enforcement groups did what every agency and private company did in Top Secret America: they followed the money. The DHS helped the Memphis Police Department, for example, purchase ninety surveillance cameras, including thirteen that monitor bridges and a causeway. It helped buy fancy video monitors that hang on the walls of a new Real Time Crime Center, as well as radios, robotic surveillance equipment, a mobile command center, and three bomb-sniffing dogs. All came in the name of river port security and protection to critical infrastructure such as bridges, dams, highways, and power stations.

Since there hasn't been a solid terrorism case in Memphis yet, the equipment's greatest value has been to help drive down local crime. Where the mobile surveillance cameras are set up, criminals scatter, said Lieutenant Mark Rewalt, as he spent a Saturday night scanning the city from an altitude of 1,000 feet. Flying in a police helicopter, Rewalt pointed out some of the numerous DHS-funded cameras below. The devices constellated the entire city; they were found in mall parking lots, in housing projects, at popular street hangouts. "Cameras are what's happening now," he marveled.

Looking at the Tennessee fusion center's website, you'd never guess that there hasn't been much terrorism around these parts.

Click on the incident map, and the state appears to be under furious attack: red icons of explosions dot Tennessee, along with blinking exclamation marks and flashing skulls. The map is labeled "Terrorism Events and Other Suspicious Activity." But roll over the icons and the explanations that pop up have nothing whatsoever to do with terrorist plots: "Johnson City police are investigating three 'bottle bombs' found at homes over the past three days," reads one description. "The explosives were made from plastic bottles with something inside that reacted chemically and caused the bottles to burst." Another told a similar story: "The Scott County Courthouse is currently under evacuation after a bomb threat was called in Friday morning. Update: Authorities completed their sweep... and have called off the evacuation." Nine years after 9/11, this map is part of the alternative geography that is Top Secret America.

Among the millions of people now assigned to help stop terrorism is Memphis Police director Larry Godwin, and he has his own version of what that means in a city where there have been more than ninety murders in 2010. "We have our own terrorists, and they are taking lives every day," Godwin said. "No, we don't have suicide bombers—not yet. But you need to remain vigilant and realize how vulnerable you can be if you let up."

Memphis wasn't about to let up, not while dollars continued to flow from DHS and crime remained high. In addition to the surveillance cameras that monitor residents near high-crime housing projects, problematic street corners, and bridges and other critical infrastructure, the federal agency helped the city pay for license plate readers and defrayed some of the cost of setting up a crime analysis center for the city. All together, since 2003, it has given Memphis $11 million in homeland security grants.

"We have got things now we didn't have before," acknowledged Godwin, who has produced record numbers of arrests using all this new analysis and technology. "Some of them we can talk about. Some of them we can't."

What he is more willing to discuss is how everything an officer does out on the street—all warrants issued, arrests made, subjects apprehended—is automatically transferred to the Memphis Real Time Crime Center, a command center with three walls of streaming surveillance video and analysis capabilities that rival those of an army command center. The tentacles of Godwin's operation reach deeply into the city's streets and neighborhoods. I got a whiff of just how deeply while riding around a Memphis public housing complex with the police department's ingenious database geek, a former cop named John Harvey who traded in his badge to become a tech guru.

Harvey, who retains arrest powers and a patrol vehicle, mostly to test and demonstrate his new gadgets, drove slowly past the cars in the parking lot in front of the rundown two-story town houses. Inside his vehicle, between the two front seats, Harvey had mounted the civilian equivalent of the Special Operations equipment used by the military—a computer that can ingest a person's name and spew back a package of data on the individual collected from various government and commercial databases. With these new tools and money from state and federal grants, Harvey and local police officers like him are building ever more sophisticated localized intelligence systems. When officers were wasting time knocking on the wrong doors to serve warrants, Harvey persuaded the local utility company to give him a daily update of the names and addresses of customers. When he wanted more information about phones captured at crime scenes, he programmed a method of storing all emergency 911 calls (which often include names and addresses) that the police could later associate with a found phone or other data and documents. He created another program to upload new crime reports every five minutes and to mine them for phone numbers of victims, suspects, witnesses, bystanders, and anyone else listed.

Then he persuaded the department to buy seventy military-grade infrared cameras to mount on the hoods of patrol cars. Now, instead of having to decide which license plate numbers to type into a computer console in the patrol car, an officer can simply drive around while the automatic license plate reader moves robotically from left to right, snapping digital images of one license plate after another and then automatically running them against the computer databases. That allowed Harvey to drive through a housing project, or park at the side of a busy street, and just wait for one of the sounds he'd programmed into the computer to signal a hit on a license number: a "boing" for lesser offenses, such as driving on a suspended license or traffic violations; a gunshot or siren for more serious alerts, including convicted gangster, sex offender, felon, murderer.

When he got a hit, the tap of a key on the keyboard brought up the name of the car's owner. Another tap brought up the owner's criminal history. If there was one, he'd hit another key, and this was when it got weird: the names of all the other people in his database who shared the same address—family, friends—would pop up, along with past offenses, aliases, Social Security numbers. Sitting in the car with him, aiming the camera at a certain car or a certain apartment, I felt like a Peeping Tom, as though I were peering through the window of a house and could see the people inside.

Harvey explained that the depth of information was valuable for officer safety. "You want to know who you're dealing with." That made sense. The data could also be used to flush out a hunch, the kind police officers are trained to feel in their gut. That man stuffing something in his jeans—is he living with his mother, or is he a convicted drug dealer? Let's watch what house he goes into and see if that address is in the database, and see if any convicted criminals live there, and if any of them are drug dealers.

The system can also track observations that may have no criminal connotation alone but which, when correlated, could be suggestive. An officer might wonder who owns the red truck parked under the bridge; by checking the system, he can see if it has ever been seen at another bridge before, and, if so, how many times. The more data captured, the more connections made.

As Harvey approached a parking lot, a young woman standing on the sidewalk noticed him. She walked around to the back of her car to block his view of her license plate. He stopped the car five feet from her and waited. She waited, too. He inched the car up a bit. She repositioned herself. He inched the car back. She moved again. "I could wait her out," he said, as she stood with her back to him, now only three feet from his bumper. But he moved on instead.

On another night, a police patrol car rolled slowly through the parking lot of a large discount store. The camera on the hood snapped digital images of one license plate after another and analyzed each almost instantly. The officers inside the car waited for a hit.

Suddenly, a red light flashed on the car's computer screen, along with the word *warrant*.

"Got a live one! Let's do it," the officer called out.

When an officer got a hit, he could pull over the driver, and, instead of having to wait twenty minutes for someone back at the office to manually check records, he could use a handheld computer to instantly call up eight databases. He might find a mug shot or a driver's license photo, a Social Security number, the status of the driver's license, traffic violations, past charges, aliases, any outstanding warrants, and even pawn shop sales—basically everything but fines on overdue library books. Such data came from throughout the state of Tennessee and was available to every law enforcement officer who had access to the databases.

The rationale for having such data available during routine traffic stops, as it applies to terrorism, is not to miss the next Mohammed Atta. Shortly before 9/11, three of the hijackers were separately stopped for minor traffic offenses. Atta, the leader of the operation who piloted one of the planes into the twin towers, was stopped and fined in Florida for driving without a valid driver's license. He failed to pay the fine, and a warrant was issued for his arrest. When he was stopped again several weeks later, this time for speeding, he was let go because the officer was not aware of the outstanding warrant. Had a nationwide or even statewide integrated computerized system been in place, he might have been detained, and history might have turned out differently.

Linking databases is a major goal for people like Napolitano and Harvey. When the technology works correctly, people doing bad things get caught. But when it doesn't work right, such reliance on technology can cause a different kind of problem, like the one encountered on the night I took a second ride with Harvey and two police officers.

I had joined Harvey, the two police officers, and *Washington Post* photographer Michael Williamson as the officers patrolled the streets with automatic license plate readers mounted on two patrol cars. They were looking for drivers with outstanding warrants and other infractions, and hoping for something more exciting than that. Alas, nothing dramatic was coming up. One of the most interesting hits, after several hours on the job, was the plate on a black car they saw in the discount store parking lot. Its registered male owner, said to be aged thirty-five, was wanted on three drug charges. The officers waited at a distance for him to come out of the store and get back into the vehicle, where they figured they would arrest him. After ten minutes, however, they were disappointed to see three teenage girls hop in the car instead.

Two other times the license plate readers beeped and the person driving the car was not the owner who had unpaid tickets but an elderly parent instead. Slightly confused and scared by the posse of police cars demonstrating a sudden interest in them, the drivers cooperated with every instruction given. (In both cases, they were poor African Americans with rundown vehicles in a town whose racial divide is more starkly apparent than in other more integrated cities.)

"It's a target-rich environment," Harvey joked as the patrol cars headed off. Even if the pullovers were false alarms, at least they provided a chance to enter more data.

The computer monitors began boinging again. The radio crackled.

"I've got five cocaine hits on this black Toyota," one of the officers announced as they moved through another parking lot. "Let's see who gets in the car."

$\star$ $\star$ $\star$

All the information from Harvey's night on patrol, down to the last license plate number, was fed into the Real Time Crime Center back at headquarters. It was plotted on a map, along with information about the other cars stopped, warrants written, and arrests made that night and every night, to produce a visual rendering. This information would help analysts predict trends so the department could figure out what neighborhoods to swarm next with officers and surveillance cameras. These police sweeps, called Blue Crush by the Memphis Police Department, sometimes netted thousands of arrests, far too many for the local jail system to handle.

"They throw them out as fast as we put them in," Harvey grunted. But that was still not the end of it, either, because the fingerprints from the crime records would also go to the FBI's data campus in Clarksburg, West Virginia. There are ninety-six million sets of fingerprints in Clarksburg, including those of all military personnel and all U.S. prisoners, and including those of citizens of Saudi Arabia and Yemen, Iraq, and Afghanistan. It's a volume that government officials view not as daunting but as an opportunity. In 2010, for the first time, the FBI, the DHS, and the Defense Department were able to search each other's fingerprint databases, said Myra Gray, head of the Defense Department's Biometrics Identity Management Agency, speaking to an industry group. "Hopefully in the not too distant future," she said, "our relationship with these federal agencies— along with state and local agencies—will be completely symbiotic."

At the same time that the biometric and fingerprinting staff are building their database in West Virginia, and the police department in Memphis is building its database, and the state of Tennessee and other states across the country are building their databases, in the nation's capital, the FBI is building an even bigger, more powerful repository of information on American citizens and legal residents with an Orwellian name: Guardian.

The Guardian database is controlled by people who work in a top-secret vault on the fourth floor of the J. Edgar Hoover FBI

Building on Pennsylvania Avenue, near the Capitol. Guardian stores the profiles of tens of thousands of Americans and legal residents who are not accused of any crime. Most are not even suspected of one. What they have done is appear, to a town sheriff, a traffic cop, or even a neighbor, to be acting suspiciously. The federal government defines a suspicious activity in a fairly loose way, as "observed behavior reasonably indicative of pre-operational planning related to terrorism or other criminal activity." In fact, the very effectiveness of this database depends on collecting the identities of people who are not now known criminals or terrorists, and on being able to quickly compile in-depth profiles of them on the theory that someday in the future a nugget of information will come in that will clarify whether the person is or is not a threat. In this way, it is a giant dragnet with which the FBI hopes to snare some gold. Like any dragnet, it is bound to sweep up at least some of the innocent.

If the new Nationwide Suspicious Activity Reporting Initiative, or SAR, works as intended, the Guardian database may someday hold files forwarded by all police departments across the country in America's continuing search for terrorists within its borders. That, certainly, is the hope.

In some places, citizens eagerly joined the fight. In Kentucky, the Office of Homeland Security released a free mobile phone application, created by the publicly held NIC corporation, that allows users to send suspicious activity reports immediately to police authorities with a description of the fishy person—represented on the app by a figure of a person fleeing—as well as a cell phone photograph, a map of the suspicious person's location, the subject's vehicle license plate number, the time of day, and a description of "the incident."

FBI officials say anyone with access to Guardian has been trained in privacy rules and the penalties for breaking them. But time and again enthusiastic local police have used the suspicion of terrorism to collect intelligence on perfectly legal protest groups, which is exactly what got the FBI in so much trouble more than three decades ago. Without appropriate training and without clear privacy guidelines, bad things happen all the time, as they did in

Pennsylvania after the state's director of homeland security, a former Army Special Forces officer with years of experience overseas but none in U.S. law enforcement, contracted with a former New York City police officer to write intelligence bulletins.

The former New York police officer, Michael Perelman, had cofounded a nonprofit security organization called the Institute for Terrorism Research and Response. Three times a week, beginning in October 2009, ITRR sent its intelligence reports to 1,800 law enforcement and homeland security offices and to state employees' email accounts. The group was supposed to monitor real threats to Pennsylvania's critical infrastructure, resources, and special events. Instead, the bulletins reported on lawful meetings and protests of groups as varied as the Pennsylvania Tea Party Patriots Coalition, the Libertarian Movement, antiwar protesters, animal rights groups, and environmental activists dressed up as Santa Claus and handing out coal-filled stockings.

After the *Philadelphia Inquirer* discovered the existence of a Homeland Security Department sole source contract with Perelman worth $102,000 and some of his intelligence reports on lawful groups, the governor ended the contract and apologized, the legislature held hearings, and Major George Bivens, the head of the Pennsylvania Bureau of Criminal Investigations, revealed that he had complained about the reports but was unsuccessful in stopping them. "I would liken it to reading the *National Enquirer*," he wrote in one email he gave to legislators. "Every so often they have it right but most of the time it is unsubstantiated gossip."

State intelligence analysts and FBI investigators say they use Suspicious Activity Reports to determine, for example, whether a person is buying fertilizer to make a bomb or to plant tomatoes; whether she is plotting to poison a city's drinking water or studying for a metallurgy test; whether, as happened on a Sunday morning in late September, the man snapping a picture of a ferry in the Newport Beach harbor in Southern California simply liked the way it looked or was plotting to blow it up.

Photographing the ferry had turned up in Suspicious Activity

Report N03821, a local law enforcement officer noting that he had observed "a suspicious subject... taking photographs of the Orange County Sheriff Department Fire Boat and the Balboa Ferry with a cellular phone camera." The confidential report, marked "For Official Use Only," noted that the subject next made a phone call, walked to his car, and returned five minutes later to take more pictures. He was then met by another person, both of whom stood and "observed the boat traffic in the harbor." Next, another adult with two small children joined them, and then they all boarded the ferry and crossed the channel.

All of this information was forwarded to the Los Angeles fusion center for further investigation after the local officer ran information about the vehicle and its owner through several crime databases and found nothing. Authorities would not say what happened from there, but there are several paths a Suspicious Activity Report can take. At the fusion center, an officer would decide either to dismiss the suspicious activity as harmless or to forward the report to the nearest FBI terrorism unit for further investigation. At that unit, the information would immediately be entered into the Guardian database, at which point one of three things could happen. The FBI could collect more information, find no connection to terrorism, and mark the file closed but leave it in the database. It could find a possible connection and turn it into a full-fledged case. Or, as most often happens, it could make no specific determination, which would mean that Suspicious Activity Report N03821 would sit in limbo for as long as five years, during which time many other pieces of information about the man photographing a boat on a Sunday morning could be added to his file: employment, financial, and residential histories; multiple phone numbers; audio files; video from the dashboard-mounted camera in the police cruiser at the harbor where he took pictures; and anything else in government or commercial databases "that adds value," as the FBI agent in charge of the database described it. The FBI is even working on a way to attach biometric data, such as iris scans and facial images, to files. Meanwhile, the bureau will also soon have software that allows local agencies to map all suspicious incidents in their jurisdiction.

Traditional law enforcement channels are not the only ones taking advantage of Guardian. The Defense Department recently transferred one hundred reports of suspicious behavior into the system. Over time it expects to add thousands more as it connects eight thousand military law enforcement personnel to an FBI portal that will allow them to send and review Suspicious Activity Reports about people suspected of casing U.S. bases or targeting American military personnel.

As of December 2010, there were 161,948 suspicious activity files in the classified Guardian database, according to the FBI. These were mainly leads from FBI headquarters and state field offices. Back in 2008, the FBI also set up an unclassified section of the Guardian database so that state and local agencies could send in suspicious incident reports and review those submitted by their counterparts in other states. Some 890 state and local agencies have sent in 7,197 reports so that far; the FBI has turned 103 of those into full investigations. From those investigations have come five arrests, the FBI said. There have been no convictions yet, but FBI agents point out it can take years for an arrest to come to trial. An additional 365 reports, explained the FBI's database manager, have added information to ongoing cases.

While the list of SAR success stories supplied by the FBI's public information office filled a page, only a few were significant. Last year, the Colorado fusion center helped the FBI's Denver office analyze information obtained through an FBI search warrant on Najibullah Zazi, an Afghan-born U.S. resident who was planning to bomb the New York subway system. The FBI was already furiously at work on the case and had used the Colorado fusion center's databases to help it quickly understand the information it had obtained. Zazi was arrested before he could carry out his alleged plot (though not before another police department, New York City's, got involved and unintentionally tipped him off to the investigation).

And in 2007, according to the FBI public affairs office, a Florida fusion center provided the vehicle ownership history that helped an ongoing FBI investigation identify and arrest an Egyptian student who later pleaded guilty to providing material support to terrorism, in this case transporting explosives. Some FBI agents said they would have eventually turned up the same information in both cases themselves, but were grateful for the help of their local counterparts.

"Ninety-nine percent doesn't pan out or lead to anything," said Richard L. Lambert Jr., the special agent in charge of the FBI's Knoxville field office. "But we're happy to wade through these things."

In practice, most SAR reports—and the names of the people included in them—don't go anywhere; they remain in the uncertain middle and just sit in the database, which feeds into the debate over the privacy implications of retaining so much information on U.S. citizens and residents who have not been charged with anything.

Most of the FBI agents who have doubts about the system won't publicly say so, given that their views are contrary to official policy. But if you asked the question another way, whether more terrorism cases come about as a result of this digital dragnet or from more focused, old-fashioned agent work, the agents responded like Richard A. McFeely, special agent in charge of the FBI's Baltimore division. Talking about the Baltimore suspect in the attempt to bomb the military recruitment center, I asked him whether the new technology had helped crack the case.

"This was good, old-fashioned police work by a lot of different police agencies coming together."

"Okay, so not so heavy on the technology?" I asked.

"That's correct."

Still, McFeely defended the large database. "We need it because you never know," he said. "And it's that one question mark that is out there."

We need it because you never know is the answer to so many questions about the size, expense, and effectiveness of Top Secret

America. But is that really an answer? "You never know" was the same as saying that all the spending, all the effort, even all the waste was worth it because, well, it might stop one attack. Nowhere else in American life has this kind of logic been an acceptable answer, except perhaps during the cold war, when a first strike by the Soviet Union could have resulted in mutual obliteration.

In every other arena, more rational cost-benefit calculations prevail. The government isn't deploying a million people and spending hundreds of billions of dollars to stop illegal drug sales and use, even though many more people die each year from drug-related violence than die in terrorist attacks, and authorities know for certain that at least as many will die from drug-related violence the following year. Most people drive cars, even though 24,474 of them died in auto accidents in 2009. Parents don't keep their children locked at home all day because they might be killed—even though 1,096 children were murdered in 2007 alone.

But if someone is taking pictures of a bridge in some city and a citizen reports it, it will probably end up in the FBI's database, said Lambert. If there's no other information connecting any of that to even a whiff of something suspicious, "that name will lie dormant there" until the same person "at a later time takes a picture of another bridge across the country or starts taking pictures of the gates at Langley [CIA's headquarters]." Explained Lambert, "Unless we have the ability to go back and look at that [information], we can't do this type of what we call predictive analysis." If the American public is worried about the privacy implications, "my message back, I guess, is that you really can't have it both ways.... We are very careful... but if we want to get to the point where we want to connect the dots, the dots have to be there. And if we're being told that the dots have to be erased every time we have contact with a dot and there's no derogatory information there," the FBI will never be able to forecast an attack.

Other democracies—Britain and Israel, to name two—are well acquainted with the sort of domestic security measures that have become increasingly commonplace in Top Secret America.

But for the United States, the sum of these activities represents a new level of governmental scrutiny of its population. Nonprofit organizations like Secrecy News, the Electronic Privacy Information Center, and the American Civil Liberties Union (ACLU) have worked around-the-clock to counter the tidal wave of new attempts to collect and mine data on Americans. Congress has held briefings, but they were never well attended. People seem not to notice the incremental changes taking place across the country, the eroding of privacy and the tabulation of personal information in government hands.

Charles Allen, who left the CIA to accept the job of leading DHS's new intelligence arm, has his own misgivings about the dragnet nature of the SAR system, and he knows other senior intelligence officials who are also skeptical. "It's more likely that other kinds of more focused efforts by local police will gain you the information that you need about extremist activities," he concluded.

Besides that, "You make mistakes," Allen said. "You put information in that's fallacious, because in the world of terrorism, counterterrorism, false reporting, exaggerated reporting seems to be a norm." As a result, he added, "I found that we were reacting, overreacting to virtually everything." Overreaction doesn't just end up wasting time and money; it also undermines morale, vigor, and credibility. American intelligence has long been haunted by its struggles to make wise connections within the enormous amount of information it has on hand. In the end, technology is only as good as the people who use it.

As with so much in the new world of Top Secret America, everything about this nationwide, technology-assisted, database-driven, distended dragnet of names relies on local police department employees to make the right decisions. The ones I met were enthusiastic, for sure. They wanted to dive into the toughest cases. In heartfelt testimony, police association representatives told Congress that they needed funds to develop ties with foreign intelligence services. They wanted security clearances and access to more and more classified information. Many departments longed to be like the New York City Police Department, which routinely sent investigators overseas when attacks occurred to look for links to Big Apple residents and terrorist networks.

Even in the smallest local police agencies, excitement over the post-9/11 national security mission was palpable. Idaho State Police sergeant Russell Wheatley, who manages the state's intelligence fusion center, did not have any international problems to investigate. The closest he got was arresting violent white supremacist and survivalist groups. Timothy McVeigh and Terry Nichols were never far from his mind. But he was ready to join the bigger fight against global terrorism anytime. Sitting in his squad car one day, his enthusiasm bubbled over. "It kinda gives me a chill to think that something a state trooper does will someday evolve into something that has to do with national security."

Most of Wheatley's colleagues had little training in terrorism analysis. They weren't FBI agents. Instead, they were often people like Lacy Craig, who was a police dispatcher before she became an intelligence analyst at Idaho's fusion center. Or they are like the detectives in Minnesota, Michigan, and Arkansas who can talk at length about the lineage of gangs or the signs of a crystal meth addict, but don't know the difference between a Shi'a and a Sunni Muslim. Yet these days, they are terrorism analysts, too.

"The CIA used to train analysts forever before they graduated to be a real analyst," said Allen, the former top CIA and DHS official. "Today we take former law enforcement officers and we call them 'intelligence officers,' and that's not right, because they have not received any training on intelligence analysis."

State fusion center officials say their analysts are getting better with time. "There was a time when law enforcement didn't know much about drugs. This is no different," said Steven W. Hewitt, codirector of the Tennessee fusion center, considered one of the best in the country. "Are we experts at the level of [the National Counterterrorism Center]? No. Are we developing an expertise? Absolutely."

Becoming expert is only partly helped by the quantity and quality of information the fusion centers receive from Washington. DHS's daily reports were meant to inform agencies about possible terror threats. But to some officials they seemed like a never-ending stream of random details—vague, alarmist, and often useless.

We reviewed nearly a thousand DHS reports dating back to 2003 and labeled "For Official Use Only" that confirmed that view. Typical is one from May 24, 2010, titled "Infrastructure Protection Note: Evolving Threats to the Homeland." It tells officials to operate "under the premise that other operatives are in the country and could advance plotting with little or no warning." Its list of vulnerable facilities seems to include just about everything: "Commercial Facilities, Government Facilities, Banking and Financial and Transportation..."

As Harvey, the two police officers, the photographer, and I traveled the streets of Memphis looking for problems, during one stop I was reminded just how all-powerful the local police can be as a seething tension quickly emerged between the officers and a young woman who had done nothing wrong at all.

It happened after the officers spotted a car several blocks away that fit the description of one they had been searching for since the week before. They drove over to the vehicle as it slowly made its way down a residential street of small, modest homes. As they drew closer, they turned on their flashing lights and the motorist, now at nearly a crawl, came to a stop. But instead of waiting in her car for an officer to approach as instructed over the megaphone, the driver opened the door and jumped out. "What's the matter?" she asked them.

Get back in your car, she was ordered.

Instead of immediately complying, the woman stiffened. "Why? What's this about? Why are you stopping me?"

"Ma'am, just get back in your car."

"Why? What did I do? This is my neighborhood."

"Ma'am, please just do as I say."

"Well, tell me what I did."

She had angled her car as if it were about to go down the driveway of the house where she had come to a stop, which happened to be her elderly father's home. He was now walking briskly toward her.

"Honey, just do as the man asks," he pleaded with his daughter, who was having none of it.

"What did I do? Why are you pulling me over?" she demanded, as one of the officers focused intently on his handheld computer while the other, hand on his gun, chest slightly thrust forward, told her again: "Get back in your car."

She looked at me and the photographer, trying to figure out what was going on and getting more incensed as the situation sank in.

"What did I do?" she demanded.

"Obstructing a lane of traffic," the officer finally said.

"What! This is my street. This is my house. Why are you doing this? I work for the city of Memphis—"

"Honey, just let the officers do their job," her father called out, clearly worried about the escalating tone of the argument, as the unequal balance of power became more and more obvious and ominous. They could make her life miserable right now. I had a powerful urge to tell the woman what they should have told her right away, that they had been looking for a car just like hers but had obviously made a mistake.

"Please give me your driver's license," the officer demanded. She handed it over.

"Is it valid?" he asked.

The young woman exploded. "Of course it's valid! I work for the city of Memphis. I work hard. You gonna write me a ticket? For what? Being in my own street. Why are you doing this? Why do you think it's okay to pull over a black person like this?"

"Whoa, whoa, whoa, you callin' us racist?" the officer demanded.

"Why are you doing this?" she tried again. "Now I'm going to have to spend a whole day off work fighting this. Why don't you go find some real crime? There's plenty of it in this city. Why are you doing this when nothing happened? This isn't right. Why do you think you can just come and do this?!'"

"Just calm down," the officer ordered.

"Honey..." her father tried again.

"Man...," she said under her breath, trying her best to maintain calm.

He wrote out a ticket and handed it to her. It would cost her a half-day's wages or at least a day off to fight it.

"Okay, here," he said, handing her the ticket. "You can pay this downtown."

"One hundred twenty-five dollars!" she yelled out. "Ahhh! For what? Being in my own neighborhood?"

"Good night, officers," her father called out. "Thank you."

The officers were already walking back to their cars. The police car doors closed. As they pulled away, a small crowd of family members and neighbors gathered around the woman.

"Can you believe it? Did you hear that?" one of the officers said as the police car rolled down the quiet street. "She called me racist. I can't believe it.... Well, we just made her day."

CHAPTER EIGHT

007s

Every police agency sending a terrorist tip in to the FBI and
every FBI bureau that began working on counterterrorism
since the 9/11 attacks created a ripple throughout the national
security bureaucracy. More tips and more counterterrorism organizations meant more intelligence analysts, more investigators,
more technical spying experts, gadget inventors, and out-on-the-
street agents. Those people, in turn, required more administrative
and logistics support: secretaries, clerks, recruiters, librarians, personnel managers, IT staff, construction workers, architects, jani-
tors, air-conditioning mechanics, security specialists, countless
guards; and every one of them, including those who emptied the
trash and processed health insurance claims, had to have a top
secret clearance.

Even organizations that did not directly perform top secret
work needed a few employees with security clearances. On Capitol
Hill, the Senate sergeant at arms, the Architect of the Capitol, the
U.S. Capitol Police, all these law enforcement officers of Congress
whose jobs are also to protect the members, they, too, have top

secret clearances so they can be briefed by the Secret Service on classified threats, and can be read into sensitive evacuation plans. The National Archives staff need clearances, too—and their own special SCIF in Maryland—in order to have access to historic classified documents.

In fact, there isn't a single federal department that doesn't have a group of employees with top secret clearances to receive sensitive threat-reporting information, to join interagency committees, and to plan for national security emergencies and participate in classified exercises using terrorist attack scenarios. This includes the National Park Service, whose newly created intelligence and counterterrorism unit protects Washington monuments and other national icons. The same is true for the Environmental Protection Agency, where law enforcement coordinators deal with sensitive information about chemical and biological agents, and for the Department of Labor, which handles health-care claims for some clandestine military employees.

The expansion of top secret clearances has been so extensive and opaque that not even the people charged with answering the public's questions always know what is happening in their own agencies. When Arkin called the U.S. Forest Service's public affairs office to ask how many employees had top secret clearances, the conversation sounded like an argument between first graders.

"We don't have anyone with a top secret clearance," the staffer told him.

"Yes, you do," Arkin said.

"No, we don't."

"Yes, you do."

"No, we don't."

"I'll email the information to you."

That was the way the conversation went at a half-dozen agencies.

Then again, for employees of other agencies, it was hard to track the influx. Even in offices long used to dealing with a cadre of top secret employees, the speed of the expansion after 9/11 made the clearance process impossible to keep up with. When Arkin compiled a chart listing the number of people with top secret clearances throughout the government—a calculation based on two years of reporting and reviewing budgets—the person in charge of clearances for most government employees (most, but not all, because no one was in charge of them all) said: "That sounds about right." Then she asked if she could use a copy of his chart for her next congressional testimony.

The huge numbers aren't unprecedented. At the height of the cold war, more Americans had held top secret clearances than at any point in history. But back then government was twice as large overall, and the military five times the size it is today. Most people granted top secret clearance were building bombers and missiles and managing a stockpile of thirty thousand nuclear weapons. The number shrank precipitously from the mid-1980s through the end of the century.

This new top secret boom was a different animal. Arkin estimated that if you added in the legions of private contractors hired after 9/11 to do work once handled by federal employees, and if you counted all the political appointees, military personnel, state and local officials, and law enforcement officers, 854,000 people held top secret clearances. This number roughly equaled one and a half times the entire population of the nation's capital.

Requests for new clearances after the terrorist attacks so overtaxed the Defense Security Service (DSS), the agency that grants clearances to industry contractors, that on April 28, 2006, DSS shut down the process altogether, sending shock waves through the nation's most dynamic business sector. DSS "will reject any requests that are submitted," read an urgent notice sent to businesses via email that day. The backlog of pending cases had grown to 700,000. DSS had simply run out of money to process any more.

A top secret clearance is a passport to prosperity for life. Salaries for employees with top secret clearances are significantly higher than those for someone doing the same thing at an unclassified level. A clearance is also almost a guarantee of permanent employment, even in economic hard times. Top secret clearances are coveted for those reasons, and also because they are a sign of acceptance into an elite corps of individuals entrusted with knowing what other citizens cannot know, and with securing the country's future. But as the tens of thousands of Americans newly ushered into the world of Top Secret America soon discovered, getting a clearance is like walking through a mirror into an alternate universe. To obtain a top secret clearance, employees must submit to intrusive background investigations. They must take lie detector tests routinely, sign nondisclosure forms, and file lengthy reports whenever they travel overseas. Not only are they extensively interviewed, but their friends and neighbors are questioned as well. Once hired, they are coached on how to deal with nosy neighbors and curious friends. They learn how not to talk about work, even within their families. Some are trained to assume false identities for one assignment, or for a few years, or an entire lifetime, giving up contact with friends, and in some cases even family, to go undercover.

These strictures spawn a tendency for the cleared not only to marry the cleared but to live around others with comparable restraints, gathered in neighborhoods populated by people like themselves in a version of a traditional military town. They are economically dependent on the federal government and culturally defined by their unique work. The difference, though, is that while the military may be an insular society, it is not a secret culture. On the contrary, soldiers and officers wear their names and ranks prominently on their uniforms. They display badges and patches that tell a personal narrative of skills acquired, places deployed to, awards received, and wars fought. They belong to huge alumni associations and openly support charitable works. They offer to put themselves in harm's way and in return receive modest salaries but high public praise. The public debate about the military's role in protecting the country and promoting American values is open and vibrant. Their mission is honored in parades; their sacrifices are glorified in public tributes, their triumphs and defeats studied by students and historians. Even their cemeteries are national places of honor.

None of this is true for the civilians of Top Secret America. A glimpse of a lanyard attached to a digital entry card is often the only clue to their status. Many are forbidden from providing a job title in public. Most are prohibited from telling outsiders what they are working on. Achievements are celebrated in closed, invitation-only ceremonies. Likewise, public debate about the role of intelligence and counterterrorism agents and analysts in protecting the country usually only takes place when something goes wrong and Congress or the Justice Department investigates, or when an unauthorized disclosure of classified information finds its way into the media.

Not being able to defend, or even discuss, your life's work, even with intimate friends or colleagues in your own agency, can often end up meaning you *have* no intimate friends, said Jeanie Burns, who knows that all too well.

Burns, a businesswoman who works in Laurel, Maryland, near the National Security Agency's cluster of government offices and private companies, has been living with a civilian with clearance for more than twenty years. He's been to war. She doesn't know where. He does something important. She doesn't know what.

She fell for him two decades ago and has had a life of adjustments ever since. When they go out with other people, she calls ahead with cautions: "Don't ask him stuff," she will say. Sometimes they get it, sometimes they don't, and when they don't, "it's a pain. We just don't go out with them again."

I met Burns at a local bar that a source had described as a popular hangout for NSA employees. As we talked, she pointed out the people in the bar who were from the agency. They were the ones, she said, whose style of dress and whose haircuts looked ever so slightly out of fashion. At one point as she sat on the bar stool scanning the room, she began to whisper. "Undercover agents come in here, too," to watch the people from the NSA, she said, "to make sure no one is saying too much." Counterintelligence agents listening to employees after work hours was just one example of the government's reach into the lives of people with security clearances.

In a world where so much is left unsaid, it's surprising how much can be inferred. Cultural clues about this world abound around the nation's capital, where more than half of the citizens of Top Secret America reside. In my years of covering intelligence agencies, I abandoned most of my preconceived notions about the people who work in intelligence, but I developed certain stereotypes. FBI agents sport very short pompadour haircuts and favor Italian food and Irish drink. When not in uniform, members of the military special forces wear cargo pants, healthy mustaches, and some version of Oakley sunglasses. They can often be spotted moving in small packs throughout the city and eating at inexpensive sandwich joints before noon, having started their workday with physical training at five in the morning.

CIA employees are less easily stereotyped; some are slovenly and fat; some are so highly polished that their fingernails and teeth glisten. A few might be taken for James Bond with their savoir faire and good looks, but most stand out in no way whatsoever, which may be a job skill. Most are easy talkers, if you can get them started. They favor red meat and boiled potato restaurants near CIA headquarters, as well as Greek and Lebanese restaurants not far away. Many retire in the same northeastern coastal or western mountain communities.

The NSA, with its historic work breaking the codes of foreign messages, employs the largest number of mathematicians in the world and is considered to have the most technically proficient people of any government agency. The NSA needs programmers, scientists, linguists, IT experts, and cryptologists. Many at the NSA brand themselves ISTJs, which stands for "introverted with sensing, thinking, and judging," a basket of personality traits identified on the Myers–Briggs personality test and summarized on one website this way: "ISTJ types are instinctively drawn toward tradition.... They have an inherent sense of duty that is virtually unshakable, making them relentlessly dependable. When they're working toward a goal that is consistent with their beliefs and obligations, ISTJs are tireless."

But it's no accident that the *I* for *introvert* comes first. "How can you tell the extrovert at NSA?" goes the joke. "He's the one looking at someone else's shoes."

All agencies within the walls of Top Secret America have common customs. A badge connotes status and rank. The pecking order is well known: blue for civilian federal employees; brown for military, which often means only a years-long rotation in any given place; green for contractors, the bottom of the pyramid. At the White House, the coveted color is tan: cleared for unlimited access.

Then there is a pecking order within the pecking order, indicated by the small letters typed on every badge showing the office an employee works in. The office is usually the source of true power: OSD for the Office of the Secretary of Defense,[1] for instance. Status awareness comes naturally to those with Type A personalities and ambitions. The fast glance-down-at-the-badge-when-the-badge-wearer-is-not-looking is an automatic reflex in the top secret workplace.

Put tens of thousands of straitlaced overachievers together, funnel them billions of dollars in contracts and salaries, build state-of-the-art office parks for them to work in, and it should be no surprise that, according to the U.S. Census Bureau, six of the ten wealthiest, best-educated counties in the United States are found within the geographic heart of Top Secret America. All that commitment, all that study, all that money, also means that despite the economic downturn, the cities and counties of Top Secret America share the

---

[1] The Office of the Secretary of Defense (OSD) contains the immediate offices of the secretary and deputy secretary of defense, both civilians appointed by the president and confirmed by the Senate; the undersecretaries of defense for acquisition, technology, and logistics; personnel and readiness; comptroller/chief financial officer; intelligence; and policy. Additional independent offices exist for special staff (legislative affairs; public affairs; intelligence oversight, etc.). The role of the secretary of defense has significantly changed since the position was established in 1947. Originally, the secretary had only general authority, shared with the civilian secretaries of the military departments. Subsequent legislation strengthened the secretary of defense's authority. Today, the secretary is the principal assistant to the president for all matters relating to the Department of Defense.

lowest unemployment rates and the highest real estate values in the nation.

Loudoun County, Virginia, ranked the wealthiest county in the country, helps supply the workforce to the National Reconnaissance Office (NRO), which manages spy satellites. Fairfax County, the second wealthiest, is home to both the NRO and the CIA. Arlington, ranked ninth, hosts the Pentagon and major intelligence agencies. In Maryland, Montgomery County, ranked tenth, is home to the National Geospatial-Intelligence Agency and the nuclear weapons program of the Department of Energy. And Howard County, ranked third, is home to eight thousand NSA employees. "These are some of the most brilliant people in the world," said Ken Ulman, the county executive for Howard County. "They demand good schools and a high quality of life."

The schools are among the best in the nation, and some of them have adopted a curriculum that teaches children as young as ten what kind of lifestyle is required to get a security clearance and what kind of behavior will disqualify them from one. To educate the next generation, Washington-area universities offer majors in the specialties required by the intelligence agencies, too — cybersecurity, emergency management, advanced IT, geographic information systems.

If there were a style to mark all this success, it would not be the glitter and bling of a Beverly Hills or the European sleekness of the Upper East Side of New York City. It would be an understated Middle Americanism of a company town where the company can't be mentioned. "If this were a Chrysler plant, we'd be talking Chrysler in the bowling alley, Chrysler in the council meetings, Chrysler, Chrysler, Chrysler," said Kent Menser, a Defense Department employee helping Howard County adjust to NSA's local growth. But in Top Secret America's suburban heart, silence and avoidance are everyday practices.

On a sunny day in Elkridge, Maryland, as housewives and their young children filled the shopping malls, a white van pulled out of a driveway and headed toward the center of the sprawling suburb. It looked like another shopper on an errand, except for the fact that five other unmarked vans followed it. Inside each one, two agents from the secretive Joint Counterintelligence Training Academy (JCITA)[2] were trying not to get lost as they careened around local roads practicing "discreet surveillance." They were learning how to follow a suspected spy, in this case someone playing the role of an army officer who was giving away secrets to a foreign contact for money.

The job of counterintelligence agents like these from the army, air force, U.S. Customs, and other government offices is to identify foreign spies targeting their organizations and to detect American traitors. Their numbers have greatly increased with the growth of foreign espionage, especially from China. They are also looking for terrorists hiding inside Top Secret America, although none have been found, except a few within the ranks of the military.

JCITA is one of the largest training academies, with some four thousand federal and military agents attending classes at the school every year, intermingling incognito in the seemingly bland suburb, as these agents were, cruising past unsuspecting civilians. On this day, I tagged along.

The agent riding shotgun, a sleek female, carried maps divided by numbered grids she used to follow the other cars' locations. As we drove, she frantically moved yellow stickies around on the map as the radio crackled with the voices of other drivers calling out a street intersection or other landmark. The goal was to have all five vans keep track of the suspect, whom they referred to as the "rab-

---

[2] The Joint Counterintelligence Training Academy (JCITA), located in Elkridge, Maryland, is the primary training organization specializing in advanced counterintelligence. Established in 2000, it is a part of the Defense Intelligence Agency. JCITA provides training to over ten thousand military and defense agency personnel around the world through in-residence, mobile training, and distance learning. Topics include discreet counterintelligence (CI) surveillance, CI investigations, CI operations, force protection, and CI analysis, as well as various technology-oriented and country-specific counterintelligence subjects.

bit," by boxing him in wherever he went. This was harder than it sounded.

Some agents gunned their engines and raced along at 60 mph, trying to keep up with the rabbit while alerting the others to the presence of local police, who didn't know that the vans weaving in and out of traffic were being driven by federal agents.

At one point, the rabbit suddenly moved a full block ahead of the closest van. He passed through a yellow light and then drove out of sight as the agents got stuck at a red light. An interminable moment passed before the light turned green.

"Go!" the female agent yelled through the windshield at the car in front of her, lingering unacceptably as the light changed. "Move! Move! Move!"

"We lost him," her partner groaned as they did their best to catch up.

After several miles of barely controlled chaos, the agents spotted the rabbit again, at a Borders bookstore in Columbia. Six men in polo shirts and various shades of khaki pants entered the store, scanning the magazine racks and slowly walking the aisles. Their instructor cringed. "The hardest part is the demeanor," he confided, watching as the agents attempted to follow the rabbit in a store filled with women and children in shifts and flip-flops. "Some of them just can't relax enough to get the demeanor right.... They should be acting like they're browsing, but they are looking over the top of a book and never move."

Before agents can even begin to learn the proper demeanor for surveillance, they have to pass the elaborate top secret security clearance process, which is supposed to take three to six months but can sometimes take more than a year. Polygraphs require polygraphers, many of whom learn their craft at the National Center for Credibility Assessment, which is also part of the Defense Intelligence Agency and located at Fort Jackson in South Carolina—credibility assessment being a fancy way of figuring out whether someone is lying.

The idea of lying or, more broadly, of deception subtly permeates the otherwise congenial atmosphere of the center. Up the lobby stairs, in front of the director's office door, a beach ball–sized plastic dome protrudes from the ceiling. Inside the dome a surveillance camera, the largest one I'd ever seen, watches—though for what, I wasn't certain. Maybe the camera was merely a way to instill paranoia in a group of people who are paid to be paranoid, to think everyone is lying.

The center's research arm, also located at Fort Jackson, experiments with ever less intrusive and more accurate ways to ferret out lies: Is a job applicant claiming not to drink heavily actually an alcoholic? Is a supposedly loyal agent passing secrets to the Chinese? Is an Iraqi going through a checkpoint in Baghdad really a neighborhood resident, as he claims? Is the terrorist suspect under interrogation telling the truth?

But as the director, William Norris, said, "This isn't like on TV. It's not like in the movies."

The setting—a typical military schoolhouse, with its institutional brown paint and flimsy furniture—sure didn't feel like the back lot at 20th Century Fox. And the work routines all seemed fairly boring, completely devoid of the tension laced through the typical spy movie script—at least until the moment when the orientation briefing was about to begin and there was nothing on the conference table except my notebook and a set of cork coasters and someone asked me: "Are you recording this?"

For a second I felt like a loser because I wouldn't have even known how to secretly record anyone. With a button-recorder concealed on my lapel? With a boxy old-fashioned cassette player in my purse? Then, remembering the large, paranoia-inspiring camera hanging over the director's office, I leaned forward and spoke directly into the cork coasters: "No. Are *you* recording this?"

Everyone laughed: the director, the assistant director, and my two escorts, who had flown all the way from Washington—one from the Defense Intelligence Agency and the other from the spooky Defense Counterintelligence and Human Intelligence Center, where the military's few truly undercover spies work.

Norris punched a big button on the remote control to start the PowerPoint command briefing.

There were 500 polygraphers before 9/11. Now there are 670 at 24 agencies. Three times a year, potential examiners come for a fourteen-week course in forensic psychophysiology, meaning the study of what the body does in response when a person attempts to deceive. Students use volunteers—soldiers stationed at Fort Jackson—as guinea pigs.

To better understand the polygraph experience, I asked to be a guinea pig. I was escorted into a small room with no windows and took a seat in a hard plastic chair. It had a pad on it that would record changes in my pulse. Two telephone cord–like tubes were strapped around my chest and stomach to measure my breathing. Gel tabs were slipped over a finger on each of my hands, and cardio cuffs were lashed around a bicep to record my blood pressure and heart rate.

The examiner, a former Secret Service agent, instructed me to lie in response to the third question so he could get a baseline reading. Even when nothing is at stake, as in this demonstration, the body gives off signals indicating deception. These translate into the movement of the needle across a scrolling paper—this bit, despite Norris's pronouncement, just like in the movies. The movements are read and recorded by another examiner sitting in the room next door.

The agreed-upon false answer pushed the needle so far up it actually left the scroll of paper altogether. The examiner said this meant I was a poor liar. That was not news: when the DIA public affairs officer asked why I wanted to visit the academy, I had to admit I wasn't sure. It was one place in Top Secret America I hoped to actually get into and describe from the inside, even though I also knew no one would be showing me anything classified top secret. My Defense Intelligence Agency escort, an earnest man who had always tried hard to answer my questions over my years of military reporting, took the chair and was questioned by the polygrapher. The procedure was the same. When it came time for my escort to utter his prearranged lie, the needle barely moved. Curious.

There has been a lot of controversy surrounding the accuracy of lie detector tests, but the Defense Department and other intelligence agencies still rely on them to grant and renew security clearances. What's generally agreed upon is that they don't work very well in foreign cultures, where the whole setup becomes too intimidating and ill-trained translators can throw off an accurate answer.

With this in mind, the academy researches new technologies in a deception laboratory on the campus. This is where the army and the intelligence agencies are hoping to strike a blow against suicide bombers, and old-fashioned loose-lips within their own agencies. Among the newest technologies was a machine that measures the movement of a subject's eyeballs. When the eye pattern deviates from the norm — say, when the face of a suspected terrorist, or an associate of the suspect's, is flashed on a screen — the machine indicates possible deceptive thoughts (because perhaps the subject recognized the face but is trying to hide it).

There was a voice stress analysis machine and what looked like a dental chair hooked up to a giant video game screen. The subject — say, an Afghan worker coming to a job at the American base in Bagram — would sit in the chair, look into the screen, and answer a series of questions. The machine would read his pupils, record his sweat response, and produce an initial credibility assessment. Another technology under study was a camera that can read the heat emitted from someone walking past, outlining places on the body's image that are devoid of heat, as would be the case if the person were carrying a concealed gun or wearing a suicide vest.

The research lab was also experimenting with an interrogation booth. *Post* photographer Nikki Kahn couldn't resist climbing inside. Nikki found a chair facing a television screen. The booth was pitch-black inside until an avatar appeared on the screen and asked her a series of questions. Kahn's face, which appeared on a screen outside the booth, was recorded by a radiometric thermal imaging camera. It translated her facial image into a rainbow of colors, each representing a biological quality such as perspiration or blood flow, changes in the colors possibly indicating deceit. Nervousness, for instance, increases the size of blood pooling near the surface of the face, especially between the eyes and on either side of the nose bridge. The camera can also see perspiration and count the pores, which open up under the stress of lying.

Researchers at the academy were also studying how changing an avatar's race, culture, gender, and physical features (hair length, eye shape, mouth size) could elicit more truthful answers from a subject of a certain race, culture, and gender. They are pairing these qualities with certain computer-generated facial expressions and voice intonations.

If the avatar is programmed to wrinkle its nose or raise its upper cheek, does that signal skepticism for persons of every ethnic background? If it raises its voice, do both the Iraqi male and the Japanese female react in the same way? Already researchers seem to agree that creating an older-looking female Hispanic avatar elicited the most honest answers from young Hispanic men.

One day, these researchers hope, a tiny screen will be attached to a soldier's helmet, allowing a perfectly designed avatar — beamed down to the screen via satellite — to ask a village elder, for instance, a question. His verbal and physiological response will be beamed back to a technician sitting in an office like this in South Carolina.

My favorite technology was the laser Doppler vibrometer, a noncontact polygraph that works by measuring reactions on the subnanometer range, which is much smaller than the diameter of a strand of hair. The operator points a tiny red laser beam at a branch of the subject's carotid artery. The beam can hear the rhythms of the entire body: the heart valves opening and closing, the lungs breathing in and out, muscle tremors and blood flow. It detects the slightest change in reaction to a question asked at a distance by a person using a megaphone: "Do you have a bomb strapped to your chest?" The subject can't feel a thing and doesn't even know he has been hit by the harmless laser beam.

The vibrometer is also of great use on the battlefield. In combat, a medic crouching behind a tank ninety feet away from a downed soldier can point the laser at the bottom of his boot and determine—through the vibrations that are picked up by the beam—whether the soldier is dead or alive.

Lying is only one of the reasons new applicants for security clearances and those wishing to renew their clearances are often denied them. Financial circumstances—debt and overspending—account for 50 percent of the reason clearances are denied by intelligence agencies and the Defense Department. Another 25 percent of the applicants denied clearances were found not to have answered the questions on the form truthfully. The remaining 25 percent are declined due to unacceptable alcohol consumption, gambling, chronic drug use, sexual misbehavior such as hiring prostitutes or viewing child pornography, or messy divorces, or because the applicant is married to, or socializes with, a citizen of a potentially hostile nation.

These claims are adjudicated in secret courtrooms around the country. Administrative judges from the Defense Office of Hearings and Appeals (DOHA)[3] hear the cases. Type "security clearance" and "lawyer" into a Google search engine and up pop the names of attorneys who make their living representing applicants who were denied clearances or denied a renewal of the one they once held, and who are trying to appeal. The actual cases and verdicts are online, too. Although the names are redacted, reading through them feels like traveling through an alternative universe where common and momentary lapses of judgment end up ruining a career in government service or top secret contracting.

---

[3] The Defense Office of Hearings and Appeals (DOHA), a component of the Defense Legal Services Agency of the Defense Department, provides legal adjudication and claims decisions in personnel security clearance cases for contractor personnel doing classified work, as well as for the Defense Department and twenty other federal agencies and departments.

After a hearing in September 2010, in a secret courtroom presided over by administrative judge Edward W. Loughran, the
applicant in case no. 09-05252 was denied a security clearance
because his risky real estate investments had gone bad. The applicant, according to court records, had bought three houses in a short
period of time "without the financial resources to handle a downturn in the market," the judge ruled. His bad luck began when one
of his renters became sick, was hospitalized, and moved out. Without the rental income, he fell behind on his mortgages. Eventually
he was forced into foreclosure. He argued in the secret court that
he had paid off one mortgage and gotten out of the real estate business and that his good character and strong prior job performance
should mitigate what the applicant believed was a decision to take a
normal business risk. The judge concluded otherwise: because of
lingering debt, his financial problems "were not resolved and were
not under control." His clearance was denied.

In another case, an Iranian who had immigrated to the United
States in the early 1980s and had become a U.S. citizen in the early
2000s was denied a clearance after having had one for several years
because he had visited Iran, did not surrender his Iranian passport, and never renounced his citizenship. By law he is not required
to do any of those things. But security officers viewed his actions
as a risk, considering Iran's hostility to the United States, its
attempt to obtain weapons of mass destruction, and its funding of
terrorism.

People can also lose their clearances for alleged criminal conduct, even if the charges are dropped or dismissed, or if a jury
returns a verdict of not guilty. This is what happened to a defense
contractor who had been previously brought before a military
court-martial eight years earlier on allegations that, as an officer,
he had participated in a gang rape of an enlisted female. Defense
challenges against the lab that performed the DNA testing, and
against the credibility of the alleged victim, resulted in an acquit-
tal. But the security clearance judge, having reviewed the record,
said it still appeared that the man had had sex with the enlisted

female, was drunk at the time, and had conspired with the two other officers to lie about what happened.

The elaborate lengths to which Top Secret America goes to keep its secrets extend to the paper they are written on, too. Every day an unmarked van slogs through rush hour traffic as it collects classified documents at each stop on a day-long circuit between the Pentagon, Fort Meade, and Boyers, Pennsylvania, a hardscrabble town of mining families fifty miles north of Pittsburgh. As the four-lane highway gives way to a two-lane mountain road, the view changes from glass, high-tech office buildings to Dollar Stores, POW flags, dog pens, mobile homes, and tiny cemeteries.

One winter day, I followed the same route into the mid-Atlantic outback. As the forest thickened and the road narrowed even further, not a single sign helped lead the way to the biggest employer in the region. The nation's largest secure bunker is announced by nothing more than a small sign that reads Plant Entrance. But one turn off the road and hundreds of parked cars appeared, as did an instruction: Stop for Vehicle Search. A guard opened the hood, trunk, and side doors before I was allowed to drive down a paved road into the gaping mouth of a towering lime-stone mountain, its face dripping dark browns as the snow melted.

The security guards did not look happy as they swung open the twenty-foot-tall gate. A driver's license was exchanged for a security badge and a fire extinguisher. Nothing was said about the fire extinguisher, so I placed it on the dashboard. At the first turn into the dark warren of two hundred fifty underground tunnels, it rolled onto the floor with a thud.

A second security badge was required to meet Kathy L. Dillaman, a lifelong Boyers resident and the granddaughter of a miner who helped carve out the 145,000-acre cavern. She works as associate director of investigations for the Office of Personnel Management, Federal Investigative Services Division.[4]

---

[4] The Federal Investigative Services Division (FISD), an element of the federal Office of Personnel Management (OPM), carries out background investigations used by govern-

The walls of her office are the rough limestone and slate of the mountain. This combination of materials makes the mountain nuclear blast–resistant, which is why the government originally took an interest in it back in the 1960s during a particularly tense period of cold war nuclear weapons anxiety. The old bunker is now owned by Iron Mountain Inc.[5] The rare lack of humidity and ultraviolet rays makes the old mine a perfect place to store Bill Gates's photo archives, Warner Brothers' movie collection, and endless stacks of classified dossiers compiled in the course of background investigations for the cast of people who, through the years, have populated Top Secret America.

Such dossiers are collected and stored here as part of the security clearance process: the applications, fingerprint cards, head shots, interview notes, polygraph results, credit and records checks, memos and adjudications. In 2010, another 2.2 million dossiers were added, some stored electronically but thousands still sent to the mountain in bright blue paper folders.

When after 9/11 so many contractors required so many security clearances that the system had to shut down, the solution was to hire private contractors who themselves needed clearances. As a result, five out of seven employees even inside the mountain work for someone other than the government.

Given the metastasis of Top Secret America, requests for top secret clearances have continued to increase at a faster rate than any other type of clearance, and they take ten times longer to complete than merely secret-level clearances. Where once there was a 392-day

---

ment agencies to determine individuals' suitability for employment and security clearances. In 2005, the Defense Security Service transferred the DoD personnel security investigative function (and about 1,600 personnel) to FISD. Most of the major agencies of the intelligence community outside DoD (for example, the CIA, the NRO, and the FBI) are responsible for their own security investigations and clearance programs.

[5] Iron Mountain Inc. is a publicly traded S&P 500 company that provides information management, storage, and protection services to more than 140,000 government and private organizations in 39 countries. Iron Mountain's infrastructure includes more than 10 data centers and 1,000 facilities, including Iron Mountain in Boyers. The government also stores patents and other valuable items inside the former limestone mine.

backlog, now a top secret clearance usually takes a little over two months to complete, Dillaman said.

While the U.S. government has spent millions to accelerate the clearance process, much of it is still done by hand by clerks from the small towns around Boyers. "It's a good job," said Chris DeMatteis, a longtime employee with the Federal Investigative Services Division. "Beats rolling pizza dough. Don't put that in. We don't want to get our pizza delivery guy mad." The pizza man has a special status at Iron Mountain because no fire is allowed inside, hence no cooking is permitted.

The offices inside the bunker have the feel of a rural postal facility. Daily, hundreds of clerks in bulky sweaters and tennis shoes shuffle, collate, and sort millions of pieces of paper sent in by local police and other agencies that are themselves not yet electronic-based. Stacks of four-by-six-inch paper fingerprint cards come in on shipping pallets and are digitally scanned and then shredded. Such stacks grew much larger after 9/11, when a new law required everyone who regularly entered a federal building, even the guy who delivers bottled water or pizza, to have his finger-prints on file.

Despite all the money and effort spent on automation, only five agencies, including the army, are able to send all files electronically to Dillaman's staff; all the others still mail in paper records. The paper records are kept in the stacks of blue folders lining one section of the cave. The folders are bar-coded, and every time a file moves through one of the twenty or so workstations in the building, its transit is logged into a computer in hopes of keeping track of it.

Near the end of the tour, Charles J. Doughty, "vice president— The Underground" for Iron Mountain Inc., escorted me to Data Bunker 220. It was located along one of the tunnels, and large stone bollards had been placed in front of the door, just in case any unauthorized vehicle made it this far into the mountain undetected.

Data Bunker 220 is Iron Mountain's state-of-the-art data center, an electronic storage room like the hundreds of others that have sprung up since 9/11 to back up, and store off-site, the millions and millions of new files that exist simply because more and more people need security clearances. The data center inside the mountain, the vice president of The Underground says, is one of the safest places on earth.

Behind steel doors and reinforced glass are the racks of servers and hard drives where the backup electronic records live.

The huge number of drives and servers found within Iron Mountain has its counterpart in the gigantic, windowless warehouselike buildings throughout Top Secret America. "There's terabytes and terabytes of data," explained Chris Crosby, senior vice president at Digital Realty Trust, a company that owns over sixteen million square feet of data center space in North America and Europe. "Data is finite. It goes somewhere. It's the infrastructure of the information age. It's our version of the railroad."

Inside Iron Mountain's Bunker 220, the Network Operations Center monitors a room of computer servers twenty-four hours a day. It has the feel of any other watch center. CNN is on one screen. On another, there are rows of boxes filled with codes. As I stood staring at the gibberish on the screen, many of the lines of data began flashing red, signaling a problem with the servers. But Doughty looked unfazed, so I tried to look unfazed, too, as I stood 250 feet underground in a hermetic bubble of limestone with only one escape exit, silently calculating my distance from the fire extinguisher sitting on the car floor.

CHAPTER NINE

The Business Card

Washington's corridors of power stretch in a nearly straight line from the Supreme Court to the Capitol to the White House. Keep going west, across the Potomac River, and the unofficial seats of power—the private, corporate ones— become visible. There, in the Virginia suburbs, are the flags of Top Secret America: the Northrop Grumman, SAIC, General Dynamics logos that define the skyline at night. Of the 1,900 or so companies working on top secret contracts in mid-2010, roughly 90 percent of the work was done by 6 percent (110) of them.

To understand how these firms have come to dominate the post-9/11 era, there's no better place to look than the Herndon office of General Dynamics. One afternoon there, software trainer Ken Pohill was watching a series of unclassified images, the first of which showed a white truck moving across a large monitor. The truck was in Afghanistan, and a video camera bolted to the belly of a U.S. surveillance plane was following it. Pohill could access a dozen images that might help an intelligence analyst figure out whether the truck driver was just a truck driver or part of a network making roadside bombs to kill American soldiers.

To do this, he clicked his computer mouse. Up popped a picture of the truck driver's house, with notes about visitors. Another click, and up popped infrared video of the vehicle. Click: analysis of an unidentifiable object thrown from the driver's side. Click: high-resolution U-2 spy plane imagery. Click: a history of the truck's movement. Click: a Google Earth–like map of friendly forces. Click: a chat window with ongoing commentary from everyone else following the truck. The whole scene would be archived on a hard drive, in case a white truck appeared somewhere else and drew suspicion.

Ten years ago, if Pohill had worked for General Dynamics, he probably would have had a job bending steel. Then, the company's center of gravity was the industrial port city of Groton, Connecticut, where men and women in wet galoshes riveted and outfitted submarines, the thoroughbreds of naval warfare. Today, the firm's commercial core is made up of data tools such as the digital imagery library in Herndon, which helps the military and intelligence agencies scan a particular piece of geography for whatever they might be looking for—white trucks, troop formations, men planting IEDs at the side of the road. They also make smaller, handheld technologies like the secure BlackBerry-like personal digital assistant (PDA) carried by President Obama. Both were developed not in the company's past industrial facilities, like those in Groton, but in carpeted suburban offices, by employees in penny loafers and heels.

The evolution of General Dynamics followed society from an industrial era to the information age: the company embraced the intelligence-driven style of warfare emerging at the end of the twentieth century. Building on its existing technological expertise, it developed small-target identification systems and equipment that could intercept communications on an insurgent's cell phone and his laptop. It found ways to sort the billions of data points collected by intelligence agencies into piles of information that a single person could analyze.

It also began gobbling up smaller companies that could help it dominate the new intelligence landscape, just as its competitors were doing. Between 2001 and 2010, General Dynamics acquired eleven firms specializing in satellites, signals, and geospatial intelligence, surveillance, reconnaissance, technology integration, and imagery.

That expansion paid off. On September 11, 2001, General Dynamics was working with nine of the sixteen major intelligence agencies. Now it has large contracts with all of them. Its employees fill the offices of the NSA and the Department of Homeland Security. The corporation was paid hundreds of millions of dollars to set up and manage DHS's new offices in 2003, including its National Operations Center, Office of Intelligence and Analysis, and Office of Security. Its employees do everything from deciding which threats to investigate to answering phones.

General Dynamics' bottom line reflects its successful transformation. It also reflects how much the U.S. government—the firm's largest customer by far—has paid the company beyond what it costs to do the work, which is, after all, the goal of every profit-making corporation. The company reported $31.9 billion in revenue in 2009, a staggering rise from the $10.4 billion it reported in 2000. Its workforce has more than doubled in that time, from 43,300 to 91,700 employees, according to the company. Revenue from General Dynamics' intelligence- and information-related divisions, where the majority of its top secret work is done, climbed to $10 billion in the second quarter of 2009, up from $2.4 billion in 2000. That division alone accounted for 34 percent of the company's overall revenue during that period of time.

The company's profitability is on display in its Falls Church headquarters. There, employees can marvel at the soaring, art-filled lobby, eat bistro meals served on china enameled with the General Dynamics logo, and attend meetings in a white auditorium with seven rows of white leather-upholstered seats, each with its own microphone and laptop docking station.

"The American intelligence community is an important market for our company," said a General Dynamics spokesman, retired rear admiral Kendell Pease. "Over time, we have tailored our organization to deliver affordable, best-of-breed products and services to meet those agencies' unique requirements." General Dynamics helps counterintelligence operators and trains new analysts. It has a $600 million air force contract to intercept communications. It makes $1 billion a year keeping hackers out of U.S. computer networks and encrypting military communications. It even conducts information operations, the murky military effort of trying to persuade foreigners to align their views with U.S. interests. In September 2009, General Dynamics won a $10 million contract from the Special Operations Command's psychological operations unit to create websites to influence foreigners' views of U.S. policy. To do that, the company hired writers, editors, and designers to produce a set of daily news sites tailored to five regions of the world. They appear as regular news websites, with names such as SETimes. com: The News and Views of Southeast Europe. The first and only indication that they are actually run on behalf of the American military comes at the bottom of the home page with the word *Disclaimer.* Only by clicking on that do you learn that "the Southeast European Times (SET) is a Web site sponsored by the United States European Command."

All of these contracts add up: in 2010, General Dynamics' overall revenue was $7.8 billion in the first quarter, Jay L. Johnson, the company's chief executive and president, said at an earnings conference call in April. "We've hit the deck running in the first quarter," he said, "and we're on our way to another successful year."

Take General Dynamics and multiply it by more than 100 to get a rough sense of the commercial mass of all the other companies divvying up the lion's share of the biggest government pie ever, demonstrating the federal government's unprecedented dependence on corporations to carry out even the basic missions of intelligence, counterterrorism, security, and the related military fields. Of the 854,000 people with top secret clearances, roughly 265,000 are not government employees; they are contractors working at for-profit companies whose bottom line is to make money. The motives of even the most conscientious, patriotic of these companies is, by definition, self-interested when it comes to working with the government.

Defense Secretary Robert Gates,[1] who has been in the private sector in between government jobs, once expressed his concerns about this tension to me: "You want somebody who's really in it for a career because they're passionate about it and because they care about the country and not just because of the money."

Employees who want to keep their corporate jobs must be attentive, first and foremost, to their company's goal of getting more business, which bothered Obama's CIA director Leon Panetta,[2] too. Contractors, he said, are obviously responsible "to their shareholders, and that does present an inherent conflict," he told me.

Private firms have long been involved with, and are often key to, helping government succeed. But the unrestricted flood of private industry into Top Secret America was a result of policy decisions within the intelligence agencies, the White House, and Congress to beef up the federal workforce quickly. At the same time, they wanted the public to believe the government was not growing during this vast period of expansion of the early 2000s. Contractors wouldn't be counted as part of an agency's workforce, and besides, by turning to the private sector, the government could avoid the rigid federal civil service rules that made the hiring process so slow.

Government executives also thought—wrongly, it turned out—that contractors would be less expensive.

The idea of saving money had been thoroughly repudiated by the tenth anniversary of the 9/11 attacks. In the intervening decade, budget analysts had plenty of time to study the issue—and what they found was disheartening. A 2008 study, published by the

---

[1] Gates stepped down as defense secretary in June 2011.

[2] Panetta became defense secretary in June 2011.

Office of the Director of National Intelligence, found that contractors made up 29 percent of the workforce in the intelligence agencies but cost the equivalent of 49 percent of their personnel budgets. Defense Secretary Gates said that defense contractors cost him 25 percent more than federal employees.

Using a contract workforce "is a false economy," said Mark M. Lowenthal, a former senior CIA official and now president of his own intelligence training academy. But that realization has done little to reverse the stunning handover of the nation's security apparatus to the private sector. In Afghanistan, the chairman of the Joint Chiefs of Staff Operational Contractor Support Task Force, which started work in July 2009, concluded that contract work accounted for over 95 percent of logistics support and developmental projects. More than 100,000 contractors, three-quarters of whom were Afghan nationals, were hired, mostly by U.S. profit-making corporations, as subcontractors.

Though Secretary Gates pledged to reduce U.S. dependence on private contractors, by the Obama administration's second year in office, its modest goal was to reduce the number of hired hands by 7 percent over two years. On paper, federal regulations say that contractors can help the government do a lot of different work but that the country's most sensitive duties must be performed only by people who are loyal, above all, to the nation's interest. For this reason, contractors are specifically prohibited from carrying out what the federal regulations call "inherently government functions." One reason for this is obvious: "Their interest is just not the interest of the government. It's the interest of their company," said Bernard Rostker, the Pentagon's former policy adviser on recruitment matters. Rostker studies government workforce issues at the Rand Corporation.

Despite these rules, in Top Secret America, contractors carry out inherently governmental work all the time in every intelligence and counterterrorism agency. What started as a clever temporary fix has turned into a dependency that calls into question whether the federal government is still even able to stand on its own.

Consider the following:

- At the Department of Homeland Security, the number of contractors equals the number of federal employees. The department depends on more than three hundred companies for essential services and personnel, including nearly twenty staffing firms that help DHS find and hire even more contractors. At the office that handles intelligence, six of every ten employees are from private industry.
- The National Security Agency, which conducts worldwide electronic surveillance, hires private firms to come up with most of its technological innovations. The NSA used to work with a small stable of firms; now it works with at least 480 and is actively recruiting more.
- The National Reconnaissance Office cannot produce, launch, or maintain its satellite surveillance systems, which photograph countries such as China, North Korea, and Iran, without the four major contractors it works with.
- Every intelligence and military organization depends on contract linguists to communicate overseas, translate documents, and make sense of electronic voice intercepts. The demand for native speakers of target languages is so great, and the amount of money the government is willing to pay for them is so huge, that fifty-six firms compete for this business.
- Each of the sixteen intelligence agencies depends on corporations to set up its computer networks, communicate with other agencies' networks, and fuse and mine disparate bits of information that might be indicative of a terrorist plot. More than four hundred companies work exclusively in this area, building classified hardware and software systems.

"We could not perform our mission without them. They serve as our reserves, providing flexibility and expertise we can't acquire," said Ronald Sanders, chief of human capital for the Office of the Director of National Intelligence. "Once they are on board, we treat them as if they're a part of the total force."

Even if an agency wanted to drastically cut the number of contractors it employs, it's not easy. Operations could suffer, if the giant Office of Naval Intelligence in Suitland, Maryland, just outside Washington, is any example. There, 2,770 people work on the round-the-clock maritime watch floor tracking commercial vessels, in science and engineering laboratories, or in one of four separate intelligence centers. But it is the employees of seventy information technology companies who keep the place humming. They store, process, and analyze communications and intelligence transmitted to and from the entire U.S. naval fleet and commercial vessels worldwide. "Could we keep this building running without contractors?" asked the captain in charge of information technology. "No, I don't think we could keep up with it."

Vice Admiral David J. "Jack" Dorsett, director of naval intelligence, said he could save millions each year by converting 20 percent of the contractor jobs at the Suitland complex to civil servant positions. It speaks to the deep dependence of the government on contractors that even though he has gotten the go-ahead, in 2010 his staff managed to convert only one job and eliminate another— this out of 589 contractor positions. Continuing to pay so many contractors "is costing me an arm and a leg," Dorsett said.

Contractors can offer more money to experienced federal employees than the government is allowed to pay them. And because competition among firms for people with security clearances is so great, corporations offer such perks as BMWs and $15,000 signing bonuses, as Raytheon did one year for software developers with top secret clearances. The result is a significant brain drain of talent, as people are lured from public service and take more lucrative private jobs.

The government has been left with the youngest intelligence staffs ever, while more experienced employees move into the private sector, often to be hired back to the agency they'd just left.

This is especially true at the CIA, where employees from over a hundred firms account for roughly a third of the workforce, or about ten thousand positions, according to senior CIA officers. Many of them are temporary hires, often former military or intelligence agency employees who left government service to work less and earn more while drawing a federal pension.

As CIA director, Panetta worried about his agency's dependence on a workforce he felt he didn't totally control. "For too long, we've depended on contractors to do the operational work that ought to be done" by CIA employees, he said—but, he added, replacing them "doesn't happen overnight. When you've been dependent on contractors for so long, you have to build that expertise over time." But Panetta was trapped: the people his agency had invested in for years had left for more money, and, lacking their expertise, he had little choice but to hire them or others with military experience back at the steeper rates.

At the CIA, private contractors have recruited spies in Iraq, paid bribes for information in Afghanistan, and protected CIA directors visiting world capitals. Contractors have helped snatch a suspected extremist off the streets of Milan, interrogated detainees once held at secret prisons abroad, and watched over defectors holed up in the Washington suburbs. At Langley headquarters, they analyze terrorist networks. At the agency's main training facility in Virginia, they are helping mold a new generation of American spies.

The extent of the contractor presence is powerfully summed up in memoriam. In June 2010, a stone carver from Manassas, Virginia, chiseled another perfect star into a marble wall at CIA headquarters, one of twenty-two for agency workers killed in the global war initiated by the 2001 terrorist attacks. The intent of the memorial is to publicly honor the courage of those who died in the line of duty, but it also conceals a deeper story about government in the post-9/11 era: eight of the twenty-two, more than one-third, were not CIA officers at all. They were private contractors.

Across the government, contract workers are used in every

conceivable way. They kill enemy fighters. They spy on foreign governments and eavesdrop on terrorist networks. They help craft war plans. They gather information on local factions in war zones. They are the historians, the architects, and the recruiters in the nation's most secretive agencies. They staff watch centers across the Washington area. They are among the most trusted advisers to the four-star generals leading the nation's wars.

And they are always in demand. When Arkin did one of his periodic top secret job listing counts, he found 1,951 unfilled positions in the Washington area alone, and 19,759 nationwide: "Target analyst," Reston. "Critical infrastructure specialist," Washington, DC. "Joint expeditionary team member," Arlington. And on and on. The need is so vast that more than three hundred companies, nicknamed "body shops," specialize in finding candidates, often for a fee that approaches fifty thousand dollars a person, according to those in the business.

The job listings Arkin kept track of each day also underlined the diversity of the national security responsibilities being put in private hands. Contractors advise, brief, and work everywhere, including twenty-five feet under the Pentagon in a bunker where they can be found alongside military personnel in battle fatigues monitoring potential crises worldwide. Late at night, when the wide corridors of the Pentagon are all but empty, the National Military Command Center hums with purpose as security-cleared personnel monitor, in real time, the location of U.S. forces everywhere in the world, as well as granular satellite images of strategic locations from Bahrain to Brazil. They maintain an open line to the White House Situation Room. The purpose of all this is to be able to answer any question the Chairman of the Joint Chiefs of Staff might have. To be ready twenty-four hours a day, every day, takes five brigadier generals and a staff of colonels and senior non-commissioned officers—and a man wearing a pink contractor badge and a bright purple shirt and tie.

Erik Saar's job description is "knowledge engineer." In one of the most sensitive places in America, he is the only person in the room who knows how to bring data from far afield—fast—from websites, government-only portals, and a mind-blowing array of web-based shared space that he is paid to keep track of. Saar and four teammates from a private company, SRA International, teach these top-ranked staff officers to understand what's available online and how to interact with it. The team's mission is to push a tradition-bound, hierarchical culture to act and think differently. They have devised classified chat rooms and classified tweets, called chirps, to get the older generation to realize the power of social media.

Like Saar, many of the contractors represent the best in American innovative thinking. Since 9/11, contractors have made extraordinary contributions to the national quest for security in an increasingly dangerous world. During the bloodiest months in Iraq, the founder of Berico Technologies, a former army officer named Guy Filippelli, working with the National Security Agency, invented a computer program and related technology that made finding the makers of roadside bombs easier. His invention helped stanch the number of casualties from improvised explosives, according to senior NSA officials.

The top secret workforce also includes companies that have revolutionized war fighting: the firms that built the unmanned Global Hawk surveillance drone and the sensors that enable it to see two hundred miles across the Pakistan, Iran, and North Korean borders; the company that equips clandestine commandos with backpack-sized surveillance kits and miniature document copiers that feed the pocket litter of captured al-Qaeda figures back to a national center in suburban Maryland for instant decoding and analysis. It includes the dozens of firms that built the transnational digital highway that carries targeting data to the Predator pilots sitting in trailers north of Las Vegas, Nevada, allowing them to hunt and, if successful, kill a suspected terrorist in Afghanistan on behalf of the U.S. government.

But private contractors have also made extraordinary blunders—blunders that have changed history and clouded the public's understanding of the distinction between the actions of officers sworn on behalf of the United States and those of corporate employees with little more authority than a security badge and a gun. Contractor misdeeds in Iraq and Afghanistan have hurt U.S. credibility in those countries as well as in the Middle East. Abuse of prisoners at Abu Ghraib, some of it carried out by contractors, helped ignite a call for vengeance against the United States that continues today. Security guards working for Blackwater (now called Xe) machine-gunned seventeen Iraqi civilians in September of 2007, adding fuel to the five-year violent chaos in Iraq and becoming a symbol of an America run amok. Guards employed in Afghanistan by Armor-Group North America, a private security company, were caught on camera in a lewd-partying scandal.

Misconduct happens at home, too. A contractor formerly called MZM paid almost a million dollars in bribes to help a San Diego businessman secure CIA contracts, sending Randy "Duke" Cunningham, who was a California congressman on the intelligence committee, to prison for eight years in 2006 for accepting bribes from a defense contractor and underreporting his income. In 2008, the number-three executive at the CIA, Kyle "Dusty" Foggo, went to prison after he pleaded guilty to steering a contract to a defense contractor involved in the Cunningham scandal.

But none of the misdeeds have even begun to slow the explosive expansion in the number of contractors working in intelligence, terrorism, and defense. The rising tide of contractors has been so overwhelming that the government still doesn't know how many are on the federal payroll. One small illustration of this came from Defense Secretary Gates. When he wanted to reduce the number of defense contractors by about 13 percent, to pre-9/11 levels, he started out by asking for a basic head count. It was harder to obtain than he would have ever imagined, because big firms often hired smaller subcontractors and didn't actually know how many employees the subcontractor had on a particular job site.

"This is a terrible confession," Gates said in his Pentagon office one day. "I can't get a number on how many contractors work for the Office of the Secretary of Defense." He was referring to the office of the department's civilian leadership, of which he was the head.

"It just hits you like a ton of bricks when you think about it," fumed a senior officer who has been in the military for nearly thirty years and was in Afghanistan when he had this revelation. "The Department of Defense is no longer a war fighting organization, it's a business enterprise. Afghanistan is a great example of it. There's so much money being made off this place."

The profit motive has a tremendous impact on policy and budgets. "The incentive for the contractor is to get more money for the contractor," said Rostker, the former Pentagon adviser. "When would you ever think of cutting back?"

The money to be made, in Afghanistan and elsewhere, isn't lost on the people at the top. Thanks to their security clearances and their access to highly guarded information, those running the most sensitive government departments and agencies possess insider information any Wall Streeter would long for and any corporate CEO would pay through the nose for; they know where the government is heading with its intelligence and counterterrorism programs, and what goods and services it needs to get there.

In fact, the counterterrorism business is such a secure, profitable ecosystem that few who enter ever really leave. Some, upon departing government, might take advantage of a teaching sabbatical or take a couple of months off to reconnect with the family, but almost always they return to the counterterrorism business. Some senior government officials argue that this rapidly spinning revolving door is a good thing: the government gains from having people with experience in the private sector's sophisticated and effective management practices, and corporations profit from those with knowledge of how government works — and all have the best of both worlds. In this view, the cozy arrangement is nothing to hide; it is something to celebrate.

Few have more to celebrate than retired rear admiral J. Michael McConnell. A navy intelligence officer, McConnell rose to become the head of intelligence for the Joint Chiefs of Staff during the first Gulf War in Iraq. After that, President George H. W. Bush appointed him director of the National Security Agency. By many accounts his four-year tenure was something less than stellar, marked by the agency's inability to adapt to the post–cold war period and its failure to adjust to the emerging communications technologies that would soon and forever change the way governments spied on one another. In fact, it was just such an NSA failure that accounted for lost opportunities to stop the 9/11 plot: American spies just weren't doing a good job snooping around websites and chat rooms used by known terrorists devising their plans and setting up clandestine meetings.

When McConnell left his government job the first time, in 1996, he was hired to run the national security branch of Booz Allen Hamilton, one of industry's top management consulting companies, which was making a big dive into intelligence contracting. A decade later, though, President George W. Bush called him back from the corporate world to become the second director of national intelligence, replacing John Negroponte. McConnell's private-sector job had been so closely intertwined with the government's intelligence and defense agencies, he announced at a news conference, that he felt like he had "never left" the intelligence business. Perhaps one of the reasons is that today, nearly 100 percent of Booz Allen Hamilton's business is with the government, making it a profit-making, nonunionized version of the federal workforce, where top managers are paid like celebrities and many mid-managers make more than the heads of the agencies they work for.

As national intelligence director, McConnell was a strong advocate for increasing the contracting work of intelligence companies like Booz Allen. They were, he argued, more efficient and innovative than government. Three years into his tenure as director of national intelligence, a period of time when all sorts of unusual intelligence practices were being unearthed by the press— including warrantless wiretaps by his former National Security

Agency—McConnell returned to Booz Allen as a senior vice president in charge of its national security business unit, making $1 million a year in salary but with a total compensation package of $4.1 million. By then Booz Allen boasted of having ten thousand people with security clearances whom it could contract out to government. "I couldn't be happier to return to Booz Allen as it continues to provide vital national security, civilian, and defense assistance to the government," McConnell said in a company announcement.

Not only can these retired generals and admirals pocket many times the paycheck they took home while in uniform, but with their personal connections, their public platform, and the credibility conferred by their rank, they can stoke the engine that keeps the machine on course. Retired air force general Michael Hayden is a good example of this. He held the positions of CIA director, NSA director, and deputy director of national intelligence before he left government and began advising corporations on how to make money in the security and intelligence business.

Hayden has lots of company: more of his colleagues from the intelligence world have followed in his footsteps than not. After 9/11, when defense and intelligence spending soared by more than 50 percent in the first five years, the stampede from the Pentagon to the nearby corporate giants raised a cloud of dust along the Beltway. Army general Henry "Hugh" Shelton, the lumbering, likable chairman of the Joint Chiefs of Staff on the day the Pentagon was attacked, joined one of the most plugged-in defense-intelligence firms around, Anteon International. Shelton's replacement as the nation's top military officer, air force general Richard Myers, who presided over the invasion of Iraq, eventually found his way to the board of directors of Northrop Grumman, the third largest defense-intelligence contractor in the nation. He also joined United Technologies, a megadefense and intelligence technology firm. When Myers's successor, Marine Corps general Peter Pace, retired from military service in 2007, he went to work for Behrman Capital. Behrman is a private equity investment firm with $2 billion under management. Pace is its operating partner on defense investments.

McConnell, Hayden, Shelton, Myers, and Pace are but a few examples of the scores of generals and admirals who have left the Pentagon since September 11 and parlayed their taxpayer-funded experience to defense and intelligence corporations making profits on contracting projects also paid for by the American public. Even the more altruistic among these senior officers have joined in the corporate moneymaking. Former marine general Anthony Zinni was one of them. Zinni railed against war profiteering when he first left the military in 2000. But after a stint writing a book, lecturing, and volunteering as a low-visibility U.S. troubleshooter in the Middle East and elsewhere, he, too, joined the corporate bonanza. The man once consumed with waning U.S. influence in the former Soviet satellite nations and with bringing peace to the Palestinians and Israelis became chairman of the board of directors of BAE Systems Inc., one of the largest defense, security, and intelligence firms in the world, with sales of $20 billion annually. He has served on several comparable boards, too, including those of DynCorp International, another security conglomerate, and National Interest Security Company (now a part of IBM), which sells advice and technological services to Top Secret America. As with most of these former generals and admirals, Zinni continues to teach, participate in security-related think tanks, and write publicly on national security.

While the revolving door has long been a tradition for the retired military, it was never a popular choice for the top managers of the Central Intelligence Agency—until 9/11. Before then, with few exceptions, top CIA officials who left the agency became college professors or security managers, or went into New York banking and finance.

The post-9/11 cash cow changed all that. As new intelligence companies sprang up and old ones greatly expanded, the very officials who failed to detect the coming of such an unprecedented plot on U.S. soil, many of whom expressed shame for such a failure, have since been richly rewarded by corporate America. At least ninety senior officers who were in charge of various CIA branches on 9/11 subsequently joined or became otherwise affiliated with corporations doing business with the intelligence community, according to the *Washington Post*'s Julie Tate. These include CIA director George Tenet; director of operations James Pavitt; the director of the agency's Counterterrorism Center, Cofer Black; and most of the directors of its analytic, technical, and paramilitary branches, as well as those in charge of the agency's geographic divisions.

The pattern has been repeated throughout the classified workforce. From the counterterrorism ranks of the FBI, the Justice Department, and the U.S. Treasury, and from their younger siblings at the Department of Homeland Security, the Office of the Director of National Intelligence, and the National Counterterrorism Center, there has been a stampede out the door. But even among this enterprising group, Michael Chertoff, the second secretary of the Department of Homeland Security, stands out.

Chertoff, affable and down-to-earth in person, spent years as a federal prosecutor and judge putting away drug dealers, mobsters, and financial crooks before the security ramp-up after 9/11 transferred him from the war against crime to the war against terror. Chertoff stayed at the DHS four years, during which time he presided over the Hurricane Katrina disaster, in which so many people died or were left homeless, in part because the agency under his leadership was too busy focusing on terrorism and not busy enough preparing for natural disasters and maintaining the nation's critical infrastructure, in this case the weak New Orleans levees.

Shortly after Chertoff left DHS, in January 2009, he and his chief of staff, Chad Sweet, formed The Chertoff Group. The company advises individuals and companies on how to handle crises, enhance corporate security, and best invest in security and other related fields, some of which were in Chertoff's government portfolio, including cybersecurity, counterterrorism, and border protection.

Besides Sweet, Chertoff raided much of the leadership of the young federal agency, including the agency's former counselor, its deputy secretary, the deputy's counselor, the head of DHS's intelligence section, the head of its science and technology branch, the head of its health affairs section, and the National Security Agency's liaison representative to DHS.

Chertoff was not even the first to strip the department's cupboards bare of leaders. The man he followed into the secretary's job, former Pennsylvania governor Tom Ridge, the first secretary of the Department of Homeland Security, had done the same thing five years earlier. Ridge, who held the position for two tumultuous years, raided the government of his chief of staff and the chief's aide, as well as DHS's special assistant for international affairs, the executive assistant to DHS's deputy secretary, and the executive director of the department's advisory council.

But Chertoff went Ridge one better. His company also hired some of the leaders of the major organizations under DHS's control, including the acting commissioner of U.S. Customs and Border Protection and a deputy chief of the Federal Emergency Management Agency. He also brought on board Michael Hayden and the NSA's number-two cybersecurity official.

Chertoff set his men up in a sleek, marbled office near K Street and advertised the close bond his partners had formed during their dramatic days in government as a selling point to potential clients. "Our principals have worked closely together for years, as leaders of the Department of Defense, the Department of Homeland Security, the Department of Justice, the National Security Agency and the CIA," the company's website says. "We've seen each other under pressure—the kind of pressure most people would never want to see, with thousands of lives or even the whole nation's security at stake, with no time to spare and usually with limited information.... We came to trust each other with our lives. We work incredibly well—together—under pressure. And once you get to know us, you'll understand how valuable we can be to securing the future of your organization."

The Chertoff Group, which continues to expand its number of offices, keeps its client list confidential, and because it is a privately held company, it is under no obligation to reveal its income. A spokeswoman said the company does not lobby and has no U.S. or foreign government clients. But the company is not shy about promoting its government experience to clients going after government business. "What sets The Chertoff Group apart is the breadth of our industry knowledge, the depth of our experience and the extent of our close contacts with industry leaders worldwide. We have personally worked with—and at one time or other, often hired or been hired by—the principals of the world's leading security and risk management firms.... We have overseen billions of dollars of technology development and acquisition for the Defense Department, the Department of Homeland Security, the Department of Justice, the National Security Agency, and the CIA."

In the shadow of swank start-ups with impeccable pedigree and unstoppable connections like The Chertoff Group are nearly two thousand small to midsize companies that do top secret work. About a third of them were established after September 11, 2001, to take advantage of the huge flow of taxpayer money into the private sector. Though most have nowhere near the star power of a Michael Chertoff, many are led by former intelligence agency officials who know exactly whom to approach for work.

Abraxas Corporation, of Herndon, headed by a former CIA spy, quickly became a major CIA contractor after 9/11. Its staff even recruited midlevel managers during work hours, making their pitch from the CIA's cafeteria, former agency officers recall. The company's revenue quickly grew to $100 million, with almost four hundred employees engaged in mostly classified intelligence agency consulting until, in November 2010, in the midst of the recession elsewhere, the giant Cubic Corporation announced it had bought Abraxas.

The counterterrorism bonanza gave some small companies a quick chance to make it big too. In June 2002, from the spare bedroom of his San Diego home, thirty-year-old Hany Girgis, who previously managed large contracts for an IT services company, put together an information technology team that won its first Defense Department contract four months later. By the end of the year, the company he called SGIS (for SkillStorm Government Integrated Systems) had opened a Tampa office close to the Central Command and Special Operations Command; it had turned a profit; and it had hired thirty employees.

Expanding, SGIS offered engineers, analysts, and cybersecurity specialists for military, space, and intelligence agencies. By 2003, the company's revenue was $3.7 million. SGIS had become a subcontractor for General Dynamics, working at the secret level. Satisfied with the partnership, General Dynamics helped SGIS receive a top secret facility clearance, which opened the doors to more work. By 2006, its revenue had multiplied tenfold, to $30.6 million, and the company had hired employees who specialized in government contracting just to help it win more contracts. "We knew that's where we wanted to play," Girgis said in a phone interview. "There's always going to be a need to protect the homeland."

Eight years after it began, SGIS was up to revenue of $101 million. It had 14 offices and 675 employees. Those with top secret clearances worked for eleven government agencies. The company's marketing efforts had grown, too, both in size and sophistication. Its website, for example, showed an image of navy sailors lined up on a battleship over the words "Proud to serve" and another image of a navy helicopter flying near the Statue of Liberty over the words "Preserving freedom." And if it seemed hard to distinguish SGIS's work from the government's, it's because they were doing so many of the same things: SGIS employees had replaced military personnel at the Pentagon's 24/7 telecommunications center; SGIS employees had conducted terrorist threat analysis; SGIS employees had provided help-desk support for federal computer systems.

Still, as alike as they seemed, there were crucial differences. For one, unlike in government, if an SGIS employee did a good job, he might walk into the parking lot one day and be surprised by co-workers clapping at his latest bonus: a leased, dark-blue Mercedes convertible. And he might say, as a video camera recorded him sliding into the soft leather driver's seat, "Ahhh...this is spectacular." (And a video of the entire scene might wind up on YouTube.)

And then there was what happened to SGIS in mid-2010, when it did the one thing the federal government can never do.

It sold itself.

The new owner is a Fairfax-based company called Salient Federal Solutions, started in 2009. It is a management company and a private-equity firm with lots of Washington connections that, with the purchase of SGIS, it intends to parlay into contracts. "We have an objective," chief executive and president Brad Antle told me, "to make $500 million in five years."

Of all the different companies in Top Secret America, the most numerous by far are the information technology firms. Some IT companies integrate an agency's mishmash of computer systems; others build digital links between agencies; still others have created software and hardware that can mine and analyze vast quantities of data. The government is all but totally dependent on these firms. I witnessed this close relationship when I attended an annual information technology conference in Phoenix put on by the Defense Intelligence Agency. The DIA expected the IT firms that it does business with to pay for the entire five-day get-together. Apparently this is another accepted tradition inside Top Secret America. This meant that the same corporations asking the government to give them contracts had to give what seemed like a nice kickback— as much as thirty thousand dollars to help fund the event—to the agencies from whom they were asking for work. In Phoenix, the kickback came to DIA employees in many forms: free happy hour food and drinks; free nightly entertainment; free massages by a couple of perky women set up in the back of the giant conference center; free shoe shines by another lovely woman; and tons of gifts—from collapsible music speakers to computer screen cleaners, light-up pens, and T-shirts. Before the heavy drinking began at the networking socials, government officials and military officers walked around like trick-or-treaters, filling their goodie bags with everything that would fit. Otherwise respectable adults dissolved into giddy children in front of some of the giveaways. (The favorite freebie seemed to be the stress-relieving sponge grenades.)

As a gold sponsor, General Dynamics spent thirty thousand dollars on the convention, just one of many it participates in each year, its spokesman said. On a perfect spring night, GD hosted a party at Chase Field, a 48,569-seat baseball stadium, reserved exclusively for the conference attendees. As government buyers and corporate sellers drank beer, ate hot dogs, and danced, a video of the director of the largest military intelligence organization in the world was displayed on the gigantic scoreboard. Digital baseballs bounced along the bottom of the screen while his morning keynote speech was broadcast.

Other companies at the Phoenix extravaganza sponsored evening socials, too. The defense-intelligence contractor Carahsoft Technology invited guests to a casino night at which intelligence officials and vendors ate, drank, and bet phony money at craps tables run by professional dealers. The McAfee network security company, a Defense Department contractor, welcomed guests to a Margaritaville-themed social on the garden terrace of the hotel across the street from the convention site, where 250 firms paid thousands of dollars each to the DIA to advertise their services and make their pitches to intelligence officials walking the exhibition hall. Tom Conway, director of federal business development for McAfee, showed me around and explained the value of rubbing elbows with government officials and potential subcontractors in such a relaxed environment. "If I make one contact each day, it's worth it," said Conway, an old hand at these kinds of affairs. Government officials and company executives said these networking events are critical to building a strong relationship between the public and private sectors. No one seemed even a bit worried about the coziness between government buyers and the corporate sellers who were paying for them to have a good time. It was all just the cost of doing business.

I asked the highest-ranking government civilian at the event what he got out of spending time at a conference such as the one in Phoenix. "Our goal is to be open and learn stuff," said Grant M. Schneider, the DIA's chief information officer and one of the conference's main draws. By going outside Washington "we get more synergy. . . . It's an interchange with industry."

Such coziness worries some people inside Top Secret America, though. "It's a self-licking ice cream cone," is the way one senior military intelligence officer described it. Another official, a long-time conservative staffer on the Senate Armed Services Committee, described the intelligence-security world that has grown up in the last ten years as "a living, breathing organism," impossible to control or curtail.

"How much money has been involved is just mind-boggling," he said. "We've built such a vast instrument. What are you going to do with this thing? . . . It's turned into a jobs program." But these officials, as senior and respected as they were, didn't dare express their criticism in public; as they confessed, laughing bitterly at the irony, if they spoke up, they wouldn't be able to work in Washington anymore.

Thomas Fingar is one of the only former intelligence officials who has not jumped into the corporate side of Top Secret America. Instead, the former deputy director of national intelligence for analysis and the longtime head of the State Department Intelligence and Research Bureau is a professor at Stanford University. The counterterrorism industry "is like cancer research," he said. "It supports more people than [cancer] kills."

The Phoenix-style government-industry get-togethers happen every week in Washington and around the country. In fact, an entire business sector of event planners has been greatly enriched off the money they make pairing up defense and intelligence contractors with defense and intelligence government officials.

Events held at the CIA and NSA are the most exclusive. No one without a top secret clearance is allowed to attend. That means no media, no watchdog group, no outside eyes to witness the exchange of gifts, which by most standards might be considered a little bribe—though not here, the government's lawyers having approved them.

Peter Coddington, chief executive of InTTENSITY, a small firm whose software configures computers to "read" documents, had glass beer mugs and pens twirling atop paperweight pyramids to help persuade officials of the DIA that he had something they needed. "You have to differentiate yourself," Coddington said, as government officials left the speakers' hall and fanned out into the aisles of the vendors section of the convention center, where rows and rows of contractors had set up booths to display their wares and their freebies and, hopefully, to attract the eye of a government buyer.

Coddington's problem was a familiar one. He needed to stop the officials from walking too quickly past his display. He needed to slow them down just long enough for him to start his pitch. His inexpensive twirling pens seemed to do the job. "It's like moths to fire," Coddington whispered, and offered a demonstration. Within minutes a DIA official with a tote bag approached. She spotted the pens, and her pace slowed.

"Want a pen?" Coddington called out.

She hesitated. "Ah...I have three children," she said.

"Want three pens?"

She stopped. She listened. In Top Secret America, every moment is an opportunity.

"We're a text extraction company," Coddington began.

On a day that also featured free ice cream and fruit smoothies, another speaker, Kevin P. Meiners, a deputy undersecretary for intelligence, gave the audience what he called "the secret sauce," the key to thriving even when the Defense Department budget eventually stabilizes and stops rising so rapidly.

Overhead used to mean paper clips and printer toner, he

explained. Now it was information technology services, the very product sold by many of the businesspeople in the audience. His solution? "You should describe what you do as a *weapons system,* not *overhead,*" Meiners instructed. "Overhead to them—I'm giving you the secret sauce here—is IT and people.... You have to foot-stomp hard that this is a war-fighting system that's helping save people's lives every day." The performance was unique: a government employee coaching private companies in how to successfully manipulate the system that he helped oversee.

Conventions like the one in Phoenix happen all over the country every week. The Annual Homeland Security Conference in Washington, DC; the Biometric Conference in Arlington, Virginia; the DoD Cyber Crime Conference in Atlanta. I attended a Special Operations Command conference in Fayetteville, North Carolina, where vendors paid for access to the uniformed officials who would decide what services and gadgets to buy for troops.

A month later, I visited the swanky Ritz-Carlton in Tysons Corner, Virginia, for a black-tie evening sponsored by the government-industry group called Intelligence and National Security Alliance (INSA) and funded through "contributions" from the same corporations seeking business from the defense, intelligence, and congressional leaders seated with them at the dinner tables. Tuxedoed waiters glided around the ballroom lubricating the already comfortable chitchat between the senior CIA, Defense Department, and NSA officials and the blue bloods among the Beltway bandits who could afford the entrance fees. Tender steak, rich seafood, and expensive wine followed at tables sponsored by the largest firms in the business, and others that someday hoped to be.

The event was the annual gala of an organization whose main purpose is to promote the symbiosis of government and private industry. The Intelligence and National Security Alliance describes itself as "the premier not-for-profit, nonpartisan, public-private membership organization that works to promote and recognize the highest standards within the national security and intelligence communities." The organization is underwritten by the major defense and intelligence corporations, including General Zinni's BAE Systems.

The organization has already advertised for its next, twenty-seventh annual gala dinner. Corporations are able to buy a "Premiere Table," where the senior-most government and corporate leaders will be seated, for $12,000 each. A "Prominent Table," with somewhat lesser officials, goes for $9,000, and a "Select Table," with warm bodies, for $6,000. The ticket price for an individual member is $350; for nonmembers, $450. Government employees are invited to hobnob, eat, and drink for free.

The honoree for 2011, a year marking the tenth anniversary of the 9/11 attacks, couldn't have been a more appropriate symbol of the new reality in Top Secret America: retired rear admiral and former director of national intelligence, now Booz Allen's four-million-dollar man, J. Michael "Mike" McConnell.

CHAPTER TEN

Managing the Battlefield
from a Suburban Sanctuary

A pilot sits at a computer controlling a CIA drone loaded with weapons powerful enough to shatter a tank and accurate enough to be airmailed through a terrorist's bedroom window. As analysts cross-reference video feeds with voice intercepts to confirm the target's location, a weapons technician calculates the probability that innocent people walking nearby might get killed as well.

As soon as a senior CIA officer, monitoring the entire scene from a separate location, gives him the final go-ahead, the pilot, who is operating from a hidden operations center in the Nevada desert, squeezes a button on the joystick, and, if the laser beam lines up correctly and he's a good shot, a cloud of debris will fly up and then settle down around a motionless human body.

When the senior CIA officer is finished issuing orders for the day, she can walk out the door and, instead of returning to a tent or a modular trailer on some desolate military base in the Middle East, get in the car and drive a couple of miles to the Capital Beltway or to the grocery store down the block, or the tanning salon or the pizza joint located along a landscaped boulevard in suburban northern Virginia—just another day at the office helping to kill terrorists five thousand miles away in Iraq, Afghanistan, Pakistan, Yemen, Somalia, and elsewhere.

Senior CIA officials guide tactical drone operations from offices that are not far from the headquarters of McConnell's Booz Allen Hamilton. Not surprisingly, the agency buildings are sealed off by fences and armed guards and monitored by dozens of cameras. The people in the homes and luxury condos nearby are not privy to what goes on inside.

Top Secret America does not just supply the contractors, equipment, and technologies to operate overseas. For the sake of convenience, it has also extended the battlefield command to "the sanctuary," as commanders call bases and offices like these in the United States. In the sanctuary, a person managing a kill in the morning can be a soccer mom in the evening or a Boy Scout troop leader on the weekend. Killer drones, the innovation that makes this surreal arrangement possible, are a particular invention of Top Secret America. No other weapon better symbolizes the revolutionary new style of one-way, remote-control warfare that arose from the desire to put as few American men and women as possible in harm's way. For military special operations, the trigger is pulled (actually, a button is pushed on a joystick-like contraption) by air force pilots working on military bases in North Carolina and Nevada. The CIA drone operations are handled out of the one north of Las Vegas, Nevada, too, from where the conventional military's Predators and their newer, more lethal cousin, Reapers, are also flown. The Arizona, California, New York, North Dakota, and Texas Air National Guards now also take part from their home bases. Although those bases are close to civilian cities, too, no secret location speaks more powerfully to the evolution of Top Secret America than the one in Virginia where the managers of the drone strikes sit.

Targeted killings—critics call them assassinations—have been conducted by the U.S. government for a decade, and drones have played a large part in the continuation and frequency of such activities. Armed Predators and Reapers have become the weapons of choice for killing individual terrorist leaders in foreign lands. The success of weapon-carrying unmanned aerial vehicles (UAVs) created a demand within every branch of the military and the CIA for as many of them as their corporate inventor, California-based General Atomics, could produce. It also spawned a development and production frenzy within the niche community of manufacturers experimenting with other types of unmanned aircraft, and with the many larger defense contractors whose technology is used to move a drone's surveillance pictures and targeting information around the world—from the battlefield to the sanctuary—in a matter of seconds.

The number of drones in the U.S. arsenal has increased from sixty to more than six thousand since 9/11. Funding for drone-related projects and activities was about $350 million in 2001, when the first CIA Predator was being flown from a trailer once used as a daycare center in the parking lot of the agency's headquarters. In ten years, spending on drones has ballooned to over $4.1 billion, and there are over twenty different types of UAVs in the government's inventory. Most of them are used for surveillance. Some of the experimental ones are as small as a dragonfly, and disguised as one, too.

In the drone war, U.S. national security agencies have maintained at least three separate "kill lists" of individuals, several sources explained. The National Security Council (NSC) kept one list and reviewed it at weekly meetings attended by the president and vice president. Another was the CIA's, with no input from the NSC or the Defense Department. A third list was the military's, but that was really more than one, since the clandestine special operations troops of the Joint Special Operations Command (JSOC) had their own list as well. Some suspected terrorists were on multiple lists. But even these highly classified kill lists were not coordinated among the three primary agencies involved in creating them. Each group had its own set of lawyers looking at legal questions. The military and the CIA each had its own set of target-ers developing the time and location of the strike. Each had its own pilots, command centers, budget process, and long logistics and personnel pipeline to maintain its own fleet of UAVs.

Permission to kill also was granted variously, depending on the agency involved and the location of the person targeted, said U.S. intelligence and military officials. Some individuals could be killed on the say-so of tactical commanders without approval from above, while others could not be killed without senior military or even cabinet-level approval; still others could not be killed without pres-idential approval. Until July 2009, the military's lethal drones tar-geted individuals in Iraq and Afghanistan, and now most of the kills take place in Afghanistan; the CIA's drones, on the other hand, killed people in countries where U.S. forces were not con-ducting military operations, including Yemen, Somalia, and Paki-stan. Presidential approval was absolutely required to operate in these countries. In Somalia, where there was no effective govern-ment, once the White House approved the overall mission, all that was needed were multiple CIA or JSOC confirmations of the tar-get's location—so the wrong person wouldn't be killed. In Yemen, where the government of Ali Abdullah Saleh had agreed to allow the CIA and JSOC to operate, authority was delegated to com-manders in the region. In Pakistan, however, in August 2010, after a number of civilians had died in drone attacks and the public there began to grow more vocal in its opposition to them, CIA director Leon Panetta announced that he would personally approve every drone strike. The director's input had not been required since the first year after 9/11.

The CIA process for putting a person on the hit list begins at Langley headquarters. There, analysts and operatives in the Counter-terrorism Center (CTC) pore over reports from informants and foreign intelligence services, as well as intercepts from the National Security Agency, whose interpreters and analysts have transformed voice files collected from sensors into English-language transcripts. They also watch hours of videotape from CIA or military special operations surveillance cameras, scrutinize satellite imagery, and collect information from observers on the ground. In the best cases, they also benefit from the forensic work of a new type of postindustrial secret agent whose expertise is the digital exhaust of captured thumb drives, hard drives, cell phones, and other electronics.

A couple of times a month, a pleasant-sounding secretary from the CIA's CTC trekked across the agency's campus to its old headquarters building, took the elevator to the seventh floor of executive suites, and handed acting CIA general counsel John Rizzo a manila envelope marked "top secret," with a standard pink routing slip attached to the outside. Rizzo was involved in daily operations in the decade following the 9/11 attacks. He had been part of the spy world for thirty-three years, and never had he found himself in such a strange and lonely position. He would remove the two-to-five-page dossier from the envelope and read it alone in his office. It was information on the habits and history of the next man whom officers at the CTC wanted to kill—without a hearing, without giving the targeted man a chance to refute the information or even to admit guilt and surrender. Instead, Rizzo, the lawyers at the CTC, and the head of the National Clandestine Service (formerly the CIA Directorate of Operations) would act as judge and jury on these terrorism files.

Rizzo is a slight man with bright blue eyes, fluffy white hair, and polished fingernails. He had already served in the agency longer than most of his colleagues when he started reviewing the nominations shortly after 9/11. He approached the job with the detachment expected of a competent attorney, although, in private, he sometimes wondered what his Irish Catholic parents would think of killings like these and his role in them. Although he led these real death-panel reviews, he had a surprisingly hard time keeping the names of people on the list straight, which he blamed on his sense that "all those names sound alike," as he would say to colleagues.

Still, it was a responsibility that weighed on him. "This was risky business," he told me. "I would be second-guessed if the wrong person got hit.

"The thought never left my mind that I was giving legal approval for killings and I had never done that before. I just had to stay focused and detached. I had no problem with the morality of it because of the continued threat al-Qaeda posed.... In moments of reflection, it was daunting to be in that position."

The duty to approve or reject putting an individual on the kill list was granted to this small group at the CIA by President Bush, and the responsibility was extended by President Obama. The agency's approval process was orderly, vetted by legions of lawyers in the White House, the National Security Council, and the CIA, and then affirmed without much discussion or controversy by eight members of Congress, known as the Gang of Eight. They included the House and Senate Democratic and Republican leaders and the chairmen and vice chairmen of the Senate and House Intelligence Committees. The CIA did not seek Congress's approval for the program or to kill a particular individual on the list. But once the covert drone program began, the agency kept Congress informed of those who had been killed.

Intelligence officials involved in the CIA selection process say there were never more than two or three dozen individuals on the list at one time. To nominate a person for "lethal action" (the term used in the original 2001 Presidential Finding that made such killings legal, in the U.S. government's view), CTC analysts would summarize the intelligence reporting they had on an individual using as much specific incriminating evidence as possible. The boilerplate request at the bottom of the case file was always the same: *Based on the above, we believe (Mr. X) poses a current and ongoing threat to the United States and therefore meets the legal criteria for lethal action pursuant to the Presidential Finding.*

Rizzo would then review the evidence contained in the file.

Because there were no written criteria or words of guidance from the Department of Justice on exactly what constituted "a current and ongoing threat," Rizzo knew the interpretation was on his shoulders, so he and his lawyers in the CTC poked and prodded the analysts about the freshness of their information, and he decided on his own that the outer edge of "current" would be information that was no more than six months old. Sometimes he and his lawyers would deny the CTC a request, usually for relying upon old and possibly outdated information.

The same was true for the renewal process. Every name on the list had to be reviewed by the lawyers every six months, and some people were taken off it because the information became outdated. The other key requirement was that the person in the file had to pose a threat to the United States—not a threat to an ally but a threat to the United States.

Being a U.S. citizen, native-born or naturalized, did not disqualify anyone from being on the list. New Mexico–born Anwar al-Awlaki was put on the CIA list sometime in 2010 when it became clear he was not just a fiery cleric spewing anti-American rhetoric but was helping to inspire and organize attacks. By then, however, Awlaki had been on JSOC's list for some time. However, another American al-Qaeda member, Adam Gadahn, was never considered for execution because in the judgment of intelligence analysts he was all talk, a Tokyo Rose.

In Pakistan, where the United States used drones beginning in mid-2008 to go after al-Qaeda and Taliban members who had fled over the Afghan border, there was an elaborate Kabuki dance between Islamabad and Washington. The Pakistani government had given the CIA approval for such strikes as long as they were kept secret—which they never were because Pakistanis and local journalists sooner or later discovered the ruins, and the wrong people, civilians, were often killed. For internal political reasons, the Pakistani government usually publicly condemned the very strikes they had approved each time one became known. Sometimes there would be a temporary halt until the tensions subsided.

In Yemen, Obama took advantage of the political void caused by the popular uprising against the regime in June 2011 by secretly ordering a dramatic increase in drone strikes against leaders of the terrorist group there, al-Qaeda in the Arabian Peninsula (AQAP). The Yemen strikes were considered bold by international legal norms not only because the United States was not at war with Yemen but because, in the absence of a Yemeni government, Obama did not seek its approval. The unilateral move symbolized just how comfortable the new president had become with remote-control warfare.

Obama's unprecedented use of drones began shortly after he took office, when he ordered an increase in lethal drone strikes in Pakistan. The strikes were facilitated by a coordination center set up near the border post not far from Peshawar, where Pakistanis sit alongside U.S. and British intelligence. With better intelligence and better coordination, the number of drone attacks increased between 2008, when there were 35, and 2009, when there were 53. They doubled in 2010, to 117.

The acceleration was aided by a number of technological advances: the more accurate Reapers had reached the region, better intercept technology was available, and Pakistan granted the United States permission to fly low-profile eavesdropping aircraft inside the country.

In all, from July 2008 to June 1, 2011, the CIA launched 220 strikes inside Pakistan, according to a senior CIA official. The agency said that some 1,400 suspected militants were killed, along with about thirty civilians.

The private Conflict Monitoring Center (CMC) based in Islamabad, which collects Pakistani and foreign news reports of casualties, had its own count. It believed that 2,052 people, "mostly civilians," were killed in the five-year campaign through June 2011, and that this number included 938 casualties in 132 drone attacks in 2010 alone.

Rizzo and his colleagues at the CTC knew they were skating on the edge of public disapproval over the accidental civilian deaths, even with all the approvals they had in hand. The motto at the CTC was: "You have to plan and execute each shot to preserve your ability to do the next shot."

Contractors were a critical part of the drone war. They remotely flew Predators and other unmanned vehicles on takeoff and landing. But they had to hand the joystick controls over to a federal employee—either a CIA officer or someone in uniform—once the vehicle got inside the kill box, meaning within range of launching its missiles. Government and military lawyers insisted that a service member or agency officer sworn first and foremost to act in the United States' interest, and not some corporate interest, push the launch button.

Killer drones were maintained in the field by another cadre of private companies. Still other contractors, a who's who of companies doing top secret work (including General Dynamics, Northrop Grumman, Lockheed Martin, and SAIC), built, maintained, and staffed the global system that carried the drones' surveillance data from overseas on to processing stations in the United States, including facilities in Virginia, California, South Carolina, Arizona, Nevada, Hawaii, and Alabama, and then on to military commands and Washington agencies and office buildings in Virginia where decisions got made.

Laid atop a map of the United States, the wiring diagram of this arrangement, called the Distributed Common Ground System (DCGS), looked like the human circulatory system. With its near-countless branches and loops, the invisible data highway became the backbone of one-way drone warfare.

The CIA's targeted killing campaign, no matter how successful, paled in comparison to the size of the drone war being waged abroad by the U.S. military, mainly through JSOC and mostly in Afghanistan. JSOC's list of people to kill was much longer and more fluid than the CIA's, and there was, in comparison, much less scrutiny of the background of the individuals on it. This is because the military is allowed—encouraged, even—to capture or kill all the people involved in an identifiable network of terrorists, not just its leaders. The military has "a lower high bar," as one commander put it, for putting an individual on the list and for being able to kill or capture all of his associates, if they can be found. Documentation was still required but in the end the military leaders in the field had to provide much less in the way of rationale.

The rationale for using drones at all involved a trade-off between risking more soldiers' lives by having them hunt and kill terrorists in ground raids, and using unmanned aircraft that involved no risk to soldiers or airmen at all. The choice was clear, given the mounting number of American casualties. But drone strikes denied the enemy a chance to surrender. That, actually, was another reason they had become so popular by 2011: there was really nowhere to put captives if the CIA didn't want to hand them over to the military and if the military didn't want to keep them in the politically unpopular prison on Guantánamo in Cuba.

Also, some JSOC operators told me that lawyers had warned them about the legal complications of killing someone face-to-face, in cold blood. This is one conversation I had on that subject with one JSOC commander: "We can kill them from the air, but the lawyers say, 'No, you can't just' "—the source put his hands together, stretched out his index fingers, stiffened his arms, and pointed his invisible pistol at my forehead—" 'blow someone away like that—pow!' "

When I tried to figure out whether any law actually said this, I got many different answers. There was no consensus, and after Navy SEALs killed Osama bin Laden at close range, the matter seemed to have resolved itself. Close-range killings, which felt more like executions than drone strikes, were permitted when they were permitted.

In June 2008, Arkin got a rare opportunity to have an inside look at the business end of these targeted killings when he scored a tour of the Combined Air and Space Operations Center in Qatar. The CAOC (pronounced "kay-ock") was the control center for the air wars over Iraq, Afghanistan, and Pakistan's tribal provinces, as well as the nerve center for a whole array of missions flown by a range of piloted aircraft and unmanned drones, all overseen from computer consoles in the CAOC.

The CAOC was a heavily guarded convention hall–sized building within a cramped, Jersey-barricaded compound inside a guarded and fenced restricted area at the sprawling Al Udeid Air Base, in Doha, Qatar. The staff of one thousand hardly ever left the facility. Arkin, who at the time was writing a study on airpower sponsored by the air force, had read a lot about these command centers. He couldn't believe he would be staying for ten days.

He was assigned a female escort, and soon he was checking into his room, a two-bedroom prefab trailer reserved for visiting VIPs. It was all of fifty steps from the dining facility, which was around the corner from the knockoff Starbucks kiosk. The grungy fitness center was in a modular building, and the communal latrine was no different from an airport public restroom; it was known jokingly as the Cadillac.

Late that night, Arkin was in the trailer when his roommate, a lanky, gray-haired officer, showed up. "Bill Holland," the man said, introducing himself. Arkin did a double take: his roommate was the highest-ranking officer at the CAOC, a two-star general who was deputy commander for U.S. Air Forces in the Central Command region. They talked about the war, Washington, and the air force, and soon the general was suggesting things Arkin should take a look at, including the overall intelligence picture inside the ops center and the Predator drone operations.

The next morning, Arkin wandered into the public affairs shop to be greeted by his escort, who fidgeted nervously and told him, with equal parts disbelief and discomfort, that she had been informed that he could sit in on the classified morning briefing. Obviously, she said, there had been some mistake.

"Yeah," he said matter-of-factly, "the general said it was okay."

" 'The general said'?" she scoffed. "What general?"

"General Holland, my roommate."

"Oh, shit," she muttered, turning to her computer, "how the fuck did that happen? *Fuck, fuck, fuck!*"

Even with a general's stamp of approval, inside the ops center Arkin was radioactive at first. But in time, he became part of the furniture, hardly noticed and left alone. One night, he found himself hanging out there trying to stay out of the way while operators with years of experience attempted to use some of the most sophisticated military technology ever created to kill a man in a mud hut.

After days of twenty-four-hour Predator surveillance—what is called "pattern of life" monitoring—special ops teams on the ground were pretty sure that they had found Gold 6—that is, the sixth most important person on the military's high-value target list for Afghanistan at the time. Still, they couldn't just pull the trigger. As Slash (the pilot call-sign name of the operations floor manager for that night's shift) explained, *if* the target didn't move, *if* positive ID could be established, *if* the visual chain of custody could be sustained, and permission could be obtained, and *if* the collateral damage estimate was accepted up the chain, well, *then* an air strike would be mounted. Such conditions had to be met in order to avoid killing civilians. Technology could only help so much. Software could show impact footprints, depending on various altitudes and angles that specific weapons were released from. In theory, the damage from a particular bomb delivered in a particular way should be neatly predictable, in reality it was anything but.

Nearby fighter jets on patrol were already being brought in as Slash's decision tree blossomed; they'd have maybe an hour's worth of fuel before they had to return to Bagram Airfield, north of Kabul. If a decision couldn't be reached before then, new planes needed to be shuffled in behind them. It was a complex, procedure-dominated operation, involving a delicate balance between moving quickly enough to take advantage of real-time intelligence and not moving so hastily that the target hadn't been fully confirmed and the collateral damage carefully considered. (This kind of operation was referred to as a "time-sensitive target," or TST.)

For the men and women of the CAOC, from the special ops liaison to the lawyer and the two-star general, Holland, the killing of Gold 6 was in most ways just another job on another night, practiced with a kind of clockwork professionalism routine in this kind of war. But, as Arkin was to learn, the plan to eliminate Gold 6 was also a brief glimpse into the inner circles of secrecy that were no longer just augmenting our war effort but steering it.

The building adjacent to the Qatar ops center compound was called the ISRD building because it housed the Intelligence, Surveillance and Reconnaissance Division. Visitors wishing to enter ISRD must surrender cell phones, pagers, laptops, and thumb drives before entering the 100,000-square-foot building, which is windowless and watched over by a military policeman, even though it is within a guarded compound inside a guarded base. Once inside, a Red Badge visitor—meaning someone who has not been cleared—is announced to all by flashing lights overhead.

In his various trips into and out of the ISRD, Arkin couldn't help but notice that right down the hall from the strategy section was the STO—the Special Technical Operations division—a secure room within a secure room, where the space and information warfare specialists toiled. A similar cipher-locked and segregated secure room was located at the rear of the main ops floor—the so-called green door through which coalition members and the uncleared couldn't go. Inside, someone told Arkin quietly, were "OGA and black SOF"—OGA for "other government agencies," which meant the CIA; black for "clandestine"; SOF for "special operations forces."

According to Sensitive Target Approval and Review (STAR) procedures, a sensitive target required going all the way up to the secretary of defense to get approval to strike. Some targets, such as electrical power grids or any locations inside Pakistan, were intrinsically designated sensitive. An estimate that more than thirty-five civilians might be killed also triggered the external approval process, which included almost any strike within an urban area. While the rules for Iraq were that all strikes (except STAR targets) could be approved by commanders on the ground, for Afghanistan, the Central Command in Tampa acted as the approval authority. And then there was the CIA and JSOC. They had their own chains of command; in other words, the CAOC was the air operations center for the entire Middle East—except for those special or secret elements that it didn't control.

As the Predator desk officer explained, both the CIA and JSOC had their own Predators, and they had other unmanned drones, their own dedicated aircraft, their own weapons, and their own target shops and review processes. Up on the big screen in the ops center, the flight path of these clandestine missions could be displayed—if needed—but usually just a few people would be notified of any potential conflicts or overlap with conventional forces. Still, the CIA and the secret military forces wanted to be in the "fur ball"—that is, to have their basic positions known, if for no other reason than to avoid friendly fire when they were out there clandestinely operating.

The Predator video feeds were in real time, broadcast on television cameras to viewers in command centers around the world, as well as to people on the ground and in the air: the army or marine unit being supported, individual special ops teams with unique laptop receivers, analysts assigned to monitor every mission, manned intelligence collection planes, nearby fighter jets, and, of course, the very deadly Special Operations AC-130 gunships.

These battlefield movies were called "Predator porn" because of the hypnotic quality of the grainy black-and-white pictures. In the early days of the Afghanistan war, thousands of airmen were glued to the Predator "idiot box," as it is also called, so much so that soon commanders yanked the feeds away from anywhere they didn't absolutely have to be.

Each Predator flight fed its video to a separate color-coded channel (blue, orange, magenta), and, at the CAOC, those videos could be called up on a kind of cable feed. When Arkin was observing, three Predators were dedicated to secret military missions, then the Brits and the Italians were each flying one, and finally there were the drones belonging to the CIA.

There were a number of very interested parties camped around screens displaying a feed showing the probable Gold 6 location. A single Predator drone flew in the precise vicinity, and it was carrying a pair of Hellfire missiles. The Hellfires were powerful, but numerous times the targeters and the CAOC directors had watched a Hellfire with its 150-pound warhead go right through its target, only to have people walk away. More powerful weapons might, of course, compensate, but their increased impact could also multiply the risk of collateral damage. That night, the nearest jets were carrying 1,000-pound bombs, and analysts determined that the blast circle radii for those bombs would include a number of structures thought to be civilian homes. A conference call was initiated between the CAOC in Qatar, the International Security Assistance Force (ISAF) headquarters in Kabul, and Central Command headquarters in Tampa, Florida.

As the generals and lawyers went through the evidence on the targeted individual, on the blast circles drawn for the weapons, and on the chain of custody, there was no discussion of whether the mud huts that were in the drone's sights actually contained civilians. As ops director, Slash decided to launch a pair of A-10 "Hogs" from Bagram Airfield. An A-10 is an attack plane that also mounts a Volkswagen-sized seven-barrel Gatling gun that can spew out sixty-five soda bottle–sized rounds per *second*. Its smaller, five-hundred-pound bomb loads also meant smaller blast circles and thus a lower probability of civilian deaths. In ISRD, the analysts drew a new set of blast circles.

The process of positive ID, a military lawyer explained, involved two parts. The first part was to positively identify Gold 6 as the particular bad guy he was suspected of being. As the lawyer explained, not only would "second sourcing" be necessary to confirm the identity of the target, but it would then have to be demonstrated that Gold 6 had been tracked in a near-perfect, unbroken chain of custody—from first identification all the way to the attack, 24/7. If Gold 6 was even momentarily lost—if he disappeared into a crowd or slipped from view under an outcropping of trees—either the entire ID process would have to be restarted, or the strike would be called off.

Within an hour, the senior intelligence officer announced that positive ID had been established. From behind the green door, word came that the National Security Agency had intercepted a confirming conversation. Approval was in hand from the command in Kabul, but the rules required that the director of operations at Central Command in Tampa also grant approval as well, which at first was a bit of a problem: on this Saturday afternoon in Tampa, the director of operations was not readily available.

Time slowed until the director of operations in Tampa was located, the strike was approved, and the two A-10s—which had received the handoff from the earlier aircraft, now heading back to base—were cleared to deliver their bombs, all under the watchful eye supplied by the overhead Predator.

Then, on the screen, clouds of debris and smoke jolted up from the ground, and the target area was momentarily obscured.

Almost instantly, the collective blood pressure in the operations center dropped. There were no high fives; such was one-way warfare. The mood was so blasé that Arkin might have even missed what happened next if he hadn't been paying attention.

It was almost imperceptible from the Predator feed, but a line of bumps seemed to emerge from the ground across the target area, like a moving underground snake. "He's strafing," someone said, referring to one of the A-10s, now spewing hundreds of bottle-sized rounds. The A-10 pilot had circled back around after dropping his precision weapons, and as everyone watched, he came back low over the target and plastered it with withering deadly fire.

"Did I just see what I thought I saw?" Arkin asked, stunned.

"It was not unauthorized," someone responded. In the many procedures laid out by the air force for pilots, one was that after all the work deciding which precision weapons to use to avoid collateral damage, the soldier on the ground calling in air support had the authority to attack again, knowing full well that doing so would unleash the most indiscriminate, lawn–mowing weapon around to do it, the A-10's Gatling gun.[1]

But it seemed that this authorized strafing undermined the entire system. After all the effort and care, after all that went into drawing blast circles and selecting weapons, in the end someone on the ground, far from the more complete process happening at the command center in Qatar, had opted to rip through the whole surgical maneuver with a machete.

The next day, Arkin learned that Gold 6 was Baz Mohammed Faizan, a man U.S. intelligence identified as the shadow Taliban governor of Uruzgan province, then a mostly unconquered Pashtun district and opium poppy center. Since he was considered an HVT, military rules had allowed the A-10 to finish the job, however brutally, to get rid of him once and for all.

A couple of days later, Arkin was sitting in an office when an officer slipped a sheet of paper across the table. He had just a moment to take it in: "Top Secret," with a bunch of code words on the top and bottom. An intelligence report from the CIA, Uruzgan province: Gold 6 had walked away.

Although Top Secret America is located in the suburbs and military bases of the United States, much of what it produces is intended for the war against terrorists overseas. Explicit in the remote nature of the new warfare was a stark trade-off: saving the lives of more American soldiers and airmen at the expense of accidentally killing more innocent civilians abroad. Or, as in the case of Gold 6, everything going according to plan but without any success. It was a trade-off never really debated in public, but one that seemed to sit

---

[1] Anyone who's ever watched a Vietnam War–era movie can picture a soldier on the ground with a radio calling in air support. These days, he's called the joint terminal attack controller, or JTAC (pronounced "jay-tack"). Once a ground commander requests "air support," the JTAC controls the aircraft. He—not the CAOC, not the pilot—has the authority to decide if the aircraft will deliver its weapons and where. And so it was in the case of Gold 6; and the JTAC on the ground was cleared to request further attacks if needed.

well with most Americans, who themselves seemed increasingly distant and distracted from the gruesome and deadly realities of the longest war in the nation's history.

No matter how good the intelligence is, or how effective the precision-guidance system, things on the ground are not always clear from the television show far away. Drone strikes have infuriated many Pakistanis, whose support for the overall U.S. war against al-Qaeda continues to wane. Fueled by the lies of their own political leaders, who insisted that the Americans were acting unilaterally and thus trampling Pakistan's sovereignty, people took to the streets—sometimes in the thousands—in opposition.

Yet as hot as public tensions grew in Pakistan over issues of sovereignty and nationalism, something fundamental had begun to shift by 2011, indicating an acceptance of this one-way, remote-control warfare. In early March, a senior Pakistani military officer, Major General Ghayur Mehmood, publicly defended the CIA program and tried to set the record straight on civilian deaths. "Myths and rumors about U.S. Predator strikes and the casualty figures are many, but it's a reality that many of those being killed in these strikes are hard-core elements; a sizable number of them are foreigners," he said at a news conference convened to address the matter. "Yes, there are a few civilian casualties in such precision strikes, but a majority of those eliminated are terrorists, including foreign terrorist elements." From 2007 to 2011, there had been 164 drone strikes and 964 terrorists killed, Mehmood told reporters. The change over time was apparent, too. In 2007, one terrorist had been killed; in 2010, 423 were killed. The general's figures were close to the CIA's count, which helped confirm their accuracy.

A subsequent flood of classified diplomatic cables released by WikiLeaks further confirmed that, as far back as early 2008, the Pakistani government had been asking the United States for more drones to support its own military operations. The American and Pakistani press had been reporting this for years, but U.S. and Pakistani officials would always deny the reports. Now, there it was in an official document: Pakistani army chief General Ashfaq Kayani requesting "continuous Predator coverage of the conflict area" in South Waziristan, where the army was trying to clean out militants.

In another cable, in November 2008, the U.S. ambassador to Pakistan, Anne Patterson, addressed the high cost of secrecy in the drone war. "As the gap between private (Government of Pakistan) acquiescence and public condemnation of U.S. actions grows, Pakistani leaders who feel they look increasingly weak to their constituents could begin considering stronger actions against the U.S., even though the response to date has focused largely on ritual condemnation."

Prior to 9/11, the idea that state-sponsored killing would become a normal part of American policy would have seemed unthinkable. But ten years after their debut, drone strikes piloted from the safety of Suburbia, U.S.A., had become an acceptable practice, even the norm. Funding Top Secret America with unlimited tax dollars during the deepest recession in memory had become normal, too, as had tacitly endorsing an incremental assault on individual privacy.

By the spring of 2011, the new way of war had become so routine that as the last cherry blossom dropped to the ground in Washington, President Obama approved the use of lethal American military drones in yet another country with which the United States was not at war: Libya. A United Nations resolution had authorized the NATO alliance to use military force to stop Libyan leader Muammar Qaddafi from brutalizing opponents to his rule. But the air strike on his command-and-control compound in Tripoli, in which one of his sons and three grandsons died, seemed to indicate he had gotten himself on a kill list, too.

CHAPTER ELEVEN

Dark Matter

Besides the damage inflicted on the enemy by the CIA's killer drones, paramilitary forces killed dozens of al-Qaeda leaders and hundreds of its foot soldiers in the decade after 9/11. But troops from a more mysterious organization, based in North Carolina, have killed easily ten times as many al-Qaeda, and hundreds of Iraqi insurgents as well.

This secretive organization, created in 1980 but completely reinvented in 2003, flies ten times more drones than the CIA. Some are armed with Hellfire missiles; most carry video cameras, sensors, and signals intercept equipment. When the CIA's paramilitary Special Activities Division[1] needs help, or when the president decides to send agency operatives on a covert mission into a foreign

---

[1] The CIA Special Activities Division (SAD) is the paramilitary element of the agency and part of the National Clandestine Service, which collects intelligence and conducts covert operations. SAD members have the skills and equipment necessary to carry out military operations, but the group is called paramilitary because military operations are not allowed to be conducted covertly. After 9/11, the SAD was first on the ground in Afghanistan, and since then it has been responsible for capturing many terrorist leaders.

country, it often borrows troops from this same organization, temporarily deputizing them when necessary in order to get the missions done.

The CIA has captured, imprisoned, and interrogated close to a hundred terrorists in secret prisons around the world. Troops from this other secret military unit have captured and interrogated ten times as many. They hold them in prisons in Iraq and Afghanistan that they alone control and, for at least three years after 9/11, they sometimes ignored U.S. military rules for interrogation and used almost whatever means they thought might be most effective.

Of all the top secret units fighting terrorism after 9/11, this is the single organization that has killed and captured more al-Qaeda members around the world and destroyed more of their training camps and safe houses than the rest of the U.S. government forces combined. And although it greatly benefited from the technology produced by Top Secret America, the secret to its success has been otherwise escaping the behemoth created in response to the 9/11 attacks.

Over a decade in which they were fighting secret battles, sometimes in countries where wars have not been declared, this group of men (and a few women) sustained a level of obscurity that not even the CIA has managed to pull off. Its commanders—headquartered at Fort Bragg and the adjoining Pope Air Force Base in Fayetteville, North Carolina—still consider the organization to be officially "unacknowledged," meaning its true purpose and everything it does is classified, and therefore, as far as the public is concerned, it does not exist.

"We're the dark matter," a strapping U.S. Navy SEAL once explained. "We're the force that orders the universe but can't be seen."

When its officers are working in civilian government agencies or U.S. embassies abroad, which they do quite a lot, they dispense with uniforms, unlike the rest of their military comrades. On the battlefield, they dress according to the mission, and when in uniform they wear no name or rank identifiers. After 9/11, they had come up with all sorts of new names to hide their secret military subunits: The Secret Army of Northern Virginia, Task Force Green, Task Force Blue, Task Force 11, then Task Force 20, then Task Force 121. In fact, they change their task force numbers so often that even their American colleagues sometimes "aren't sure who we are," one officer explained, acknowledging that obscurity was the goal.

All these task forces are part of JSOC, which sits at the center of the secret universe as the dark matter that shapes the world in ways that are usually not detectable. Like the CIA, the Joint Special Operations Command has become the president's personal weapon against terrorists, one both Presidents Bush and Obama have wielded often over the years, with little or no input from Congress or the larger public policy community that has weighed in on life-and-death policy options since the beginning on what is now the country's longest war, the war against al-Qaeda.

JSOC's parent organization, the U.S. Special Operations Command, located in Tampa, describes the unit's mission in a deceptively vague way: to "study special operations requirements and techniques...ensure interoperability and equipment standardization." They decline to offer any more information.

After a JSOC SEAL team killed bin Laden in Pakistan on May 2, 2011, the White House never cracked the door even an inch on this ultrasecret unit, describing them only as "a small U.S. team" and "U.S. military personnel." The word *JSOC* was never uttered as details flowed out about the operation. But except for that one time, its operations are never revealed to the media. Its leaders don't speak in public. Its public affairs officers answer no questions. It has no external website.

The first time I ran into JSOC was in a warehouse on Qatar's massive air base in the middle of the night in early 2002. I was sitting on a crate next to some army soldiers, waiting for a seat on a cargo plane that would take us to a larger base in Kuwait and then back home to Washington, DC. Three young men with unkempt beards and dirt on their hands came in and sat down. They reminded me of a pack of German shepherd pups, with their boundless enthusiasm for each other and whatever they were up to.

Their name tags were gone, their shoulder patches replaced by blank Velcro. Their uniforms were not quite right, either, and one of them still had a black weapons strap around his thigh. I wanted to ask, "Who the heck are you?" but settled instead for making eye contact with the hope that might lead to a conversation. It didn't. They looked right past me.

When I got to Kuwait, I described their appearance to an army officer I knew well. "Probably black SOF," he said.

White SOF I knew. They lived in their own safe houses; regular army soldiers didn't know much about them, and they worked, in small teams called ODAs, for Operational Detachment-Alphas, in the hinterlands of Afghanistan, Kosovo, and elsewhere. During the initial invasion of Afghanistan, the ODAs teamed up with the remnants of the U.S.-backed Northern Alliance and then rode on horseback with them to call in U.S. air strikes against the Taliban. They had been the first military units on the ground—or so I thought. It took just 316 U.S. Army Special Forces soldiers all of 49 days, with the help of local tribal and warlord forces and U.S. air power, to vanquish the Taliban, recapture Kabul, and chase al-Qaeda into the mountains and across the border into Pakistan. JSOC troops had been there, too, I learned later, serving as bodyguards for the man who would become Afghanistan's first postwar president, Hamid Karzai, as he moved around the country during the U.S. invasion, and as partners with the CIA paramilitaries working with the Northern Alliance to form a fighting force against al-Qaeda and the Taliban.

Shortly after the invasion of Afghanistan, JSOC troops also took part in the now infamous Tora Bora operation to capture bin Laden. As it turned out, hunting bin Laden and other al-Qaeda leaders was their main mission, and their rules of engagement were carefully and secretly constructed for their use only.

★   ★   ★

JSOC's core is built of the army's Delta Force, Navy SEAL Team 6,[2] the army's 160th Special Operations Aviation Regiment,[3] the army's 75th Ranger Regiment,[4] and the air force's 24th Special Tactics Squadron.[5] Its subunits are many, and its task forces are custom-built for a given mission and range in size from a half-dozen to several hundred people.

After 9/11, everything within JSOC grew in size and complexity. It acquired all of the pieces of a self-sustaining secret army, including a personnel pipeline, an equipment and technology acquisition branch, and a research arm. It has its own intelligence division, numbering three thousand staffers who can research and make models of targets, including 3D walk-throughs of locations where JSOC will conduct raids. It has its own drones, its own reconnaissance planes, even its own dedicated satellites in its own space unit. JSOC has its own cyberwarriors, too, who conduct operations like embedding sensors in computer keyboards to follow

---

[2] SEAL Team 6 is the "sea-air-land" special mission and counterterrorism unit assigned to JSOC, sometimes known as the Navy Special Warfare Development Group (DevGru), and located in Dam Neck, Virginia. On missions, they come together in task forces (TFs) combining operations, intelligence, logistics, etc.

[3] The 160th Special Operations Aviation Regiment—nicknamed the Night Stalkers, and headquartered at Fort Campbell, Kentucky—are assigned to Army Special Operations Command. With one-of-a kind helicopters and specially trained pilots and crew, the 160th is called upon for armed helicopter support to white special operations commands and to JSOC. They are supplemented by Air Force Special Operations Command aircraft that also support longer-range infiltration and exfiltration missions, gunship support, and combat search and rescue.

[4] The Army's 75th Ranger Regiment, with battalions at three U.S. locations—Fort Benning, Georgia; Hunter Army Airfield, Georgia; and Fort Lewis, Washington—is 2,500 strong. They are the premier airfield seizure and raid unit in the army and are used to support JSOC and general purpose forces in ambush, reconnaissance, airborne and air assaults, and perimeter.

[5] The 24th Special Tactics Squadron (STS), located at Pope AFB, North Carolina, provides special operators who are experts in landing zones, tactical and close air support, targeting, and providing trauma care and air medevac for injured personnel. They are assigned to JSOC.

what suspected terrorists type, or creating fake online identities in order to trap suspects and elicit information. But, most essential to its identity and core mission, JSOC has the rare authority to decide which individuals to add to a kill list, and then to kill them.

JSOC existed for decades before the 9/11 terrorist attacks, but in a much paler form. The idea of a super-elite clandestine force dates from 1977, when Lufthansa Flight 181 was hijacked by four members of the Popular Front for the Liberation of Palestine and was flown to Mogadishu, Somalia. A German antiterrorist squad, GSG 9, stormed the plane and rescued the crew members and passengers with help from Somali commandos. Impressed, the U.S. government took note that it had no similar capability. Months later, a U.S. hostage rescue unit was activated, and spent two years training.

In 1979, soon after it was approved to become operational, a group of Iranian students overran the U.S. Embassy in Tehran and kidnapped its occupants. Five months later, President Carter sent a covert hostage rescue team made up partly of the new unit to bring the Americans home. Operation Eagle Claw, as it was known, instead became an embarrassing failure, defeated by poor planning, bad communications, lack of teamwork between units, a sandstorm, mechanical failure, and a collision of aircraft that killed eight service members and an Iranian civilian. This fiasco led to the creation of the Special Operations Command, a permanent command led by a four-star general or admiral, the highest military rank. The command's main purpose would be to integrate the various elite forces of the army, navy, and air force charged with freeing hostages, deploying behind enemy lines, and fighting alongside foreign surrogates worldwide on clandestine operations. JSOC would be the only truly clandestine unit of the new command, and it quickly became nearly autonomous from its parent organization.

Prior to the attacks of 9/11, special operations forces were rarely used for counterterrorism operations or manhunting missions. In fact, they were rarely used at all. This was mainly because regular military commanders were suspicious of their independence (General Norman Schwarzkopf famously denied much of a role to special operations for this reason during the first Gulf War, in 1991). But more than that, sending small teams into hostile territory was nearly impossible because the kind of detailed intelligence they would need to operate secretly was always lacking. Neither the mind-set nor the methodology for gathering such information existed in any sophisticated way.

JSOC took its central place in the post-9/11 era under Defense Secretary Donald Rumsfeld, who smarted from the CIA's ability to move first into Afghanistan and vowed never to be outdone by the agency again. Before he left office, Bush briefly sent JSOC into Pakistan. To soothe the worries of U.S. Ambassador Anne Patterson about the mounting civilian deaths JSOC raids elsewhere had produced, and to prove how carefully its missions were conducted, commanders brought a Predator control console to Patterson's Islamabad embassy office so she could witness a raid in real time. But the brief forays still became a point of public outcry in Pakistan, and U.S. officials canceled future missions there after only three raids, though the CIA continued to conduct drone strikes.

As the secret organization killed more people and dismantled more terrorist networks, decision makers in Washington gave it more money, more troops, and greater responsibility. Its headquarters doubled in size, as two permanent task forces were established overseas, each commanded by a general officer. From 1,800 troops on September 11, 2001, JSOC grew to a force sometimes as large as 25,000 today. Most of the force provides equipment, logistics, analysis, and everything else needed by the raid parties: the trigger pullers, the snipers, the manhunters.

As JSOC's role grew more crucial, other organizations that weren't as lethal or meaningful tried to attach themselves to the organization's rucksack. It had its pick of partners and swallowed up the ones it wanted. It acquired or teamed up with half a dozen organizations, including the ultrasecret Technical Operations

Support Activity, or TOSA[6]—one of several names for an organization previously known as the Intelligence Support Activity, The Activity, and Grey Fox—which had helped kill drug kingpin Pablo Escobar in Colombia in 1993 and which has its own extraordinary eavesdropping and aviation abilities.

JSOC also partnered with the National Security Agency's new expeditionary force, with Britain's SAS,[7] and with the special forces equivalents in Jordan, Australia, and Poland, all of whom have taken orders from the Americans, and have also been wounded and killed under their command.

If killing were all that winning wars was about, the book on JSOC would be written. In the first months of the war in Afghanistan, according to senior JSOC leaders who were there, the raid teams killed thousands of people. In the first *weeks* of the war in Iraq, they helped kill hundreds on the march to Baghdad. As Iraq descended into chaos in the summer of 2005, JSOC leaders pushed their troops to the breaking point to execute 300 raids a month there. As a result, over 50 percent of JSOC Army Delta Force commandos now have Purple Hearts. They were killing dozens and capturing more, and the toll it exacted on the force reminded its commander at the time, General Stanley McChrystal, of Lawrence of Arabia's description of "rings of sorrow," the emotional toll casualties took on small groups of warriors. Greatly influenced by Lawrence's life story, McChrystal thought of his JSOC troops as modern-day tribal forces: dependent upon one another for kinship and survival.

But no war in modern times is ever won simply by killing enough of the enemy. Even in an era of precision weaponry, acci-

---

[6] The Technical Operations Support Activity (TOSA) is an army-owned intelligence, surveillance, and reconnaissance (ISR) organization that supports special operations, JSOC, and other short-term intelligence collection efforts that demand close-in presence.

[7] The British Special Air Service (SAS), the UK equivalent to the United States' Delta Force (the Special Boat Service is the equivalent of SEAL Team 6), is the special mission and counterterrorism unit that operates closely with JSOC. Much of the JSOC organizational style of squadrons and flights is taken from the SAS.

dents happen that often create huge political setbacks. In Afghanistan and Pakistan in particular, every JSOC raid that also wounded or killed civilians, or destroyed a home or someone's livelihood, became a source of grievance so deep that the counterproductive effects, still unfolding, are difficult to calculate. JSOC's success in targeting the right homes, businesses, and individuals in its prolific night raids was only about 50 percent, according to two senior commanders. Given the difficulty of gathering intelligence on a terrorist and then striking at the moment he is home, commanders considered this rate a good one.

When they made mistakes and the wrong person was at home or the wrong home was invaded, U.S. commanders and civilian leaders, including Presidents Bush and Obama, offered apologies and money, but these measures didn't neutralize the anti-American feelings the attacks fueled. Eventually, as local folklore grew about men in black with green eyes and laser beams, the commandos' reputation for violence grew larger than life, and they were blamed for deaths and torture they did not commit. Al-Qaeda and the Taliban were quick to seize on these sentiments and sometimes planted evidence that made JSOC's raids and mistakes look worse than they were. U.S. diplomats and the regular army troops in daily contact with the people whose countries they occupied were left to soothe tensions, and they were often inadequately prepared for that task.

"Sometimes our actions were counterproductive," McChrystal told me. "We would say, 'We need to go in and kill this guy,' but just the effects of our kinetic action did something negative and they [the conventional army forces that occupied much of the country] were left to clean up the mess." But such mishaps were considered exceptional; more routine were the invisible successes.

Predictably, as JSOC achievements mounted, the number of private companies working on weapons, sensors, logistics, electronics, and information technology for it soared; a contractor village now hugs the perimeters of JSOC's North Carolina compound and the Tampa headquarters of the Special Operations Command.

By Arkin's calculation, there are about 5,000 civilian contractors and 49 companies doing top secret work for JSOC: developing unique equipment, conducting primary analysis for targeting, or performing the large administrative tasks required to keep the organization hidden.

JSOC has more eavesdropping and surveillance technology, more translators and cybersnooping equipment, than any clandestine espionage outfit, and yet the White House and the Defense Department do not view it as an espionage organization. Instead, the spying done by JSOC and its member units is called reconnaissance, or "recce" (pronounced "reh-key") and labeled "intelligence preparation of the battlefield," which is a way to shoehorn clandestine intelligence-gathering into Title 10 of the U.S. Code,[8] the law that governs traditional military activity. Under Title 10, Congress does not have to be briefed on JSOC activities, and JSOC is not considered to be carrying out covert actions, although many people in the CIA and elsewhere think it should be. All traditional espionage and covert operations, usually undertaken by the CIA, are governed by Title 50,[9] which requires congressional notification and the involvement of the director of national intelligence. (JSOC's shut-

---

[8] Alfred Cumming wrote this succinctly in an April 6, 2011, Congressional Research Service report titled "Covert Action: Legislative Background and Possible Policy Questions." As he explains, there is no legal definition of "clandestine" activity. A covert action is one in which the government's participation is unacknowledged, while a clandestine activity, according to senior defense officials, is one that, although intended to be secret, can be publicly acknowledged if it is discovered or inadvertently revealed. Being able to publicly acknowledge a clandestine activity provides the military personnel with certain protections under the Geneva Conventions. Those who participate in covert actions, however, could jeopardize any rights they may have under the Geneva Conventions. Also, he wrote, "Some observers suggest that Congress needs to increase its oversight of military activities that some contend may not meet the definition of covert action, and may therefore be exempt from the degree of congressional oversight accorded to covert actions. Others contend that increased oversight would hamper the military's effectiveness."

[9] Title 50 of the U.S. Code, War and National Defense, is that compilation of laws relating to national defense. It includes covert action, defined in statute as an action by the U.S. government to influence conditions abroad where the role of the United States is not acknowledged. A covert action first requires a written Presidential Finding, and Congress must be briefed, although not always beforehand.

ting down of nearly every overseas jihadist website on September 11, 2008, was not considered a covert action, even though it would have been if the CIA had done the very same thing. It was considered a defensive act of war, and thus a traditional military activity.)

In 2003 testimony initially classified top secret, the former Special Operations Command leader General Peter J. Schoomaker told the 9/11 Commission that without precise intelligence, it was impossible for even the best-trained forces to work discreetly abroad. As an example, he told the panel, before 9/11 he had been asked to capture a man leaving Iraq using a small JSOC team. The administration told him, however, that the team could be on the ground for only a short while. The problem, he said, was that no one had a photograph of the man. No one knew what he looked like, what hotel he was supposed to be staying in, or whether he was planning to leave the country by airplane or boat. Schoomaker could launch the mission, he explained, but not with a small team. He would need people at various locations and for a longer period of time to locate the right man. It was the same reason—lack of precise intelligence— that inhibited JSOC from hunting terrorists. Without good information, it was impossible to get close enough to kill or capture them. That is why, up until the 2001 attacks, the weapon of choice against terrorists had either been precision-guided cruise missiles launched from hundreds of miles away or, in even rarer instances, arrest by the FBI for legal trial in the United States when possible.

The 9/11 attacks changed all that. Three days afterward, Pakistani president Pervez Musharraf agreed to allow JSOC to secretly run operations into Afghanistan from Pakistani bases. Oman granted permission to host the unit's deadly AC-130[10] Spectre gunships and rear headquarters, according to an account by army general Tommy Franks, who was in charge of the U.S. military's first

---

[10] Air Force Special Operations gunships, nicknamed Spectre and Spooky, have a combination of small (25 mm and 40 mm) Gatling guns and cannons and one large (105 mm) cannon. With a crew of fourteen, the AC-130 employs strike radars and eavesdropping equipment for target detection and identification. The aircraft, though heavily armored, operate primarily at night.

counterattack overseas. In its first post-9/11 iteration, JSOC was a blunt killing machine that paid only moderate attention to the second- and third-order effects of its actions. It pursued al-Qaeda leaders with snipers, helicopter assaults, nighttime raids, and the terrifying AC-130s with side-firing weapons that were a standard part of its assault forces. Its rules of engagement required commandos to announce their presence at raids to give the enemy a chance to surrender; in Afghanistan, though, the men they hunted usually did not surrender, according to commandos who took part in the missions. JSOC's rules also allowed units to kill civilians traveling with high-value targets, if necessary, which they did quite often in the early days.

Often working with CIA teams, JSOC troops killed hundreds of people in Afghanistan, along the border with Pakistan, and, with the help of indigenous special forces, in the Philippines and elsewhere, according to military officers familiar with JSOC's operations.

The early lethality of JSOC was demonstrated in the failed December 2001 mountain battle at Tora Bora, in which bin Laden and many of his followers are believed to have escaped across the border into Pakistan. Some fifty JSOC troops of Task Force 11 arrived on December 8 to operate independently of both the overt army Special Operations teams and the Afghan Eastern Alliance. Every night, while Afghan troops and the Special Operations teams accompanying them would withdraw from their forward positions to eat and regroup, JSOC would continue to pummel the 3,000-strong al-Qaeda force. On the nights of December 13 and 14, for example, JSOC killed so many enemy forces that, according to the army's official history of the war, "dead bodies of al-Qaeda fighters were carted off the field the next day" by the truckload.

On the other side of the border, meanwhile, another JSOC team had its hands full helping Pakistanis round up a large group of al-Qaeda prisoners who had escaped during transport. In that incident, Colonel Michael A. Longoria, commander of the 18th Air Support Operations Group[11] assigned to a JSOC task force, facing intense gunfire from snipers and assault by local tribesmen and prisoners, helped a trapped Pakistani convoy fend off the attacks. Longoria killed two enemy snipers, helped recapture the escapees, moved wounded Pakistani casualties, and tended to seventeen dead Pakistani soldiers in what the Pentagon called "the bloodiest escape and firefight in Pakistan during Operation Enduring Freedom." For his efforts, he was awarded the Bronze Star in a private ceremony.

In contrast to its successes, which usually went unpublicized, JSOC's mistakes reverberated around the world. In what the Rand Corporation labeled "the single most serious errant attack of the entire war," on July 1, 2002, a JSOC-operated AC-130 gunship fired upon and killed at least forty-eight civilians in the small village of Kakarak in the Deh Rawod area of Uruzgan province. The incident took many inside the Pentagon by surprise, a senior air force officer said at the time, as most people had already shifted their attention to preparing for war with Iraq. JSOC Task Force 11 had been hunting Taliban leaders in villages seventy miles north of Kandahar in the most intense manhunt since Tora Bora. When a reconnaissance team came under attack, they called for AC-130 gunship support, which subsequently fired on six sites in the vicinity, according to a Pentagon account at the time. The estimates of civilian deaths ranged from forty-eight to hundreds. Villagers told the *Washington Post* that American soldiers wearing beards came soon after the strikes, inspecting the dead and treating some of the wounded. They said the forces detained seven men and took them away in vehicles with guns mounted on top.

---

[11] The Air Force 18th Air Support Operations Group, headquartered at Pope AFB, North Carolina, is the headquarters for all combat controllers assigned to conventional military units. Combat controllers are responsible for liaison between air and ground units and for the provision of close air support and combat search and rescue. The 18th ASOG oversees a network of nineteen geographically dispersed units and supplies combat controllers for JSOC missions as well.

The unclassified summary of the investigation declared the sites hit as "valid targets." But the report also said that neither the reconnaissance elements nor the AC-130 gunships were initially able to identify who specifically was present at the six targets. From the sky, the summary noted, "it is...not possible to distinguish men from women or adults from children." The "wedding party incident," as it became known because a wedding party at one of the six sites was fired upon, came to symbolize American disregard for Afghan civilians. It would be the first American attack to be publicly condemned by President Hamid Karzai. He summoned Lieutenant General Dan McNeill, overall ground commander for U.S. forces in Afghanistan, for an explanation. Secretary Rumsfeld called the incident a "tragedy," and President Bush "expressed his sympathies" in a telephone conversation with Karzai.

It was the nature of this war, and of the extraordinary freedom offered to JSOC, that this pattern of condemnation and apology would replay itself frequently as the number of lethal operations grew. In 2010, JSOC forces killed five innocent Afghan civilians in another bungled raid. McChrystal's successor, Vice Admiral William H. McRaven, admitted at the time that his team had committed "a terrible mistake," and he visited the victims' relatives to ask for forgiveness. McRaven took two sheep to the village in Paktika province where the raid occurred and offered to sacrifice them in accordance with Afghan tradition. The offer of sacrifice was declined by village elders, but they did accept thirty thousand dollars in cash, according to an eyewitness quoted in the *Times* of London.

McRaven told the father of two of the victims, "I am a soldier, I have spent most of my career overseas away from my family, but I have children as well and my heart grieves for you." After the mishap, McRaven ordered that all units use the bright-green laserlike lights on AC-130 gunships that often accompany assault forces on the nighttime raids. While it fractionally reduced the element of surprise, the lights identified the aircraft as American and were often enough to persuade insurgents to give up rather than draw their weapons.

In 2003, JSOC soldiers were among the first troops in southern Iraq, riding in with the protection of an armored task force of the 3rd Infantry Division. According to three senior JSOC commanders, these troops helped the division kill upward of five thousand Iraqis in perhaps the bloodiest portion of the war, the march to Baghdad. "It sounded like World War II, there was so much noise," said a JSOC commander who was there. The gunners on the armored vehicles faced human waves of Iraqi army forces, fedayeen, and their ragtag civilian supporters. They were ordered to kill anyone who got up on the vehicles. "That's the dirty little secret, the dark underbelly of the war," he said. "There were bodies everywhere." Troops eventually shot dogs to keep them away from the carcasses. Such armored vehicles also delivered the JSOC commandos on their own missions to capture or kill senior Iraqi Baathists loyal to Saddam Hussein and to find and secure weapons of mass destruction that were, it turned out, not there.

While JSOC troops worked well with CIA operatives and analysts in small teams in Afghanistan, the civilian CIA's inability even with its paramilitary elements to safely move around an increasingly violent Iraq created an intense fissure between the two organizations. JSOC's relative ease of movement, made possible by the fact that it is a military unit with the best combat training and equipment in the world, and its high enemy-killed-in-action numbers spurred the unit and its civilian supporters in the Pentagon to plan even more missions.

Some of those plans were not without controversy. At the time of General Schoomaker's testimony to the 9/11 Commission in 2003, just before the war in Iraq began, JSOC and the CIA were in a roiling dispute over whether the military unit could legally conduct missions outside of a war zone and whether the law required the Defense Department, on JSOC's behalf, to seek permission for these operations directly from the CIA, as the head of the intelligence community. "The bureaucratic mess is onerous," Schoomaker told the commission, according to a declassified copy of his testimony. Predictably, Schoomaker believed the secretary of defense should have the authority to order clandestine antiterrorism missions.

Unknown to Schoomaker, who had long since ended his career in JSOC, on September 16, 2003, three days before his testimony, Defense Secretary Rumsfeld had signed an order that hit JSOC's Fort Bragg headquarters like a lightning bolt. Labeled "EXORD"[12] and "CJCS War on Terrorism Execute Order," the approximately eighty-page document created a new category of top secret, compartmented activities, which were to be tightly controlled under the code name Focal Point. These were aimed at disrupting, capturing, and destroying the al-Qaeda network and its supporters anywhere in the world. In military terms, it was the equivalent of a Presidential Finding, the written rationale and approval the president was required to send to Congress when authorizing a CIA covert action. There was one big difference: JSOC would not need to notify Congress because, its lawyers argued successfully, it conducted traditional military operations with a traditional chain of command—no matter how untraditional its operations appeared.

The EXORD listed fifteen countries where these operations could occur. Next to each country was a list of activities permitted under various scenarios with the preapprovals needed to carry them out. In Iraq and Afghanistan, where declared wars were under way, authority to prepare for and take lethal action against al-Qaeda members was granted without additional approval from the president or secretary of defense. In the other countries in which they might operate—among them Algeria, Iran, Malaysia, Mali, Nigeria, Pakistan, the Philippines, Somalia, and Syria— JSOC forces would, in most cases, need at least tacit approval from the country involved, and a sign-off from some higher authority in

---

[12] An execute order (EXORD) is the specific order that directs a commander to initiate military operations, defines the time to initiate, and provides guidance for operational plans. The president or secretary of defense can authorize the chairman of the Joint Chiefs of Staff to issue an EXORD. Execution continues until the operation is terminated or the mission is accomplished or revised. Some military operations, particularly counterterrorism operations, are conducted under standing, or open-ended, EXORDs.

its chain of command. In the Philippines, for example, JSOC could undertake psychological operations to confuse or trap al-Qaeda operatives but would need approval from the White House for lethal action. To attack targets in Somalia required at least approval from the secretary of defense, while attacks in Pakistan and Syria needed the president's sign-off.

The EXORD also included a lengthy description of the rules of engagement for each scenario, including which types of munitions and electronic surveillance should be used for nighttime and daytime assaults, and what extra care was required to minimize the possibility that civilians would be killed or injured. Assaults likely to result in large numbers of civilian casualties needed increasingly higher levels of approval.

Creation of the EXORD had taken many months and dozens of meetings between the various, and jealously competitive, national security agencies. The CIA didn't want JSOC encroaching on its turf; the State Department was worried about the ramifications to diplomatic relationships if these missions went awry or were somehow discovered and made public. But with Bush's full support, Rumsfeld signed off and the other agencies relented. The next day, when the order became official, JSOC began its journey toward superseding the CIA as the center of an opaque universe, the dark matter that would shape the global war against al-Qaeda and, in the process, mold relations between countries.

By then it was mid-2003, the hunt for bin Laden was going nowhere, and Iraq was in the hands of the coalition. Major General Dell Dailey, the JSOC commander at the time, worried about the toll of constant overseas deployment on such an elite, ever-ready unit. He proposed decreasing the number of forces overseas: bringing them home, where they would be ready to surge into hot spots when needed. McChrystal, then on the Joint staff, listened in silence as Dailey spoke to the chairman of the Joint Chiefs. Three months later, when he became JSOC's new commander, McChrystal immediately reversed course, and JSOC would never be the same.

McChrystal had learned a lot about Washington from his work

as the vice chief of operations on the Joint Staff. He had been shocked by the acrimony between Rumsfeld and some generals on the Joint Staff and between the various intelligence and military organizations all trying to accomplish the same things. He decided there was a natural aversion to decision making at the top of government. No one wanted to be wrong, so they either asked more questions or added more layers to the process, sometimes without even realizing it. The result was that the process of getting approval for action slowed to a crawl.

The buzzwords after 9/11 had been "sharing" and "interagency cooperation." But those were just words. Practically, it meant the meetings were bigger and longer and, given the increased compartmentalization, included people who either couldn't actually talk to each other or were mutually in the dark about essential details, making the process less productive than it should have been. Also, any one of a multitude of agencies could stifle action until it was too late. Top Secret America, in other words, had become inert under its own weight and size.

Although JSOC's new power had come from Washington, McChrystal believed that in order to be successful, he had to move it as far away from the capital as possible, "to slip out of the grip" of Washington's suffocating bureaucracy, he told associates.

Under McChrystal, JSOC would become the adaptable, innovative counterterrorism organization that Top Secret America was supposed to be, too. He embraced the new freedoms the White House had given to its secret units to aggressively target individuals from the air or with raids on the ground. But he achieved this only by outright rejecting at least four of Top Secret America's defining characteristics: its enormous size, its counterproductive duplication, its internal secrecy, and its old-fashioned, hierarchical structure.

During McChrystal's first orientation trip overseas, in October 2003, the new JSOC commander found 20 of his men in Afghanistan conducting occasional raids, and 250 men in Iraq who, using one surveillance drone, were trying to find Saddam Hussein and his loyalists. He flew by helicopter from Baghdad to Mosul and

Ramadi, where several other JSOC troops were stationed in virtual isolation. His 12 men in Mosul, he discovered, were totally cut off from the others, with no effective way to communicate or to share information about the enemy. And there was no way to stay on top of what the CIA or embassy staff was working on.

"We needed to become networked together," he said in an interview. To make this happen, he began a campaign to coax other agencies to help him out, and to acquire the technology, and force the cultural change, to make this possible. McChrystal eventually moved his headquarters to Balad Air Base, forty-five miles northeast of Baghdad, and worked inside an old concrete hangar that had once housed Saddam Hussein's fighter jets. There he constructed a warren of three connecting command centers: one dedicated to fighting al-Qaeda in Iraq, one dedicated to fighting the Shi'a extremists in Iraq (established only in 2006), and a third for himself, so he could oversee JSOC's worldwide operations, including those in Afghanistan.

Inside, young techies from the National Security Agency and their peers from the National Geospatial-Intelligence Agency worked alongside old hands from the State Department and the CIA and starched FBI agents deployed to gather evidence and keep it untainted from the chaos of battle for use in Iraqi courts. Computer screens hung from the ceiling, some of them replaying footage of the falling World Trade Center towers for motivation. Photos of the faces of wanted terrorists were tacked to the walls. Everyone had the necessary clearances, and, with McChrystal's prodding, they talked to each other—which meant they could actually get some work done.

For some inside government, this emphasis on sharing information and brainstorming problems as a group might have been seen as pie-in-the-sky thinking, a kumbaya kind of notion. But McChrystal was anything but a kumbaya type of leader. His legend preceded him. Stories were passed that he ate just one meal a day and ran at least ten miles every day. He was impatient, chewed his nails, was intolerant of sloppiness, got bored easily. He certainly looked the part of the manic commander, with his taut, bony face, intense eyes, and thin physique. Shortly after his arrival in Balad, a sign went up inside the wire: "17-5-2." This was McChrystal's prescription for time management: seventeen hours for work, five hours for sleep, two hours for eating and exercise. Three meals a day meant twenty minutes for each, one hour to exercise, and another to clean up and organize. That was it.

When McChrystal addresses civilian audiences now, he sometimes begins by showing a photograph of his father, General Herbert J. McChrystal Jr., "the soldier I wanted to be." McChrystal was the fourth in a family of five boys and one girl. All Herbert's children grew up to serve in the military or marry into it. McChrystal graduated from West Point in 1976, during the army's post-Vietnam crisis, and after that ascended through the ranks of the elite, secretive wing of Special Operations. He served as a staff officer and an operations officer in the first Gulf War and spent time on a fellowship at Harvard University and the Council on Foreign Relations in New York, where he ran a dozen miles each morning to its Upper East Side offices.

Mixed with his legendary work ethic was his Scotch Irish exuberance and common-man demeanor. He seemed almost naïvely trusting (which would become his undoing years later, after he and his staff made inappropriate comments about his civilian leaders to a *Rolling Stone* magazine reporter; he offered to resign, and Obama accepted). He viewed beer calls with subordinates as an important bonding exercise. He made people call him by his first name. He told them what he thought. "When I asked him a question, he actually gave me an answer," said one of his top advisers, Graham Lamm, a Brit. He told people that he considered his Ranger vow never to leave a fallen comrade behind more binding even than his marriage vows. His colleagues both civilian and military describe him as a force of nature, a personality so strong and persuasive that he convinced his ever-widening circle of teammates that to be successful would mean casting off another trademark of Top Secret America—its compartmented secrecy.

Within the confines of this highly classified world, McChrystal exposed the guts of his operation to everyone involved in it. His subordinates learned to share information with one another because he ordered them to do so. Sharing, he told them, made it more likely that the organization would function better. "The more people you shared your problem with, the better you'd do in solving it," he would say.

To push this idea further, McChrystal ordered the creation of what became a simple PC-based common desktop and portal where troops could post documents, conduct chats, tap into the intelligence available on any target—pictures, biometrics, transcripts, intelligence reports—and follow the message traffic of commanders in the midst of operations. By the summer of 2004 it was in place. Now, not only would every single troop in JSOC have access to this real-time picture of evolving targets on the battlefield, but so would the unit's historical rivals: the CIA, the NSA, the FBI, the Defense Intelligence Agency, and even certain elements within the State Department, including several ambassadors with whom McChrystal worked closely. He wanted them all to become a part of the JSOC intelligence-gathering apparatus and was willing to show enough of his hand to convince them to come along.

The goal of such an integrated process was overdue by the time McChrystal took command of the relatively small JSOC corner of Top Secret America. While much of the lumbering intelligence community in Washington continued along its dysfunctional path, McChrystal began salting every relevant national security agency in the capital region with JSOC liaison officers. These were not members of the B Team, as they were in many organizations— they were the smartest, most worldly troops in the unit, and sometimes even its most senior. For example, when relations between the CIA and JSOC were rough in the beginning of the Iraq deployment,

McChrystal gave the agency his chief intelligence officer, Colonel Michael Flynn, to work in the Baghdad station.

McChrystal made sure that all the key administration and DoD players had a JSOC liaison on their personal staff, including Richard Myers, chairman of the Joint Chiefs of Staff; CIA director George Tenet; General John Abizaid, commander of the Central Command; Ryan Crocker, U.S. ambassador to Afghanistan; and Anne Patterson, U.S. ambassador to Pakistan. In all, McChrystal pushed out more than 75 liaison officers to Washington and another 100 in the field. They rotated every four months so none would become bureaucrats, disconnected from combat.

For the most part, McChrystal's liaison offensive worked as intended, though there were some in the target organizations who did not appreciate the gesture, and thought of the liaisons as spies for an organization that was already too important. Nevertheless, those suspicions did little to derail JSOC's spectacular rise. Even the nature of the new war contributed. The Iraq conflict's heavy reliance on modern technology gave tech-savvy JSOC teammates an advantage they did not have in Afghanistan, where few people used cell phones, laptop computers, or even landline telephones, all devices that JSOC, with the help of the National Security Agency and TOSA, would eventually learn to monitor and locate. Before the Iraq push, the NSA was focused on tracking movements and conversations of world leaders and key terrorists to learn their plans and intentions, not on tracking single individuals on the battlefield simply to discover their location. It rarely shared the raw product of its monitoring directly with combat units—that, it was felt, was the job of the service-level military intelligence units. But the NSA wanted in on the action, too, and soon was sending representatives to McChrystal's Balad headquarters.

The collaboration paid off handsomely. By September 2004, the NSA had figured out how to geolocate cell phones even if they were off. "We just had a field day," said a senior JSOC commander. "We did thousands of them." When they hit on a hot phone— "The Find," as they called it—someone could send a plane to watch the building where the phone had lit up, and a raid would be mounted if appropriate. Using a new computer linkup called the RTRG,[13] for Real Time Regional Gateway, they would feed in every bit of data or piece of paper they captured and would soon get back a set of new phone numbers and new leads.

Lacking actual informants and eyes on the ground, aerial surveillance of the enemy became the primary means of tracking terrorists and Saddam loyalists. Lacking enough aircraft and impatient with Washington's acquisition process, McChrystal's team improvised. They turned two captured four-seater Pilatus aircraft that had been used for drug smuggling into camera surveillance planes. They mounted cameras on their UH-60 helicopters and on a DH-7 leased aircraft. They cajoled six planes out of the National Guard, outfitted them with sensors, and began using them, too. Their surveillance fleet, a hodgepodge of fifteen types of aircraft, grew from one aircraft to forty in a matter of a year or so.

Another tool they perfected was the use of dogs before and during raids. They rigged cameras on the animals' backs and trained them to run a perimeter or through a house or compound fast enough to avoid being shot. "They were fearless," said one senior JSOC commander. They would go down holes, point out trip wires, sniff out explosives, pick up the scent of humans; the dogs even learned to fast-rope out of helicopters harnessed to their handlers and to do parachute jumps in tandem with them. Some were killed, and others were wounded multiple times. The commandos nominated several for Purple Hearts, and when officials denied them real medals, they created their own version to honor their canine teammates.

Most Afghans and Iraqis feared dogs. Their presence was almost

---

[13] The NSA's Real Time Regional Gateway is a network created during the Iraq and Afghanistan wars to speed up the delivery of signal intercepts from collectors to users on the ground. Called an "interactive national repository," RTRG allows users to see all signal intelligence that collectors are working on in real time. This includes ground collectors, Air Force RC-135 Rivet Joint and Liberty planes, SIGINT-equipped drones, and SIGINT satellites operated by the NRO. RTRG has provided a tenfold increase in the speed with which intercepts are provided to operators on the ground.

as controversial as drones, and Afghan president Hamid Karzai complained bitterly about the animals. Once he even called Secretary of State Hillary Clinton as she flew across the globe to tell her that one had bitten a young boy. "We're keeping the dogs," she brusquely told him, according to one person who overheard the conversation.

The early 2000s were a period of rapid commercial invention inside Top Secret America; many accessories for America's high-tech war were introduced: drones as small as dragonflies, robots of astonishing variety, sensors that could be implanted somewhere and spew out information about nearby movements for as long as a year, tiny radio and computer sets and miniature tracking devices that could pinpoint the location of individual soldiers wherever they were in the world.

One of the most useful innovations was what some in JSOC dubbed the Electronic Divining Rod, a sensor worn by commandos that could detect the location of a particular cell phone. Wearing the device, JSOC troops entering an apartment building, for example, could follow the beeping noise from the monitor into a room full of people. Like a coin-sweeper used on the beach, the device would get louder as the soldier carrying it came closer to the person carrying the phone in question.

Killing the enemy was always the easy part, JSOC commanders said; finding him was the hard part. But thanks to a man named Roy Apseloff, JSOC's intelligence collection improved dramatically. Apseloff, who had introduced himself to McChrystal and his chief intelligence officer, Michael Flynn, one day when they were visiting CIA headquarters, managed a small office called the National Media Exploitation Center, located in an odd-shaped building in Fairfax, Virginia. He explained how he could help them mine and analyze the pocket litter—literally, the trash in a suspect's pockets—as well as documents and electronic equipment his troops were seizing in raids.

At the time, these items were bagged up and left for translators to work on in their spare time. Apseloff, however, showed McChrystal and Flynn how his team of thirty people, using special technology to download the contents of locked and/or damaged computers, could extract names, phone numbers, messages, and images, and then, using specialized software, could process and store that data and link it to other information—information that might help analysts find not just one more bad guy but an entire network of them. McChrystal and Flynn were impressed, and a long, close partnership began.

The major challenge McChrystal and Apseloff confronted was how to find the gems in the trash quickly enough to be useful. This was an old problem. What was about to change was the speed with which connections could potentially be made. The time between the capture of information and its interpretation had been reduced from weeks in World War II, to days in the first Gulf War, to hours in Kosovo, to minutes and even seconds in Afghanistan and Iraq.

The key was more bandwidth, the size of the electronic pipeline that carried information like email and telephone calls around the world. In transcontinental communications, bandwidth can be increased in only two ways. A pipeline for digital information can be laid under the ocean floor in the form of a glass-filled fiber-optic cable, or it can be built in the sky using an orbiting satellite to receive the information on its way up from one spot and beam it back down to another, often in another country. Both pipelines are expensive to build and inherently limited in how much they can carry—the satellite method especially so.

The value of bandwidth was first realized during the Kosovo air war in 1999, when commanders began using video-teleconferencing to allow communication between participants in different countries and on ships at sea, and when Predator drones mounted with cameras were first used to film Serb paramilitary forces on the ground. To reposition the finite number of military satellites available so that they could transmit information from Kosovo required borrowing the digital pipelines used by other military commands, such as those the Pacific Command used to track the civil war in East Timor and missile developments in China and North Korea. Ever since, vicious battles have been waged between the military services and individual commanders over bandwidth access.

Luckily for the military, the attacks of 2001 coincided with an entirely unrelated economic development: the dot-com bust. The economic downturn created a glut in commercial satellite pipelines already available and now underutilized. The military quickly bought up private companies' excess capacity, which only fed its craving for more and more information requiring ever more capacity.

According to commanders, in the early days of the Afghanistan war, the Special Operations Command, including JSOC, spent $1 million a day on commercial bandwidth. Within a year after McChrystal's arrival, JSOC had linked sixty-five stations around the world to enable viewers to participate in the twice-daily, forty-five-minute video teleconferences that he held. By 2006, JSOC had increased its bandwidth capability by one hundred times what it had been just three years earlier, according to senior leaders. All that information flowing through the pipeline wasn't just sent to Washington; it was also pushed down to Delta Force troops, Navy SEALs, and the 160th Night Stalker pilots at their bases around Afghanistan and Iraq.

The other challenge JSOC faced was a human one: how its troops were interrogating and treating detainees. Shortly after McChrystal took command in September 2003, he visited the JSOC detention facility in Iraq, a place separate from the larger Abu Ghraib prison that would become notorious for prisoner abuse at the hands of low-level army soldiers. There was a skeletal staff of about thirteen people, meaning they had no time to try to cajole detainees into divulging important intelligence. There was little or no information about individual detainees for interrogators to use to question them in a more productive way. As a result, interrogators didn't know what questions to ask or how to ask them to get a response.

Worse, some JSOC Task Force 121 members were beating prisoners—something that would before long become known to Iraqis and the rest of the world. Indeed, even before the Abu Ghraib prison photos began circulating among investigators, a confidential report warned army generals that some JSOC interrogators were assaulting prisoners and hiding them in secret facilities, and that this could be feeding the Iraqi insurgency by "making gratuitous enemies," reported the *Washington Post's* Josh White, who first obtained a copy of the report by retired colonel Stuart A. Herrington.

That wasn't the only extreme: in an effort to force insurgents to turn themselves in, some JSOC troops also detained mothers, wives, and daughters when the men in a house they were looking for were not at home. These detentions and other massive sweep operations flooded prisons with terrified, innocent people—some of them were more like hostages than suspects—that was particularly counterproductive to winning Iraqi support, Herrington noted.

Another investigation of JSOC detention facilities in Iraq during a four-month period in 2004 found interrogators gave some prisoners only bread and water, in one case for seventeen days. Other prisoners were locked up for as long as seven days in cells so cramped they could not stand up or lie down while their captors played loud music to disrupt sleep. Still others were stripped, drenched with cold water, and then interrogated in air-conditioned rooms or outside in the cold.

As the Iraqi insurgency intensified and pressure mounted to stop it, JSOC interrogators converted one of Saddam Hussein's torture cells—complete with eighteen-inch hooks attached to the ceiling—into a jet-black, garage-sized interrogation booth they named the Black Room. There, according to the *New York Times,* interrogators beat some prisoners with rifle butts, spit in their faces, and used them for target practice in a game of paintball. Posters at the center advised, "NO BLOOD, NO FOUL," meaning interrogators couldn't be prosecuted if they didn't make a prisoner visibly bleed. The CIA and FBI were concerned enough about the tactics that they barred their own personnel from participating in JSOC interrogations. The Special Operations Command disciplined thirty-four JSOC task force soldiers involved in five cases over a one-year period beginning in 2003.

McChrystal's first tour of the Baghdad detention center shocked him. Several detainees were being kept naked, and dogs were being used to guard their cells. "This is how we lose. This is our Achilles' heel," he told associates.

In response, McChrystal set out to professionalize the interrogation system by training interrogators how to best question prisoners and by teaching others how to collect information about a detainee and the details of his capture to prepare for the first interrogation session. By the summer of 2005, JSOC had what Michael Flynn once called "industrial-scale, capture-interrogation-exploitation operations." Interrogation booths at Balad were just around the corner from the large warren of rooms where specialists mining thumb drives, computers, cell phones, documents, and translations of other interrogations sat. Twenty people were tasked with collecting and analyzing the information needed to effectively interrogate a single detainee. Flynn insisted that the assault leader join the interrogation team of each detainee he captured, ensuring that someone who knew precisely who had been found in which room of each house and with what evidence—cell phones, CDs, and so forth—could determine what incriminating piece of evidence belonged to whom.

The army's technical paper maps were torn down from the walls of the Balad command center and replaced with flat-panel screens and Google Earth–type maps. Detainees willing to cooperate were taught how to use a mouse to fly around their own virtual neighborhoods; some became so fascinated with the technology that they would eagerly zoom in and out of streets and buildings, showing interrogators safe houses, weapons caches, and back alleys.

Egyptians and Saudis were occasionally brought in to interrogate their own nationals, to more easily appeal to them in their own dialect and culture. Family members were connected by videoconferencing to help convince their sons or brothers to cooperate. When the foreign delegations balked at returning, videoteleconferencing was set up so a prisoner could be questioned and pressured by someone back home. Following McChrystal's crackdown, JSOC still had to use the rules laid out in the Army Field Manual to interrogate detainees; but its interrogators were permitted to keep them segregated from other prisoners and to hold them, with the proper approvals from superiors and sometimes Defense Department lawyers, for up to ninety days before they had to be transferred into the regular military prison population. They still are permitted to do so.

The new interrogation system included an FBI and judicial team that put together evidence needed for trial by the Iraqi Central Criminal Court in Baghdad. From early 2005 to early 2007, the teams sent more than 2,000 individuals to trial, said several senior military officials.

The U.S. military and JSOC were not the only organizations that had invaded Iraq. Al-Qaeda was quick on their heels. Al-Qaeda used the U.S. invasion of Iraq as a call to arms to terrorists and recruits throughout the Middle East who flooded in from Tunisia, Libya, Egypt, and Saudi Arabia — as many as two hundred of them a month at the high point. They set up safe houses from al-Qa'im, on the Syrian border, to Baqubah, northeast of Baghdad, Fallujah, and Ramadi. Realizing that it wasn't necessary to risk another attack inside the United States, the terrorists hoped to defeat the enemy in a land whose culture and language these foreigners, they assumed, couldn't begin to understand. Saddam Hussein had been decidedly secular in orientation, his regime unfriendly to groups like bin Laden's. Now with Saddam gone and the country in chaos, al-Qaeda moved to fill the vacuum. Thus JSOC's mission, in part, became solving a problem in Iraq that President Bush's decision to invade had actually created.

Having been surprised to discover, following the initial invasion, that there were no al-Qaeda in Iraq, military commanders were reluctant to believe it when operatives actually did arrive in force several years later. By then JSOC had discovered hard evidence that an intricate terrorist web actually existed and was mounting continuous, deadly operations against the Iraqi population and American troops. Their evidence was gathered using a combination of the rapid analysis of material seized in raids and more effective, less coercive interrogation methods, with one set of detainees leading to another set of operations, which led to more captures and more detainee interrogations. By the end of 2005, a shocking picture emerged: Iraq was infested with semiautonomous but highly organized al-Qaeda networks. There was one in the Ramadi-Fallujah area; another along the Tigris River Valley, another in Mosul; another in Haditha and al-Qa'im. Al-Qaeda had divided Iraq into sections and put a provincial commander in charge of each. That commander further divided his territory into districts and put someone in charge of each of those, too. There were city leaders within those areas, and cells within each city. There were leaders for foreign fighters, for finance, and for communications, too.

In the spring of 2006, using the magic of bandwidth and the constant surveillance of unmanned aircraft, JSOC executed a series of raids, known to troops as Operation Arcadia, in which they collected and analyzed 662 hours of full-motion video shot with more than one aircraft flying overhead at all times over seventeen days (almost 40 hours analyzed for each 24-hour period). They also netted 92 compact discs, twelve SIM cards, and barrels full of paper. Those finds led to another round of raids at 14 locations. Those raids yielded 14 hard drives, 11 thumb drives, and a basement stacked with compact discs, 704 of them, including a representation of the entirety of al-Qaeda's sophisticated marketing campaign (it included pictures of civilians wounded or killed by what the organization asserted were American actions). It was all a precursor to the capture of Iraq's top al-Qaeda operative, Abu Zarqawi, by JSOC's Delta Force on June 7, 2006.

During this time, JSOC's Balad headquarters was busier than ever before and included nearly 100 CIA employees and 80 from the FBI. JSOC's EKIA (enemy killed in action) list grew longer, too. In 2008, in Afghanistan alone, they struck 550 targets and killed roughly 1,000 people, along with 17 civilians. In 2009, they executed 464 operations and killed 400 to 500 enemies, some al-Qaeda but mostly Taliban, according to internal sources.

Because of JSOC's many successes on the battlefield, the Defense Department gave the unit a bigger role in several nonmilitary assignments as well. JSOC worked to trace the secret flow of money from international banks to finance terrorist networks. It became deeply involved in "psychological operations," which later became "military information," because it sounded less intimidating. JSOC sent small teams of soldiers out of uniform into embassies around the world to help with what it called media and messaging campaigns. With a formidable production unit at its North Carolina headquarters, it could build websites whose U.S. sponsorship was sometimes obscured. It could distribute cell phones and radios to friendly forces, create magazines and video programs, and produce radio programs for broadcast into any country in the world, including those that actively seek to jam outside communications.

When Obama came into office, he cottoned to the elite organization immediately. (It didn't hurt that his CIA director, Leon Panetta, has a son who, as a naval reservist, had deployed with JSOC.) Soon Obama was using JSOC even more than his predecessor to conduct secret targeted killing of al-Qaeda and Taliban leaders in Afghanistan and elsewhere, primarily Pakistan and Iraq. In 2010, Obama secretly directed JSOC troops to Yemen to kill the leaders of al-Qaeda in the Arabian Peninsula. Several dozen troops were sent over a six-month period to kill scores of people on JSOC's hit list, among them six of the fifteen individuals U.S. intelligence had identified as top regional commanders.

In Yemen, JSOC joined an interagency team, led by the ambassador, and including the CIA. U.S. troops did not take part in any actual raids but helped plan missions, developed tactics, and provided U.S. weapons and munitions. They also shared some of the most sensitive electronic and video surveillance, as well as three-dimensional terrain maps.

Cooperative efforts with Yemen to fight terrorism dated from the attacks of 2001, when CIA director Tenet coaxed Yemeni president Abdullah Saleh into a partnership that would permit the CIA and military units to hit Yemeni terrorist training camps and al-Qaeda targets. Saleh agreed, in part because he believed his country, the ancestral home of Osama bin Laden's father, was next on the U.S. invasion list, according to an adviser to the Yemeni president. Tenet gave Saleh's forces helicopters, eavesdropping equipment, and 100 Army Special Forces to train an antiterrorism unit. American commandos also crafted a media campaign in support of Saleh that portrayed him as an anticorruption activist, giving rise to a certain irony by mid-2011, when the Arab Spring forced him into exile, in part because of his corrupt ways. Saleh used the campaign without attribution to its U.S. authors before the elections, though the messages did not overtly ask citizens for their vote; that kind of political campaigning could only be carried out by the CIA, because secretly influencing the politics of another country is considered a covert action.

Besides deepening the secret relationship with Yemen, Obama sent JSOC forces elsewhere as well. A helicopter assault force was deployed to Somalia to kill Saleh Ali Saleh Nabhan, who was involved in several bombings in Kenya, including the attack on the U.S. Embassy in 1998.

Obama's national security team worked in secret to maintain and deepen the bilateral intelligence relations forged in Yemen during the era of CIA director George Tenet. A steady stream of high-ranking officials visited the president beginning in 2010. In April, Saleh boasted on his government's official website of a visit by JSOC commander McRaven, who was rarely seen in public. Saleh's government posted a photo of a meeting on its official website as proof. The unacknowledged JSOC was stunned by the announcement.

When Yemeni citizens joined the Arab Spring, JSOC was forced to cease operations while the chaos settled. Having backed Saleh, an autocrat who was ruthless with political opponents, the U.S. government had to suspend its actions, too, and wait out the shake-up.

"I don't think it's my place to talk about internal affairs in Yemen," Defense Secretary Robert Gates told reporters traveling with him in Moscow in March 2011. "We are obviously concerned about the instability in Yemen. We consider al-Qaeda in the Arabian Peninsula, which is largely located in Yemen, to be perhaps the most dangerous of all the franchises of al-Qaeda right now. So instability and diversion of attention from dealing with AQAP is certainly my primary concern about the situation."

With so many new targets and so many target packages awaiting execution, the frustration inside JSOC mounted as turmoil from the Arab Spring forced the president and his clandestine commandos to be patient. In the meantime, the organization turned its attention elsewhere and continued its march ahead of the rest of Top Secret America: in a thirty-thousand-square-foot office building turned command center, JSOC began to replicate the intelligence analysis and targeting model that had worked so well in Afghanistan, Iraq, and Yemen to fight one of its most recalcitrant foes.

The intelligence team was assembled. So was the target development group and envoys from the CIA, the FBI, the NSA, the Defense Department, and the National Media Exploitation Center, the facility that was so helpful to McChrystal when he was beginning the secret unit's transformation eight years ago. This task force is not located in a former dictator's bunker or in some godforsaken part of the world. It is across the highway from the Pentagon in pristine suburban splendor, near a popular buffalo burger restaurant and a five-minute drive from McChrystal's home office and the former general's favorite beer call restaurants.

As its name implies, the focus of Joint Special Operations Task Force–National Capital Region (JSOTF-NCR) is not the next terrorist network to have sprung up in some far-off corner of the world but another of JSOC's lifelong enemies: the Washington bureaucracy. Some fifty battle-hardened JSOC warriors and a handful of other federal intelligence and law enforcement agencies work in the operations center every day. Its mission is to replicate McChrystal's model for operations under consideration in other countries.

Mexico is top on its list of priorities. JSOC is eager to apply its targeted killing model—with night raids and armed drone attacks—to help destroy the drug and weapon networks worming their way into the United States and infecting Mexico's political and social fabric. Although the CIA is leading a quickly expanding counter-narcotics effort there, so far the Mexican government, whose constitution limits contact with the U.S. military, is relying on the other federal agencies—the CIA, the DHS, the Drug Enforcement Agency, and Immigration and Customs Enforcement (ICE)—for intelligence collection, fusion, analysis, intercepts, surveillance, targeting, equipment, and training to help them stop the cartels. More aggressive proposals, including some that would allow the CIA and JSOC to help the Mexican government conduct targeted killings, have been discussed at the White House, Langley, and the Pentagon, and in other offices of Top Secret America.

But JSOC's National Capital task force is not just sitting idly by, waiting to be useful to its southern neighbors, either. It is creating targeting packages for domestic U.S. agencies that have sought its help. It has put together plans for raids and investigations for the U.S. Immigration and Customs Enforcement agency, which is the latest federal agency to make a big play for a larger counterterrorism role. ICE plans to use its vast number of U.S. law enforcement authorities and its contacts in immigration detention jails and smuggling pipelines. The second largest federal law enforcement group in the nation, ICE increased the number of its counterterrorism investigations and arrests in 2011, making a run at what had been the FBI's sole purview. Not surprisingly, it was doing so on its own, without coordinating with the bureau.

JSOC has brought the data mining that was so helpful to making lightning-fast raids overseas to its work for U.S. federal agencies. The National Capital task force has its own supercomputer that can crunch billions of data points to narrow searches for particular people, telephone numbers, and locations of interest. Its database includes numbers from nearly every U.S. phone book, as well as commercially available data on U.S. citizens and residents. To abide by rules limiting the military's access to information on Americans, the computer automatically masks the identity of any U.S. citizen or resident from the gaze of its military operators. That information can only be unmasked in certain circumstances permitted under U.S. law, said military and law enforcement officials. JSOC, which for so long stayed as far away from Washington as possible, has arrived in force to take on the slow metabolism of Top Secret America's obese body, to infiltrate its command and control centers, to push its leaders to make decisions that use JSOC's unique skills, and to be ready to pounce anywhere in the world once they do.

Beyond the Fear of 9/11

The squadron of Navy SEALs had been back with their families for only three weeks from their umpteenth deployment to Afghanistan since December 2001 when they received the call to hurry back to JSOC's off-site training facility near Fort Bragg for an exercise. As they waited for a briefing in a conference room, they were surprised to see JSOC commander Vice Admiral William H. McRaven walk in.

"This isn't an exercise, is it?" one of the commandos piped up.

For more than six months, the president's cabinet had met secretly to decide what to do about the possibility that al-Qaeda leader Osama bin Laden might be hiding in a compound in Abbottabad, Pakistan. Just a week earlier, Obama had made the risky decision to send in a team that was so secret that its cover name, the Naval Special Warfare Development Group — DevGru for short — sounded just like that of any other paper-pushing office in Top Secret America. The cabinet members debated various options and were divided over what to do, given that the best estimate the terrorist leader was actually there was 45 to 55 percent. Defense

Secretary Gates, who remembered the failed 1980 rescue attempt of U.S. hostages in Iran, was not in favor. Secretary of State Hillary Clinton was firmly supportive of authorizing the mission. Marine General James Cartwright, the vice chairman of the Joint Chiefs, advocated a missile strike that would risk no American lives. Panetta was cautiously in favor of inserting a small commando team.

To help him decide, Obama had finally asked the CIA analyst in charge of the Osama bin Laden team whether he thought bin Laden was in the compound, knowing the analyst could not be certain but also that this one person had a better sense of the likelihood than anyone else. "Yes, I do," the analyst replied.

The intelligence trail that led to HVT #1 had not begun with the thousands of analysts working in Top Secret America whose job was to sift through a dragnet of information on people who may or may not have acted suspiciously, or even with one of the names on the more limited list of known terrorists kept by the National Counterterrorism Center. It began with a tiny team of experienced CIA analysts who had been tracking bin Laden for nearly ten years; who had collected and who remembered every scrap of information about his background, his family, his habits, his voice intonations, and his physical appearance, and about every person he may have trusted.

Working at the CIA's Counterterrorism Center, they had started with a nom de guerre for one of bin Laden's couriers that had come up during an agency interrogation of a detainee. That nickname led them to a real name, which led them to a cell phone number, which led them in August 2010—with the help of colleagues and equipment from the National Geospatial-Intelligence Agency, the National Security Agency, and the National Reconnaissance Office—to a town thirty miles northeast of the capital, Islamabad. Electronic intercepts, satellites, drones, surveillance planes, 3-D models, tools that measure vibrations and can see through foliage, all were deployed to determine the inhabitants and to visually dissect the compound, which had been expertly designed to mask views of the inside from a distance.

Among senior JSOC operators, the consensus was that a raid would ensure that they could kill or capture bin Laden if he were there. The risk of civilian casualties would be far fewer than with a bomb or missile attack, although the risk to the team would obviously be greater. They had executed hundreds of similar raids in Afghanistan and Iraq over the years, and this one seemed much less dangerous than a lot of those, since there wasn't going to be an armed mob waiting for them, as there was sometimes. Just as important to the commandos, who had lost so many comrades and who had been awarded so many Purple Hearts as survivors, a raid and contact at close quarters would send an important message: that the United States was willing to risk American lives to get him.

Obama and his team decided not to tell the government of Pakistan, which in some ways had become a foreign version of Top Secret America's bloat, a place that sucked so much money from Washington with so little accountability that U.S. officials had actually lost track of how much they had spent there. The best estimate was $21 billion in less than a decade, a sum quoted by Bruce Riedel, a former CIA officer who had chaired a White House policy review of Pakistan in 2009. Besides, if the troops needed to go in and get out without capturing or killing bin Laden, the administration wanted to be able to deny that anything had taken place. These requirements amounted to a covert action, so the CIA was put in charge. It was agreed that Panetta would be in charge of decisions made at the cabinet level, while McRaven would be in charge of everything that happened below that, which meant the entire operation. And below McRaven, the entire burden lay on the shoulders of the SEALs and pilots, who would ultimately have to use their experience and judgment.

To limit the number of people who knew about the plans, the decision about the chain of command did not go through the normal plethora of White House, CIA, State Department, and military lawyers. To keep decisions rolling, and to minimize bureaucratic jealousies that might result in a leak, the circle of participants was minuscule until the operation was nearly ready to proceed. Admiral

Eric Olson, McRaven's boss, was told just a month before and only then because McRaven insisted. General David Petraeus, commander of the Central Command, was informed less than a week earlier, and the U.S. ambassador to Pakistan, Cameron Munter, who had replaced Ambassador Anne Patterson in October 2010, got the word just four days prior. The government of Pakistan was informed only afterward.

In the division of labor that had developed over a decade of war, the SEALs had always worked in Afghanistan, while the army's Delta Force operated predominantly in Iraq. In this operation, planners decided to keep the force extra small, without the overhead security provided by the AC-130s that normally accompany raid parties. Surprise and speed would be key—the team had forty minutes to get in and get out—so they opted for a stealth version of a Black Hawk troop-carrying helicopter flown by the 160th Night Stalkers. The plan called for one helicopter to land in an animal pen inside the compound and another elsewhere in the yard. One assault force would enter the main building from a first-floor door, while the other would be set down on the roof and enter the third floor, where analysts believed bin Laden was living.

Those planning the raid knew from surveillance that there were more than a dozen children and a few women inside, so they rehearsed how to get them safely out of the way. They practiced what to do if a helicopter crashed, or if Pakistani authorities or an unruly crowd arrived and wanted to get into a firefight. What they feared most was an attack by the Pakistani military. The team chief was instructed to announce over a bullhorn, if confronted, that he and his men were U.S. forces engaged in a mission, and to instruct the Pakistani commander to immediately call his headquarters, which by then would be on the line with its U.S. counterparts. The last thing anyone wanted was an armed international incident, with U.S. and Pakistani forces shooting at each other. A group of senior U.S. officials would be monitoring the event from the embassy in Islamabad, and from the White House and CIA headquarters, as it unfolded.

The mission was set for Sunday, May 1, Pakistan time. In Washington, it was April 30, the night of the White House Correspondents' Dinner, the main media social event of the year. The SEAL team joked about how funny it would be if the president announced the raid as part of his humorous monologue, only to have the entire press corps blow it off as a joke.[1] The more serious question, though, was what would happen if none of the national security invitees showed up at the dinner. Wouldn't that draw attention?

The date was dictated by nature. On that night, there would be no moon to illuminate the helicopters or the raid party. The date was altered by nature, too. It was too cloudy on the chosen night, so they rescheduled for the next night, May 2. If they couldn't go then, it would be another month before it would be safe for a night raid, and everyone was worried that, by then, with a greater number of people in the know, even this secret would not hold.

On the flight, the stealth helicopters went undetected. But one encountered mechanical problems due to the unexpected heat as it tried to land in the animal pen. To avoid rolling, which causes most serious injuries, the pilot dug his nose down into the earth. The SEALs jumped out, along with Cairo, the Belgian Malinois shepherd whose job was to sniff out bodies—dead or alive—that might be hidden in the building.

The first movement the team encountered was a man, who turned out to be the courier, Abu Ahmed al-Kuwaiti, running from the main building to a second structure to get his weapon. He was shot as he came outside with it. Some twenty-four SEALs were inside the compound walls, seventeen of them shooters who ran into the main building, knowing it might be booby-trapped to immediately explode. But no explosion occurred. Bin Laden's son, his son's wife, and another male were killed inside. On the first floor, the SEALs herded a dozen children into a corner and kept

---

[1] In his speech that night, Obama began one joke with what would turn out to be the understatement of the year: "What a week. As some of you heard, the state of Hawaii released my official long-form birth certificate...")

them there until the raid was over. On the second floor, commandos similarly restrained two men and another half-dozen or so women and children.

As three or four SEALs continued up the stairs to the third floor, one of them saw a head poke out from around the corner. "Motherfucker, it's him," one of them thought, as he recounted to teammates later. They rushed the room, only to find two women in long robes, their hands obscured from view, standing in front of bin Laden. One lunged at the nearest commando. She was shot in the leg, as was the second woman. This was followed immediately by a shot to bin Laden's forehead and another to his chest, a classic kill by a veteran SEAL in his midforties who had been fighting in Afghanistan, off and on, for more than nine years. It was over in seconds. A pistol and an AK-47 rifle sat untouched on a nearby ledge.

The women were given first aid and left behind with the children. It took fifteen minutes to rig the downed helicopter with enough explosives to destroy its frame and incinerate its unique stealth skin. In the meantime, SEALs inside the house were loading into bags the biggest surprise of the evening: a trove of CDs, thumb drives, and computers that would be sent immediately to the National Military Exploitation Center in Fairfax County for unlocking, downloading, and analysis. They were shocked at how much there was: 2.4 terabytes of data, they later learned.

Bin Laden's body was flown to Bagram, Afghanistan, transferred to a twin-rotor Osprey helicopter, and flown to the USS *Carl Vinson,* waiting in the northern Arabian Sea.

After a decade of scraping together clues about the government's secret activities, on May 2, 2011, I discovered a treasure trove of them in one place. A source pointed me to a building in Cranberry, Pennsylvania, north of Pittsburgh. I had started the long drive from Washington early the previous evening and stopped at a Days Inn next to the Pennsylvania Turnpike at night. As I climbed into bed, my BlackBerry began buzzing: Osama bin Laden was dead.

"Congrats!" I texted to a half-dozen people I knew who had spent a decade chasing him. Some were out of government, still recuperating from the relentless grind their lives had become. "For the first time since I left, I wish I was there!" a former CIA official typed back at 11:36 p.m.

Bin Laden's death was not the end of terrorism or even al-Qaeda. But it was a bold punctuation mark, the period at the end of a decade-long story. As his body was pushed into the sea off a U.S. aircraft carrier, a chapter in the nation's history slid in after it. An era in which the fear of bin Laden's theatrical brand of terrorism turned rational people irrational also sank to the ocean's bottom along with the cleansed and weighted corpse. We hope.

With his death and the demise of so many other al-Qaeda leaders, it was no longer rational to think that the terrorist network could continue to thrive. Having devoted so much time and money to looking for al-Qaeda in the United States, it was no longer rational to act as if terrorism was a greater threat to Americans than the violent crimes that kill and traumatize more than a million people each year. After so many false starts and dead ends, it wasn't rational, either, to think that finding terrorists was easy—nor was it clearheaded to keep spending billions of dollars on unproven, broad-brush monitoring that swept up innocent people in its wake. It wasn't rational in a time of economic disintegration to continue to pay for so many private contracts so numerous that nobody could keep proper track of them, and whose effectiveness no one could assess. There were still secrets to be kept, but one of the biggest that didn't need keeping from the American public was the truth about Top Secret America.

Top Secret America had been born of fear and panic ten years earlier, yet the nation's leaders still were unable to have a fact-based dialog with the public, free of fear-mongering, about terrorism and the withering, criminal organization named al-Qaeda that brought it to our shores. "I think we need to keep a very cool head," Defense Secretary Robert Gates told me months before bin Laden's death. "There's a lot of talk about the growth of radicalization. Yes, there has been growth. But between September eleventh, 2001, and December thirty-first, 2009, we had forty-six cases prosecuted...and about a hundred twenty-five people involved. So I would say the numbers of extremists are very small. Let's stay calm."

The next morning I continued up I-76 and got off at the Cranberry exit. Turning left onto a small side street off the main thoroughfare, I passed a FedEx office, a Bravo Cucina Italiana restaurant, and a Red Roof Inn, then arrived at my destination.

There, I was asked to leave my computer and cell phone outside the operations room, which my host entered by scanning his retina at the door and then keying in a pass code. Inside, three analysts were hunched over, staring intently at computer screens. A large server sat on the other side of an interior window, churning through millions of files of data.

Rick Wallace, director of special operations, pulled up a chair so I could sit next to him and view his screen. Thin, with wire-rimmed glasses and unruly hair, he looked like the frazzled computer nerd in a television crime series, the one who breaks the code to find the bad guy for the cool squad of detectives. "Okay, watch this," he said.

Wallace began opening his saved document files. The first one was from TRW, the megadefense contractor now owned by Northrop Grumman, for the SBL IFX Project, a space-based laser designed to shoot down missiles. On the cover sheet of the document, it said the material had to be kept "in areas protected by cipher locks" and then "inside a locked container." But here it was, right before my eyes.

He pulled up another file he had stored for himself called Pentagon Secret Backbone. It was a detailed diagram of the Defense Department's Secret Internet Protocol Router Network, SIPRNET, in which all documents and emails classified secret were kept. It revealed all the vulnerable spots where a thief or spy might try to penetrate the system.[2] He pulled up details of First Lady Michelle

---

[2] The Defense Department immediately took it down once the company told them of its find in 2007.

Obama's convoy route for a 2009 event and the location of various U.S. Secret Service safe houses. He accessed tax returns from a senior JSOC officer; the personnel roster for the army's 1st Signal Brigade, which listed hundreds of troops by name, Social Security number, and security clearance; and a list of the names of the army's 3rd Special Forces Group troops. This one included the names of their children, too.

He had a January 2010 top secret Intelligence Summary of Afghanistan, laying out who was cooperating with whom; and a National Security Agency handbook, marked "For Official Use Only," and another document consisting of 21,000 names from the army's promotion list, with every kind of data a foreign spy might need in order to find new recruits.

Wallace had classified records from every component of the Department of Homeland Security. The Transportation and Security Administration, he explained, was the worst at losing control of its documents. Sensitive TSA material he pulled up detailed the places on an airplane that were routinely not searched. Another listed ways to defeat airport screening procedures. There were dozens of other secret documents he was able to access with a few clicks.

Wallace was not doing anything illegal. He wasn't hacking into anyone's computer. He hadn't stolen anyone's pass code. No one had slipped him something he should not have had. And yet here was document after document of classified, sensitive, very personal information about government secret activities and individuals' lives.

Wallace doesn't have a top secret clearance. He's not a counterterrorism or law enforcement official. In fact, he doesn't work for the government at all. He is employed by Tiversa, a small Pennsylvania firm. It sells a service to protect the data of individuals and companies and to help them find information about themselves already floating around in cyberspace without their permission, often because a client's child has installed peer-to-peer file-sharing software to share music and videos. Most parents and file-sharing users are unaware that the software automatically opens the door for strangers to come in and browse through every other file on the computer and any other computers linked to it, which usually meant the parents'. It is like leaving the back door to your house wide open so the twenty million people throughout the world who have similar software can walk in, make themselves at home in every room, and steal whatever they want.

Tiversa calculates that the people worldwide who know about this trick are conducting 1.7 billion searches every day through other people's data, including some searches that are run automatically, twenty-four hours a day, against all open doors. They are looking for more than the latest hit song. Some of them are foreign governments. Some are probably WikiLeaks activists. Some are scam artists and criminals, others simply voyeurs.

As Tiversa scanned the Web to find leaks of corporate and personal data for its clients, its technicians were "catching dolphins in the tuna nets," as Wallace described it, stumbling upon these classified documents. In following the trail of these leaked files, Tiversa can often identify who, or what computer, has grabbed other people's sensitive information. In 2009, the company found a file of blueprints and avionics for the presidential helicopter, *Marine One,* being traded on the Gnutella file-sharing network. It traced the trades to a computer in Iran. In 2007, it found more than two hundred classified documents in just a few hours of searching the networks. These included a document from a contractor working in Iraq that detailed the radio frequency the military was using to defeat improvised explosive devices. More recently, company sleuths said they had traced the footsteps of WikiLeaks. Wallace believed the organization had found some of the documents it has been publicly posting using the same methodology.

When Wallace or someone else in the company calls a government agency to tell them about the documents they have found floating around, he said that much of the time the person on the other end verbally shrugs it off, leaving Wallace and his colleagues disappointed in their government's understanding of the security threat from such simple, common software.

Tiversa was not just a fascinating discovery. It makes an essential point about the shifting ground we stand on. As the government works tirelessly to expand the blanket of secrecy over everything having to do with terrorism and intelligence (except when it is politically useful, as in the now-disproven details of Saddam Hussein's mobile biolabs or, more benignly, Osama bin Laden's killing), the wider culture is stampeding into a new, anything-goes era of flash mobs, tweet-olutionaries, Facebook communities, file sharing, YouTube intelligence and surveillance, hacktivists, WikiLeaks, and twenty-four-hour-a-day Internet media. There are a thousand other ways technology spreads information cheaply across the globe, reordering political power in the process.

Even our reporting on Top Secret America fit into this category. Arkin had put together his massive database using information in the public domain, a good portion of it on job boards and obscure government websites. When Kat Downs, the *Washington Post*'s digital designer, and Ryan O'Neil, the programmer, had figured out how to code it and display it online, we showed officials from twelve intelligence agencies the list of organizations and private companies doing top secret work. Most officials were stunned. Some agencies didn't have such a list themselves. And many had no clue that there was so much information on their cherished secrets out in the world.

In this era of involuntary transparency, there was evidence everywhere that the more a nation comes to rely on secrecy to maintain its form of government and its relations with other countries, the more vulnerable it is to political turmoil once those secrets are revealed. This became apparent throughout the Middle East and Southeast Asia, where people living under corrupt and autocratic regimes are able to share the truth about their governments. Through the stories and pictures of repression and brutality that citizens so quickly learned to distribute to their countrymen and the outside world via the Internet, revolutions have been born. In Tunisia, Egypt, Libya, Yemen, Iran, Iraq, the West Bank and Gaza,

Pakistan, Afghanistan, Mexico, and elsewhere, the power of the truth to change history and the frailty of governments based on secrets are being demonstrated on a daily basis.

Top Secret America's obsessive reliance on secrecy has made the United States vulnerable, too. In its most benign form, too much secret information gums up the very system it was created to serve. In its most dangerous form, secrecy is allowing the people in the know, those with security clearances, to hide their own malfeasance, or to unintentionally chip away at democracy—the very system Top Secret America is there to protect, one built on individual privacy and rights.

Ten years after the attacks of 9/11, more secret projects, more secret organizations, more secret authorities, more secret decision making, more watchlists, and more databases are not the answer to every problem. In fact, more has become too much. The number of secrets has become so enormous that the people in charge of keeping them can't possibly succeed. That is one lesson from the WikiLeaks disclosures. The leaked State Department cables were allegedly first available to a disgruntled army private with a history of instability because the government wasn't giving even a basic level of protection to those documents, and because his colleagues allowed him to bring a rewritable CD-ROM with Lady Gaga's music into work, not realizing it could act as the black bag into which a quarter of a million sensitive diplomatic cables could be dumped and carted away.

In the government-wide security and counterintelligence investigation that has followed the WikiLeaks disclosures, government experts have learned that most federal agencies have little understanding of how to protect their sensitive information, according to people involved in the review. They don't know what information is unprotected, who can access secret data who shouldn't be able to, or who has already done so and how much they have stolen. Many agencies know exactly where their computer systems are leaking but haven't installed the proper patches in three years, either because managers don't fully understand the importance of fixing the problem or because the agencies don't have technicians knowledgeable enough to do it, according to the review. And even if they began now to address these issues, it's too late: no one expects the leaks to stop or the hundreds of government computer systems to ever become secure enough. Besides, as Google CEO Eric Schmidt noted in 2010, "Every two days now we create as much information as we did from the dawn of civilization up until 2003."

Or, as a report by the American Bar Association and the government's Office of the National Counterintelligence Executive noted: "There is a shadow race between those trying to keep information secret and those seeking that information—and the seekers are rapidly gaining the upper hand.... The nature and scale of this challenge calls for a careful assessment of the U.S. government's traditional approach to counterintelligence and its dependence on secrecy as the key to gaining and maintaining a competitive advantage."

The smarter and safer route is to design policies and construct foreign relationships based on operating forthrightly, in a way that won't embarrass us or harm anything of value when it is revealed. That would cover 99 percent of the matter in the political universe and allow for the likelihood that few secrets can truly be kept. That leaves the other 1 percent of information that truly deserves protection, like the Osama bin Laden operation.

One afternoon I sat in the living room of a top counterintelligence official, a person who has spent a lifetime thinking about how adversaries can put the United States at a disadvantage. We played a game about secrets. Start with a world in which there are none, and then put into a box the things that must truly be kept secret. What would those things be?

The definition of *top secret* was written for a completely different era, he pointed out, when the emerging missile and nuclear technology seemed so precious and unique that letting it out would, in fact, cause "exceptionally grave harm" to our national security. But we could not think of a case in the last ten years in which some secret had leaked out that had actually caused grave harm. Certainly some intelligence sources had dried up; and some foreign informants may even have been killed or otherwise silenced. But since the cold war, the world had become so technologically advanced that loss of any particular technology that would have had a severe impact on U.S. capabilities back then would these days likely just prompt a new round of innovation to replace it; and nothing, in fact, would be irreparably harmed. The same was true for relations between countries. Although countries might stop cooperating temporarily (usually for public relations more than anything else), globalization and the presence of transnational threats like terrorism and drug smuggling had prompted even provisional allies to stick together where it mattered most. That is certainly the lesson from the unauthorized disclosures of the CIA's covert prisons that so angered allies in Europe—for just a while. So into the imaginary box went nuclear codes and weapons production, bioweapons pathogens and other lethal, unique technologies, and high-level sources who were irreplaceable—but not much else.

But that is not the way things were going. In fact, more information was being classified every day. At the same time, though, the managers of Top Secret America, who range in age from forty-five to sixty-five years old and therefore may not be conversant with the simplest technologies of the information era, still did not realize the seepage that was eroding the foundation of their world every day. The most glaring example was the colossal intelligence failure of 2011. It wasn't another terrorist plot the government had failed to unearth. It was something much harder to have missed: the Arab Spring, the dynamic political change sweeping across the Middle East and carrying with it predictable instability. Tunisia, Egypt, Yemen, Syria, Jordan, Libya, Algeria, Saudi Arabia, and Palestine—these were the same countries that U.S. intelligence agencies were supposed to be watching closely for terrorist rumblings and for political instability that could make it easier for al-Qaeda to operate. The government's utter failure to notice the revolutionary wave swelling in one country after another had left the United States scrambling to figure out how to help push the forces of change toward democracy and away from theocracy of the Islamic fundamentalist variety.

It felt like a repeat of the other giant surprise: the collapse of the Soviet Union back in the day when a paler, less technologically sophisticated version of Top Secret America existed. Had those managers in their forties, fifties, and sixties not been so intent on throwing layer upon layer of inexperienced analysts at the same terrorism problem, and had a true leader of the intelligence agencies actually been managing the kind of intelligence that was being collected in such a way that every agency didn't run after the same narrow terrorist targets, then the intelligence operatives following Tunisia might have noticed that leaders there were being disparaged in an enormous flood of public tweets, chats, and website traffic and that those newly emboldened voices were promoting dramatic change. Or they would have noted the huge increase in the number of young Egyptians watching their soul mates to the east on their iPhones, BlackBerrys, and laptops. They might even have picked up on the uptick in iPhone sales before that. Instead, what was hiding in plain sight took the intelligence community completely by surprise, again. As the Muslim Brotherhood moved to capitalize on the social and political void in Egypt, the most strategically important U.S. ally in the evolving Middle East, Washington's gigantic intelligence apparatus did nothing to warn policymakers, who were then completely unprepared to promote a palatable alternative. Top Secret America had become so focused on undoing one terrorist at a time that no one was seeing the big, strategic picture, and that was because, at the bottom of it all, it had grown so big and so unwieldy and no one, still, was actually in charge.

Secrets aren't just hard to keep; they can also become toxic to the system they try to protect. As Top Secret America spread to state and local government, state troopers, county sheriffs, and city police, eager to become part of the response to a grave national security threat, sought to learn more about terrorism, which they were also now being empowered to fight. They sought trainers, experts in terrorist ideology and practices, to teach them more about the Islamic communities in which allegiance to radical imams often took hold. Billions of dollars had been poured into the Department of Homeland Security, but very little of it went to training all those frontline foot soldiers who would be counted upon to recognize a potential threat, or even to develop a rudimentary knowledge of the cultural background so many terrorists shared. Without help from the Department of Homeland Security, local law enforcement departments and agencies found their own teachers. One of them was Ramon Montijo.

He has taught classes on terrorism and Islam to law enforcement officers all over the country. "Alabama, Colorado, Vermont," said Montijo, a former Army Special Forces sergeant and Los Angeles Police Department investigator who is now a private security consultant. "California, Texas, and Missouri," he continued.

What he tells them is always the same, he said: most Muslims in the United States want to impose Sharia law here. "They want to make this world Islamic. The Islamic flag will fly over the White House—not on my watch!" he said. "My job is to wake up the public, and first, the first responders."

As is increasingly the case, the first responders will be sheriffs and state troopers. These aren't FBI agents, who have years of on-the-job and classroom training. Instead, they are often people like Lacy Craig, the police dispatcher who became an intelligence analyst at Idaho's fusion center, or the detectives in Minnesota, Michigan, and Arkansas who can talk at length about the lineage of gangs or the signs of a crystal meth addict. Now each of them is a go-to person on terrorism as well.

Into this training vacuum come self-described experts whose grasp of the facts is considered wildly inaccurate, even harmful, by the FBI and others in the intelligence community. Like Montijo, Walid Shoebat, who describes himself as a onetime Muslim terrorist and convert to Christianity, also lectures to local police. He, too, believes that most Muslims seek to impose Sharia law in the United States. To prevent this, he said in an interview, he warns officers that "you need to look at the entire pool of Muslims in a community." When Shoebat spoke to the first annual South Dakota Fusion Center Conference in Sioux Falls in June 2010, he told his audience of police officers, sheriff's deputies, firefighters, and first responders to monitor Muslim student groups and local mosques and, if possible, to tap their phones. "You can find out a lot of information that way," he said.

The next year, 2011, he was invited back. "You've been infiltrated at all levels," Shoebat warned the audience. "Are all Muslims who interpret for the U.S. military terrorists? Of course not. But that doesn't mean you play Russian roulette." Shoebat's trip and honorarium were paid for by a grant from the Department of Homeland Security, according to the *Rapid City Journal,* which covered his visit.

"The critiques and evaluations that came back highly recommended that he come back again," South Dakota's director of Homeland Security, Jim Carpenter, told the newspaper. "We acted on those, and that's why he came back."

Shoebat and Montijo aren't the only people sharing such fear-inducing expertise with local law enforcement officers. In the neo-conservative Center for Security Policy's publication *Shariah: The Threat to America,* its authors describe a "stealth jihad" that must be thwarted before it's too late. Among the book's multiple authors are such notables as former CIA director R. James Woolsey and former deputy undersecretary of defense for intelligence and JSOC commander Lieutenant General William G. Boykin, along with the center's director, Frank Gaffney Jr., a former Reagan administration official. They write that most mosques in the United States already have been radicalized, that most Muslim social organizations are fronts for violent jihadists, and that Muslims who practice Sharia law are actively but stealthily trying to impose it on this country.

Gaffney said his team has spoken widely, including to many law enforcement forums. "Members of our team have been involved in training programs for several years now, many of which have been focused on local law enforcement intelligence, homeland security, state police, National Guard units, and the like," Gaffney said. "We're seeing a considerable ramping up of interest in getting this kind of training." Gaffney asserts that the three hundred campus chapters of the Muslim Student Association are really practicing stealth jihad, as is the Council on American-Islamic Relations, which is probably the most vocal antidiscrimination organization. "Here we are, some nine years after 9/11, and people are only now, whether they're police chiefs, or whether they're FBI agents, or whether they're military intelligence, or other intelligence officers, beginning to be exposed to this kind of information," Gaffney told me. He says not all Muslims are the enemy but that many are. "Muslims who attend mosques that aren't owned and operated by the Saudis are, by and large, I think, not a problem, at least not yet."

Gaffney's views are ridiculed by many experts on terrorism and Islam. Philip Mudd is one of them. For three decades, Mudd drove the CIA's effort to stop al-Qaeda and other international terrorists. For four years after that he worked with the FBI to do the same. He has read the interrogation transcripts of captured terrorists. He's studied the research on what makes so many young men turn violent. He's even interviewed young terrorists sitting in Middle Eastern prisons. He disagrees completely with the ideas that people like Gaffney and Boykin, who describes himself as a fundamentalist Christian activist, hold and are trying to spread. "I think this is a fundamental misunderstanding of the phenomenon we face," Mudd said. Eric Rudolph, the Olympic Park Bomber, "who assassinated someone under the guise of Christianity, was not a Christian; he's a murderer.... This is nonsense. It's nonsense wrapped around rubbish.... I don't buy that this is about Islam, I just don't buy it."

Inculcating the counterterrorism effort with the idea that Islam itself is responsible for violent extremism "is extremely dangerous," Mudd added. "Our ability to absorb these [American Muslim] kids feeds into our capability to prevent terrorism. The more we go down a road to saying, when there's an attack, let's go firebomb a mosque, the more we feed a sense that after someone takes an oath to America he's still not a real American. This'll kill us."

DHS spokeswoman Amy Kudwa said the department does not maintain a list of terrorism experts; nor does it intend to start one. Who were they, she asked rhetorically, to tell local authorities which instructors were good and which were not, and to drive the bad ones out of business? But after being questioned about these problems, she said the department is working on guidelines for local authorities wrestling with the topic. At the moment, Muslims were the target of these ill-informed experts. But, according to DHS and FBI documents we obtained, the FBI and local homeland security officials already had become more interested in certain groups; African Americans once in prison, because jailhouse conversions to Islam could be a growing threat; animal and environmental rights activists because some of them had committed violent acts; recent immigrants and U.S. residents from Somalia, Yemen, Iraq, Iran, Afghanistan, Pakistan, Saudi Arabia, Nigeria, North Africa, and elsewhere because they could be a pipeline for their terrorist countrymen. Local law enforcement groups were also passing around warnings about peaceful demonstrators, sent to them from state intelligence fusion centers. Other groups, especially antiwar protesters, appeared often in the pages of these Law Enforcement Sensitive bulletins.

Given all the new war-inspired surveillance technology and databases that Top Secret America's private contractors had developed, it is inconceivable that authorities would not start using them for broader purposes. What would happen if the next president elected to lead the United States believed that there was nothing wrong with using these systems to examine peaceful, lawful political protest groups more carefully, just in case?

"You know, the Constitution defends all of us against unreasonable search and seizure," said former NSA director Hayden, who engaged in the questionable practice of wiretapping in the United

★　　★　　★

States without proper legal warrants after 9/11. "What constitutes reasonableness depends upon the threat."

John Rizzo, the dapper CIA general counsel, had watched the latest president take office with a bit of apprehension. Having personally signed off on all the agency's most controversial covert programs—harsh interrogations, renditions, and secret prisons—he took note when candidate Obama blasted those measures. His guard went up when he heard Obama's team would be conducting a review of every covert action still on the books.

But then Rizzo got a message from the new team, even before Inauguration Day. "His people were signaling to us, I think partly to try to assure us that they weren't going to come in and dismantle the place, that they were going to be just as tough as, if not tougher than, the Bush people."

Swiftly, Obama declassified Bush-era directives on interrogations and then banned the harsh techniques. He announced that he would close the military prison at Guantánamo, but he backed off on this under political pressure. He promised to try alleged terrorists in criminal courts but backed down on that too. The covert action review proceeded as planned.

When it was finished, the new administration had "changed virtually nothing," said Rizzo. "Things continued. Authorities were continued that were originally granted by President Bush beginning shortly after 9/11. Those were all picked up, reviewed, and endorsed by the Obama administration."

Like that of his predecessor, Obama's Justice Department has also aggressively used the state secrets privilege to quash court challenges to clandestine government actions. The privilege is a rule that permits the executive branch to withhold evidence in a court case when it believes national security would be harmed by its public release. From January 2001 to January 2009, the government invoked the state secrets privilege in more than one hundred cases, which is more than five times the number of cases invoked in all previous administrations, according to a study by the Georgetown Law Center on National Security and the Law. The Obama administration also initiated more leak investigations against national security whistle-blowers and journalists than had the Bush administration, hoping, at the very least, to scare government employees with security clearances into not speaking with reporters.

And the growth of Top Secret America continued, too. In the first month of the administration, four new intelligence and Special Operations organizations that had already been in the works were activated.[3] But by the end of 2009, some thirty-nine new or reorganized counterterrorism organizations came into being. This included seven new counterterrorism and intelligence task forces overseas and ten Special Operations and military intelligence units that were created or substantially reorganized. The next year, 2010, was just as busy: Obama's Top Secret America added twenty-four new organizations and a dozen new task forces and military units, although the wars in Afghanistan and Iraq were winding down.

Some contractors were bracing for harder times, but by now their relationship with government felt like a long, comfortable marriage. A divorce was unthinkable. Each side identified itself as one half of a couple. The video shown by the Defense Intelligence Agency to a ballroom full of contractors in Phoenix described the relationship in Hollywood terms. The government-contractor couple was like "Fred and Ginger," "Ben and Jerry," "Sonny and Cher," "Butch Cassidy and the Sundance Kid," the video cooed.

In many companies, profits and expansion continued. CACI,

---

[3] They were the navy's Cyber Warfare, Exploitation & Information Dominance (CWEID) Lab, the Coast Guard Maritime Intelligence Fusion Center Pacific (MIFC–PAC), Combined Forces Special Operations Component Command Afghanistan (CFSOCC–A), and an air force GEO-Spatial Intelligence Office (AFGO) inside the National Geospatial-Intelligence Agency.

one of the most important players, recorded $36.4 million in profits in the third quarter of fiscal 2011. It hired four hundred new employees and was looking for another four hundred. Analysts attributed its success to the swelling cybersecurity and intelligence markets and to its lucrative contracts with the army for intelligence and information warfare services.

The outcome of American military and covert actions around the globe was still uncertain, but by the tenth anniversary of 9/11, another big attack on the United States seemed improbable. Even in the capital region, where fear had taken hold after 9/11, ordinary Americans were feeling safer than they had in years. The air force's Combat Air Patrols weren't running night sorties much anymore. Color-coded alerts had disappeared, along with police checkpoints and roadblocks on Capitol Hill. No one talked about stocking up on gas masks or building safe rooms. None of the people with top secret clearances were quietly arranging to move their families out of the area or buy hot-air balloons or kayaks for a quick escape, as they had a decade earlier. In fact, the city was booming with business investment, nightlife, and touring high school students whose parents were no longer afraid to let them visit the White House, the most obvious terrorist target.

All this was good news, and yet President Obama had not altered the size or even begun to attack the inefficiency of Top Secret America. In fact, he made sure it continued to receive more and more taxpayer money, despite an enormous federal deficit and an ever-growing $14 trillion national debt that threatened to undermine the nation's financial security.

The only small indication that something might budge was a vague announcement on February 10, 2011, by James R. Clapper Jr., who had been promoted to director of national intelligence. "We all understand that we're going to be in for some belt-tightening. And given, you know, the funding that we have been given over the last ten years since 9/11, that's probably appropriate." The details of the reduction hadn't been worked out, he said. But as soon as they were, they would be classified.

ACKNOWLEDGMENTS

Many people who helped make this book possible do not wish to be named here, but we thank them deeply for their willingness to answer questions, provide insight, even read chapters for accuracy. Without them this book would still be just an idea.

We are happy to be able to acknowledge the senior editors of the *Washington Post,* Marcus Brauchli, Liz Spayd, and Raju Narisetti, who gave us the encouragement and time to write the series, "Top Secret America," that inspired this book. Our teammates at the *Post* were steadfast and creative and we thank them too: Lauren Keane, Kat Downs, Sarah Sampsel, Ryan O'Neil, Justin Ferrell, Laura Stanton, Jennifer Morehead, Jennifer Jenkins, Nathaniel Vaughn Kelso, Greg Manifold, Karen Yourish, Stephanie Clark, Ben de la Cruz, Whitney Shefte, Dan Drinkard, Anne Ferguson-Rohrer, Robert Kaiser, Laris Karklis, Jacqueline Kazil, Todd Lindeman, Doris Truong, Amanda Zamora, and especially our editor David Finkel, our researcher Julie Tate, and the only news photographer we know who actually likes to turn buildings into pictures, Michael S. Williamson. We add Phil Bennett, who encouraged us from the beginning; and Donald Graham because he's a great and caring newspaperman.

And a warm call-out, too, to those who became our legal team at the *Post,* Eric Lieberman, Jim Kennedy, Kevin Baine, and Jeffrey Smith.

Tom Shroder, our calm and thoughtful editor for the next-to-final draft, was critical to making this happen at every step and of great moral support.

We could not have done this so quickly and efficiently without the supportive and professional help from the team at Little, Brown and Company: Publisher Michael Pietsch; copyeditors Janet Byrne and Peggy Freudenthal; legal counsel Eric Rayman; in publicity Nicole Dewey and Carolyn O'Keefe; Heather Fain and Amanda Tobier in marketing; Digital Publisher Terry Adams; Digital Managing Editor Liz Kessler; and especially our very talented editor Geoff Shandler and his hardworking new star, Liese Mayer.

Finally, our stellar agent, Gail Ross, helped in so many ways, as a sounding board, a negotiator, and, most important, a friend.

Dana wishes also to thank Anne Priest, Cissy delaVallee, Anne Hull, David Finkel, Bruce McWilliams, Bonnie Jo and Matisse Mount, Michael Kirk, Jim Gilmore, Margie, Janet, Colette, Irene, David, Karen deYoung, Haley Goodfellow for keeping me on track in every way; Nicholas Goodfellow for lightening up the moments when I wasn't working; and Bill Goodfellow for too many things to list here.

From Bill: The funny thing about working on the edges of *Top Secret America* is that the well-being of my own friends depends on those friendships and our contacts remaining undisclosed. I would like to thank the many people who have helped me to understand the military and the intelligence world, people who have scratched their heads with me in trying to fathom the government's size and conduct, people who fact-checked, people who passed along nuggets of data or documents, people who argued and debated what it all means, people who gossiped about our common interests and obsessions, people who kibitzed all the way through.

Thanks again to Phil, Steve, John, John, Dave, Gary, Bob, and Dan for the years and the inspiration.

Outside government, I'd like to first acknowledge Chuck Gundersen and Peter Pringle, always there; Tom Cochran, Chip Fleischer, Hans Kristensen, Matthew McKinzie, Stan Norris, Tom Powers, John Robinson, and Bob Windrem, colleagues and collaborators extraordinaire. Thanks, Sondra and Ron, Danny and Jamie. Thanks to the many journalists who share information with me in spite of potential competition, trusting and knowing that what goes around comes around, particularly Sy, Eric, Greg, and Mark. Thanks, Kevin and Cory, Julia and Reed, Philene and Darren; and Steve and Hannah: I'm warmed to know you're there. Thanks, Kimberly. To my attorney, Jeff Smith, thanks for almost three decades(!) of backup. To Rikki and Hannah, I love you. To Luciana, Olivia, and Galen: it's out of the bunker and into the badger den.

Three institutional giants came together to make this book, and its enhanced digital form, a deeper experience for readers than it would have been otherwise. Their easy collaboration is worth celebrating. So thank you, Little, Brown; the *Washington Post;* and Public Broadcasting Service's *Frontline*.

NOTES ON THE DATABASE AND WRITTEN SOURCE MATERIAL

The interconnecting databases developed for this project involved the review of hundreds of thousands of documents. The basic questions we sought to answer were which agencies do work at the top secret level within the U.S. government, what type of work it is, where this work physically takes place, and what private contractors are involved. Then we asked how much of this effort began after 9/11, and how much had efforts under way before 9/11 expanded since then.

The databases included:

- Government entities engaged in top secret work, by agency, address(es), and type of work. This included military and civilian agencies of the federal government, followed by agencies at the state and local government level.
- Corporate entities doing top secret work, by company, government client, location, and type of work.
- Locations where top secret work was being done, by government entity, contractor, and type of work.

We mined four basic sources of data to build these databases and ultimately used the following feeder sources (from the hundreds of thousands collected)

for the Top Secret America website (http://projects.washingtonpost.
com/top-secret-america/):

- Some 3,000 government contracts and task orders that specified the requirement for the contractor to work at the top secret level, by government sponsor, company, type of work.
- Some 38,000 job announcements from private companies requiring a top secret clearance, by company, location, client, and type of work.
- Some 12,700 job descriptions and announcements from some 1,200 government entities requiring a top secret clearance, by location and type of work.
- Some 1,500 résumés and biographies where individuals stated they did top secret work, for whom, and where.

In total, 112,000 individual files totaling 520 GB of data were collected. The databases we built describing over 700 government entities and 1,900 companies included 640,000 fields. Over 10,000 locations were geocoded; at the *Washington Post,* web specialists, researchers, interns, and copyeditors helped with input, design, and fact-checking.

For additional information on the methodology used in the project, see: http://projects.washingtonpost.com/top-secret-america/articles /methodology/.

Books

James Bamford. *A Pretext for War: 9/11, Iraq, and the Abuse of America's Intelligence Agencies* (New York: Doubleday, 2004).
———. *The Shadow Factory: The Ultra-Secret NSA from 9/11 to the Eavesdropping on America* (New York: Doubleday, 2008).
Gary Berntsen and Ralph Pezzullo. *Jawbreaker: The Attack on Bin Laden and Al-Qaeda: A Personal Account by the CIA's Key Field Commander* (New York: Crown, 2005).
George W. Bush. *Decision Points* (New York: Crown, 2010).
Richard Clarke. *Against All Enemies: Inside America's War on Terror* (New York: Free Press, 2004).
Steve Coll. *Ghost Wars: The Secret History of the CIA, Afghanistan and Bin Laden, from the Soviet Invasion to September 10, 2001* (New York: Penguin Press, 2004).
Bob Drogin. *Curveball: Spies, Lies, and the Con Man Who Caused a War* (New York: Random House, 2007).
General Tommy Franks (with Malcolm McConnell). *American Soldier* (New York: HarperCollins Publishers, 2004).

Roger Z. George and Harvey Rishikof. *The National Security Enterprise* (Washington, DC: Georgetown University Press, 2011).

Bradley Graham. *By His Own Rules: The Ambitions, Successes, and Ultimate Failures of Donald Rumsfeld* (New York: Public Affairs, 2009).

Rebecca Grant. *The First 600 Days of Combat: The U.S. Air Force in the Global War on Terrorism* (Washington, DC: IRIS Press, 2004).

Benjamin S. Lambeth. *Air Power Against Terror: America's Conduct of Operation Enduring Freedom* (Santa Monica, CA: Rand Corporation, 2005).

Matt J. Martin (with Charles W. Sasser). *Predator: The Remote-Control Air War over Iraq and Afghanistan: A Pilot's Story* (Minneapolis, MN: Zenith Press, 2010).

General Richard B. Myers, USAF, Ret. (with Malcolm McConnell). *Eyes on the Horizon: Serving on the Front Lines of National Security* (New York: Threshold Editions [A Division of Simon & Schuster, Inc.], 2009).

Sean Naylor. *Not a Good Day to Die: The Untold Story of Operation Anaconda* (New York: Berkley Publishing Group, 2005).

Bruce Reidel. *Deadly Embrace* (Washington, DC: Brooking Institution Press, 2011).

James Risen. *State of War: The Secret History of the CIA and the Bush Administration* (New York: Free Press, 2006).

Donald Rumsfeld. *Known and Unknown: A Memoir* (New York: Sentinel, 2011).

Tim Shorrock. *Spies for Hire: The Secret World of Intelligence Outsourcing* (New York: Simon & Schuster, 2008).

Gary C. Shroen. *First In: An Insider's Account of How the CIA Spearheaded the War on Terror in Afghanistan* (New York: Ballantine Books/Presidio Press, 2005).

George Tenet (with Bill Harlow). *At the Center of the Storm* (New York: HarperCollins Publishers, 2007).

Paul Thompson. *The Terror Timeline* (New York: HarperCollins Publishers, 2004).

Bob Woodward. *Bush at War* (New York: Simon & Schuster, 2002).

———. *Obama's Wars* (New York: Simon & Schuster, 2010).

———. *Plan of Attack* (New York: Simon & Schuster, 2004).

———. *State of Denial: Bush at War, Part III* (New York: Simon & Schuster, 2006).

Government Reports

We utilized countless budget books from various national security agencies; Congressional hearings and committee reports; and reports of the General Accountability Office, Congressional Research Service, and the Inspector General's offices of the Defense Department, the military services, the Department of Homeland Security, and the Department of Justice. At the federal and state levels, we collected well over 1,000 warnings and intelligence reports from intelligence community members and state fusion centers. In addition:

The 9/11 Commission Report: Final Report of the National Commission on Terrorist Attacks Upon the United States, Authorized Edition (New York: W. W. Norton and Company, 2003).

Commission on the Intelligence Capabilities of the United States Regarding Weapons of Mass Destruction

Office of the Director of National Intelligence, National Intelligence: A Consumer's Guide, 2009.

Report on the U.S. Intelligence Community's Prewar Intelligence Assessments on Iraq

U.S. Air Force (CENTAF), "Fast and Final: Operation Iraqi Freedom," 22 March 2004, Unclassified Powerpoint Briefing.

U.S. Army Special Operations Command, Weapon of Choice: ARSOF in Afghanistan (Ft. Leavenworth, KS: Combat Studies Institute Press, 2003).

U.S. Army Special Operations Command, All Roads Lead to Baghdad: Army Special Operations Forces in Iraq (Ft. Bragg, NC: USASOC History Office, 2005).

U.S. Army, The United States Army in Afghanistan: Operation Enduring Freedom.

U.S. Special Operations Command (SOCOM), History of SOCOM, 6th edition, 31 March 2008.

We also used various published and unpublished papers of the National Defense University and the war colleges and specialized higher education institutions of the Defense Department and the intelligence community.

Other Sources

We also found invaluable the near-daily newsletter produced by Steve Aftergood of the Federation of American Scientists, called SecrecyNews.

EXTENDED ENDNOTES

Most of the work for *Top Secret America* involved original research and reporting; that is, the compilation of data from primary documents and interviews with hundreds of confidential sources. The *Top Secret America* website (found at http://www.topsecretamerica.com and http://projects.washingtonpost.com /top-secret-america/) provides thousands of additional pages profiling federal government agencies, state and local government organizations, and corporate entities.

Chapter 1: Top Secret America
p. 5: President Bush, in an address on 16 September 2001, used the phrase "war on terrorism," a war that he said was "going to take a while." See White House, "Remarks by the President Upon Arrival, the South Lawn," 16 September 2001.

National Security Presidential Directive No. 46/Homeland Security Presidential Directive No. 15, "U.S. Strategy and Policy in the War on Terror," 6 March 2006 (classified top secret), rescinded all earlier counterterrorism directives and defined the objectives of the war on terror. The directive also provided that the attorney general, acting through the FBI and in cooperation with other federal departments and agencies, coordinate law enforcement activities to detect, prevent, preempt, and disrupt terrorist attacks against the United States.

The military implementation of the war on terror was codified in the SOCOM (Special Operations Command) Global Campaign Plan for the WOT (also known as CONPLAN 7500). (Note: In these early documents, WOT, for War on Terror, was a more commonly used acronym; GWOT, Global War on Terror, came later.)

p. 5: Post–9/11 supplemental budgets. On 28 September 2009, the Congressional Research Service (CRS) reported that Congress had approved an estimated $944 billion for military operations, base security, reconstruction, foreign aid, embassy costs, and veterans' health care for the war on terror and the Afghanistan and Iraq operations initiated since the 9/11 attacks. Of that total, the CRS estimated that Operation Iraqi Freedom would receive about $683 billion (72 percent) and Operation Enduring Freedom about $227 billion (24 percent). See CRS Report for Congress (Amy Belasco), *The Cost of Iraq, Afghanistan, and Other Global War on Terror Operations Since 9/11*, 28 September 2009, RL33110.

Bob Woodward first reported President Bush's Presidential Finding on al-Qaeda in the *Washington Post*. The original "Memorandum of Notification" said the objective was to attack bin Laden's organization and to kill or capture those responsible for the 9/11 attacks and their supporters. See Bob Woodward, "CIA Told to Do 'Whatever Necessary' to Kill Bin Laden; Agency and Military Collaborating at 'Unprecedented' Level; Cheney Says War Against Terror 'May Never End,'" *Washington Post*, 21 October 2001, p. A1.

p. 8: Windermere Group. In March 2005, Essex Corporation announced its acquisition of The Windermere Group LLC, then a privately held company headquartered in Annapolis, Maryland. Essex was then acquired by Northrop Grumman (see http://projects.washingtonpost.com/top-secret-america/com panies/northrop-grumman/), and the former management team from Windermere established KEYW Corporation (http://projects.washingtonpost.com /top-secret-america/companies/keyw-corporation-the/).

Chapter 2: All You Need to Know

p. 13: On September 26, 2002, the House and Senate Intelligence Committees invited Cofer Black, former head of the CIA's Counterterrorist Center, to testify; see *Joint Investigation into September 11th: Hearing Before the Joint House-Senate Intelligence Committees*, 109th Congress, 2002; statement of Cofer Black, former chief of the Counterterrorist Center, Central Intelligence Agency.

The formal name of the center at the time of 9/11 was the DCI Counterterrorist Center, having been established in the Clinton administration as a multi-agency intelligence community center under the Director of Central Intelligence (DCI). The CIA Counterterrorist Center (CTC) continues today within the CIA, but many of the interagency counterterrorist functions have been transferred to the newly created National Counterterrorism Center (NCTC), which reports to the Director of National Intelligence (DNI).

pp. 13–14: Biographies of J. Cofer Black can be found at http://cambridgeforecast.wordpress.com/2006/09/30/cofer-black-bio/ and http://www.greatertalent.com/CoferBlack/.

pp. 14–15: Predator. The MQ-1 Predator unmanned aerial vehicle (UAV) is a medium-altitude, long-endurance, unmanned aircraft system. The crew for the Predator is one pilot and two sensor operators. They fly the aircraft from inside a ground control station via a satellite data link for beyond-line-of-sight flight. The aircraft is equipped with a color nose camera (generally used by the pilot for flight control), a day variable-aperture TV camera, a variable-aperture infrared camera (for low light or night), and other specific mission sensors that can be switched on (weight permitting). The cameras produce full-motion video (FMV).

The basic MQ-1 Predator carries the Multi-spectral Targeting System, which integrates electro-optical, infrared, laser designator, and laser illuminator into a single sensor package. The aircraft can employ two laser-guided AGM-114 Hellfire missiles. The military version of the Predator was first used in Kosovo in 1999 to provide real-time images to commanders through the use of two-color TV cameras and a Spotter high-resolution forward-looking infrared (FLIR). In 2001, the Predator B was first put into use by test-firing a Hellfire missile. In November 2002, a CIA-operated Predator killed six suspected al-Qaeda members in Yemen by firing a Hellfire missile at their car as it traveled through the desert. A naturalized U.S. citizen was among those killed.

At the beginning of the Iraq war, the military was operating twenty-two Predators capable of sustaining three twenty-four-hour combat air patrols (CAPs). Three Predator-type operational orbits (known as "patrol lines") in 2003 grew to eighteen by 2007 and thirty-one by 2008 and are slated to reach sixty by 2012. One twenty-four-hour Predator-class combat air patrol requires 174 service members and four drones.

Since 9/11, additional Predator types have been introduced, including the army's Gray Eagle, and civil agencies, including Customs and Border Protection, the Coast Guard, and NASA, have begun flying Predator variants.

See also Reaper, below.

pp. 15–16: high-value targets (HVTs). The Defense Department defines a high-value target simply as "a target the enemy commander requires for the successful completion of the mission. The loss of high-value targets would be expected to seriously degrade important enemy functions throughout the friendly commander's area of interest." See *Department of Defense Dictionary of*

Military and Associated Terms, JP 1-02, 8 November 2010; available at http://www.dtic.mil/doctrine/dod_dictionary/.

U.S. Army Combat Studies Institute, *On Point II: Transition to the New Campaign: The United States Army in Operation IRAQI FREEDOM, May 2003–January 2005*, by Dr. Donald P. Wright and Colonel Timothy R. Reese (2008), chapter 5, "Intelligence and High-Value Target Operations," provides the most concise description of Iraq-based HVT operations to capture Saddam Hussein and his sons.

pp. 16–17: enhanced interrogation techniques. The first press report of the systematic abuse of detainees was by Dana Priest and Barton Gellman, "U.S. Decries Abuse but Defends Interrogations; 'Stress and Duress' Techniques Used on Terrorism Suspects Held in Secret Overseas Facilities," *Washington Post*, 26 December 2002; http://www.washingtonpost.com/wp-dyn/content/article/2006/06/09/AR2006060901356.html.

See also later: Priest, "CIA Puts Harsh Tactics on Hold; Memo on Methods of Interrogation Had Wide Review," *Washington Post*, 27 June 2004, p. A1, http://www.washingtonpost.com/wp-dyn/articles/A8534-2004Jun26.html.

pp. 19–20: Greystone operations. Greystone was first described by Dana Priest using its unclassified nickname, GST, in the *Washington Post* on 30 December 2005, http://www.washingtonpost.com/wp-dyn/content/article/2005/12/29/AR2005122901585.html.

p. 20: Controlled Access Programs (CAPs). The Controlled Access Program is explained by the Special Security Center of the Director of National Intelligence at http://www.dni.gov/ssc/capco.htm. The original directive creating the program—Director of Central Intelligence directive 29, subject: Controlled Access Program Oversight Committee (effective 2 June 1995)—is online at http://www.fas.org/irp/offdocs/dcid3-29.html.

pp. 23–24: WMDs in Iraq and the Curveball episode. In addition to Bob Drogin's book *Curveball* (see Notes on the Database and Written Source Material for complete publication information), in February 2011 the *Guardian* newspaper published the confession of Rafid Ahmed Alwan al-Janabi, who was Curveball in flesh and blood. See Helen Pidd and Martin Chulov, "Curveball's Lies—and the Consequences; Details of What the Iraqi Defector Said About WMD, and How It Was Used by Germany and the United States," *Guardian* (UK), 15 February 2011, http://www.guardian.co.uk/world/2011/feb/15/curveballs-lies-consequences-iraqi-defector?INTCMP=ILCNETTXT3487; and Martin Chulov and Helen Pidd in Karlsruhe, "Defector Admits to WMD Lies That Triggered Iraq War," *Guardian* (UK), 15 February 2011, http://www.guardian.co.uk/world/2011/feb/15/defector-admits-wmd-lies-iraq-war.

pp. 25–26: Special Access Programs (SAPs). Within the government, there are three types of formal SAPs: acknowledged, unacknowledged, and waived. An acknowledged SAP may be openly recognized or known (e.g., the F-22 fighter); however, specific details of technology within the SAP will be classified. A waived SAP is authorized by the secretary of defense to be excluded from regular reporting requirements to Congress. Within a SAP of any kind, subcompartments may also be established to limit knowledge of extremely sensitive aspects of a program.

A SAP is expensive to maintain and is supposed to be justified at numerous levels, from command to service or agency and then approved by at least the deputy secretary (in both the Department of Defense and the Department of Homeland Security). With the designation of a program as a SAP also come specific reporting requirements to Congress.

Based on Director of National Intelligence and DoD regulations, all SAPs require, as a minimum:

- Legal review for compliance with U.S. law, treaty, policy, directive, and regulation
- A program security guide
- A security classification guide
- An approved "billet" list (by position), with a ceiling established, and an up-to-date personnel access roster (by name)
- An indoctrination and debrief process
- An operations security (OPSEC) plan and TEMPEST countermeasures review
- A counterintelligence (CI) assessment
- A treaty plan (if applicable)

SAPs that contract for goods and services outside of normal channels are called carve-out programs. In this case, the term refers to the Defense Security Service being carved out of its normal industrial-security roles and reviews.

If the association of a nickname or code word with a specific classified activity is compromised, or is suspected of being compromised, the program is required to establish a new nickname or code word.

Post 9/11, SAPs have not only migrated outside the acquisitions, intelligence, and Special Operations communities to departments such as Homeland Security and Commerce, but they also have been joined by a number of formalized SAP-like programs, each of which employs some of the compartmentalization and security of SAPs but avoids many of their otherwise onerous administrative, security, and reporting requirements. (Military services regulations published since 2001 dealing with SAPs formally include these other programs.) Two of the most important SAPs are "sensitive activities" and "special activities," each of which has a specific meaning depending on the agency using it, but this is not well understood even within each agency.

According to a definition used by the navy (see below), a "sensitive activity" is any activity that may involve: "(1) The potential for public controversy or embarrassment; (2) Unusual or significant risks to...property and/or personnel; (3) Adverse military or diplomatic reactions or consequences; (4) Issues of unlawful or improper conduct; or (5) Issues regarding the...[service] and its relations with or support to other military departments or government agencies."

"Special Activities," as defined by Executive Order 12333, the same order that governs covert action, are "(a), activities conducted in support of national foreign policy objectives abroad which are planned and executed so that the role of the United States Government is not apparent or acknowledged publicly, and functions in support of such activities, but which are not intended to influence United States political processes, public opinion, policies or media, and do not include diplomatic activities or the collection and production of intelligence or related support functions."

The army describes these as including "sensitive support to other Federal agencies; clandestine or covert operational or intelligence activities; sensitive research, development, acquisition, or contracting activities;...and other activities excluded from normal staff review and oversight because of restrictions on access."

For background, see:

- DoD Instruction 5200.01, "DoD Information Security Program and Protection of Sensitive Compartmented Information," 9 October 2008 (Incorporating Change 1, 13 June 2011).
- DoD Directive 5205.7, "Special Access Program (SAP) Policy," 5 January 2006; Army Regulation 380–381, Security: Special Access Programs (SAPs) and Sensitive Activities, 21 April 2004.
- SECNAVINST 5000.34D, "Oversight and Management of Intelligence Activities, Intelligence-Related Activities, Special Access Programs, Covert Action Activities, and Sensitive Activities Within the Department of the Navy," 3 December 2008.
- William M. Arkin, *Code Names: Deciphering U.S. Military Plans, Programs, and Operations in the 9/11 World* (Steerforth, 2005).

p. 29: Operation Mountain Storm began in Afghanistan on 13 March 2004. In the two months of Mountain Blizzard that preceded it, the coalition conducted

1,731 patrols and 143 raids and cordon-and-search operations. They killed twenty-two enemy combatants and discovered caches with 3,648 rockets, 3,202 mortar rounds, 2,944 rocket-propelled grenades, 3,000 rifle rounds, 2,232 mines, and tens of thousands of rounds of small-arms ammunition, the Department of Defense said. Mountain Storm was the next in the continuing series of operations in the south, southeast, and eastern portions of Afghanistan designed to destroy terrorist organizations and their infrastructure while continuing to focus on national stability and support. See various DoD and Central Command (CENTCOM) press releases at the time.

pp. 31–32: Jordan. William M. Arkin first reported on secret military operations taking place in Jordan: "Hiding Jordan," WashingtonPost.com, 15 July 2002, http://www.washingtonpost.com/ac2/wp-dyn?pagename=article&node=&contentId=A6091-2002Jul15&notFound=true; the full article can be read at http://www.casi.org.uk/discuss/2002/msg00974.html.

p. 33: Secret prisons. Dana Priest, "CIA Holds Terror Suspects in Secret Prisons," *Washington Post*, 2 November 2005, http://www.washingtonpost.com/wp-dyn/content/article/2005/11/01/AR2005110101644.html, described the secret-prisons apparatus of the Greystone program.

Chapter 3: So Help Me God

p. 36: 2009 inauguration background information:

FBI/Department of Homeland Security, Joint Threat Assessment, (U//FOUO) 56th Presidential Inauguration, 7 January 2009; DHS Inspector General, United States Secret Service After-Action Review of Inaugural Security (Redacted); OIG-10-04, October 2009.

DHS, United States Secret Service, *United States Secret Service Fiscal Year 2009 Annual Report* (2010).

District of Columbia Homeland Security and Emergency Management Agency, 2009 Presidential Inauguration, 17–21 January 2009, *Regional After-Action Report Summary*, 31 August 2009.

Two execute orders (EXORDs) were issued for Department of Defense support to the presidential transition and specifically the inauguration.

p. 39: Military forces on alert for the inaugural. Joint Task Force 29, a collection of National Guard units from sixteen states under the command of the 29th Infantry Division of the Virginia National Guard, mobilized into forward-support positions preparing for possible catastrophic events involving the inauguration. The forces operated under an operations order for Valiant Shepherd. To prepare for its role as a joint task force with regional responsibilities during the inauguration, the 29th Infantry Division actively trained for more than two years. See various press releases of the National Guard Bureau, the Virginia

National Guard, and the Department of Defense, as well as the After-Action reports references above.

p. 40: Secret Service. The Secret Service, as the lead agency for the National Security Special Event (NSSE) declared for the inauguration, set up the Multiagency Coordination Center, a large operations center that could accommodate the heads of all the agencies involved. Information feeds from all of the organizations came into the center and were forwarded to the Joint Task Force National Capital Region (JTF NCR), the area's Northern Command (NorthCom) representative and the highest-level military command.

p. 40: F-22. The air defense plan for Washington during the Obama inauguration involved air patrols by Air Force F-22 Raptors from the 1st Fighter Wing, Langley AFB, Virginia. This was the first use of the F-22s in the United States for a potential real-world mission.

p. 40: RC-26. The RC-26 Condor is an Air National Guard (ANG)–owned dedicated, light-manned intelligence, surveillance, and reconnaissance (ISR) aircraft that generally supports Special Operations Forces. Within the domestic mission, the RC-26 is the ANG's primary aircraft for Incident Awareness and Assessment for all National Special Security Events (NSSEs), to support military and civilian counternarcotics missions, for homeland security, and for response to natural or man-made disasters. The aircraft fly from eleven locations inside the United States.

p. 41: Cheyenne Mountain. For additional information on the Northern Command (NorthCom) and North American Aerospace Defense Command (NORAD) Cheyenne Mountain complex, see http://www.norad.mil/about /cmoc.html.

pp. 42–43: *The 9/11 Commission Report.* The full text of the National Commission on Terrorist Attacks upon the United States (the 9/11 Commission) report is online at http://www.9-11commission.gov/report/index.htm. See also Testimony of Richard A. Clarke, before the National Commission on Terrorist Attacks upon the United States, 24 March 2004.

George Tenet directly responded to the 9/11 Commission's criticism of his "we are at war" memo in his autobiography: "The 9/11 Commission later said that I declared war but that no one showed up. They were wrong"; *At the Center of the Storm*, p. 119 (see Notes on the Database and Written Source Material for complete publication information).

pp. 46–47: Al-Shabaab. The Canadian news media also reported on the potential al-Shabaab threat to the 2009 inaugural. See Colin Freeze, "Bogus Plot Threatened Obama Inauguration; Short-lived Panic over Threat of Somali Terrorists from Canada Threatened to Derail Ceremony," *Globe and Mail*, 5 January 2010; Allison Jones, "Officials Investigated Perceived [Canadian] Border

Threat on Inauguration Day in 2009," *Canadian Press*, 5 January 2010, http://www.google.com/hostednews/canadianpress/article/ALeqM5g1BsPpqumvpov_m2FQGlRzACzIdw; and QMI Agency, "RCMP Says It Helped in Tip about Obama Attack," *Toronto Sun*, 5 January 2010.

The various potential threats to the inauguration are discussed in the following documents obtained by the authors:

- Washington Regional Threat and Analysis Center, Daily Summary #2009-036, Friday, 16 January 2009; UNCLASSIFIED//FOR OFFICIAL USE ONLY//LAW ENFORCEMENT SENSITIVE; 2009 INAUGURATION.
- Washington Regional Threat and Analysis Center, Daily Summary #2009-033, Wednesday, 14 January 2009; UNCLASSIFIED//FOR OFFICIAL USE ONLY//LAW ENFORCEMENT SENSITIVE; 2009 INAUGURATION.
- Department of Homeland Security Office of Intelligence and Analysis Warning, "(U//FOUO), Potential Threat to Inauguration 19 January 2009"; prepared by DHS/I&A Intelligence Watch and Warning Division and the FBI Counterterrorism Division, January 2009.

Before the inauguration, the United States had launched several strikes against al-Shabaab and considered it a serious threat to U.S. and European interests overseas. In May 2008, the United States quietly ordered a Tomahawk sea-launched cruise missile attack on a safe house in a remote town of central Somalia, killing the al-Shabaab leader Aden Hashi Ayro. After the attack, al-Shabaab stated it would target all U.S., Western, and U.N. personnel and interests. In October 2008, five synchronized suicide bombing attacks were launched in Somalia against local government, Ethiopia, and U.N. offices.

pp. 47–48: Washington Regional Threat and Analysis Center (WRTAC). The WRTAC is the district's citywide all-hazards intelligence fusion center. A governance board, composed of district and federal agencies, oversees its management. Formerly the Metropolitan Washington Fusion Center (MWFC), operated by the Metropolitan Police Department and established in 2006.

pp. 48–49: FBI weapons of mass destruction crisis management mission. A classified annex to National Security Presidential Directive (NSPD)-46 /Homeland Security Presidential Directive (HSPD)-15, the United States Policy and Strategy in the War on Terror designates the FBI as lead federal agency for the operational response to terrorist incidents, including the use of a weapon of mass destruction in the United States.

Nimble Elder is elliptically described in the voluminous budget justification material of the various agencies enlisted in the program: the Departments of Defense, Homeland Security, and Justice, and even the Environmental Protection Agency. See also Tammy P. Taylor, Ph.D., P.E., Office of Science and Technology Policy, "Role of National Science and Technology Council," 2009 National State Liaison Officers Conference, 18 August 2009.

p. 49: Attribution Working Group. See Tammy P. Taylor, "Role of National Science and Technology Council," cited in the previous note.

The FY 2005 Defense Department budget also states: "In the 'Domestic Nuclear Event Attribution' (DNEA) Program, develop a deployable lab: install classified interagency communications system/communications terminals at critical agencies; perform the first simulated nuclear event field exercise; formally integrate program plans and improve technical/operational procedures at the national level through support to DTRA's [Defense Threat Reduction Agency] FBI customer co-chair of the National Security Council [NSC] formed sub-Policy Coordination Committee Attribution Working Group; brief the program to the Vice President" (Exhibit R-2a, RDT&E Project Justification, Program Element 0602716BR, Project BD—Weapon Effects Technologies, February 2004).

p. 50: Sensitive Compartmented Information Facility (SCIF). The number of SCIFs is seen in a description of the responsibilities of the army's headquarters for the Military District of Washington (MDW). There, it states that the MDW is responsible for supervising the operation of over 350 SCIFs in the District, Maryland, Virginia, and southern Pennsylvania. This does not include any SCIFs operated by the intelligence agencies, all of which are under the authority of the individual agencies.

p. 50: Joint Worldwide Intelligence Communications System (JWICS). JWICS is the intelligence community's top secret, Sensitive Compartmented Information (SCI)–cleared high-speed multimedia global communications network, delivering secure information services to national and defense intelligence components. All U.S. government TS (Top Secret)–SCI networks run off the high-capacity JWICS backbone, which is used to handle data, voice, imagery, and graphics.

pp. 53–54: Joint Special Operations Command (JSOC) in Washington. The first post–9/11 report of military Special Operations involvement in contingency plans for the national capital region was Eric Schmitt, "Commandos Get Duty on U.S. Soil," *New York Times*, 23 January 2005, p. A1, based on the Power Geyser program described in William M. Arkin's book *Code Names: Deciphering U.S. Military Plans, Programs, and Operations in the 9/11 World* (Steerforth, 2005).

For more information on the Director of National Intelligence, its activi-

ties, and its contractors, see the Top Secret America project page: http://projects
.washingtonpost.com/top-secret-america/gov-orgs/dni/.

p. 55: On 21 January 2009, shortly after assuming office, President Obama
issued a Memorandum for the Heads of Executive Departments and Agencies
titled "Subject: Transparency and Open Government" and setting forth three
basic principles for agencies of the executive branch to pursue as the normal
course of business: transparency, participation, and collaboration. On 8 December 2009, the Office of Management and Budget issued an Open Government
Directive detailing specific time lines, goals, and requirements for each executive branch agency to meet in support of the president's goals.

Chapter 4: An Alternative Geography

pp. 57–61: Defense Policy Analysis Office (DPAO). The document clues about
DPAO were contained in:

- U.S. Congress, House of Representatives, *National Defense Authorization
  Act for Fiscal Year 2004*, House Report 108-106: Part 1.
- Defense Logistics Agency, Operation and Maintenance, *Defense-Wide
  Fiscal Year (FY) 2005 Budget Estimates*, Budget Activity #4: Defense-
  Wide Other Logistics Programs, p. 27.
- *FY 2004 Emergency Supplemental Appropriations Act* (P.L. 108-106), Restoration of the Defense Policy Analysis Office (DPAO) Funding.
- Defense Logistics Agency, Operation and Maintenance, *Defense-Wide
  Fiscal Year (FY) 2007 Budget Estimates*, p. 17; and Office of the Secretary
  of Defense Fiscal Year (FY) 2006/FY 2007 Budget Estimates, February
  2005, Vol. 1, *Justification for FY 2006/FY 2007, Operation and Maintenance, Defense-Wide*, U.S. Court of Appeals for the Armed Forces, Office
  of the Inspector General, Former Soviet Union Threat Reduction,
  Overseas Humanitarian, Disaster and Civic Aid, Support for International Sporting Competitions, p. 303.

pp. 57–58: J39. A J39 information operations staff organization (within the
J3 Operations Directorate), sometimes called the Special Technical Operations
Division (STOD), is assigned to every combatant command and most military
intelligence organizations supporting classified operations. The J39 is responsible for all offensive information warfare programs and activities coordinated by
the Joint Staff but, because of its unique handling of Special Access Programs
(SAPs), high clearances, and special communications, is also called on to deal
with most compartmented cyber and intelligence operations, with the exception of Special Operations.

The Special Technical Operations (STO) office or organization of military commands and units is the place for planning and executing compartmented capabilities. The Joint Staff, unified commands, and intelligence agencies all have STO organizations, most (but not all) collocated with J39. They uniquely communicate through the Planning and Decision Aid System (PDAS), also known as Island Sun.

CJCS Instruction 3120.08B, *Integrated Joint Special Technical Ops (S/NF)*, February 2003, explains that STOs are the means by which SAP capabilities are generally integrated into theater campaigns and conventional military operations.

p. 59: air force XOIWS. According to internal air force briefings, obtained by the authors, the Influence Operations Division is responsible for policy, guidance, and management, to include training of air force influence operations. Influence operations consist of military deception (MD), psychological operations (PSYOP), and operations security (OPSEC): "Influence operations allow the commander to convey selected information and indicators to target audiences, shape the perceptions of decision-makers, secure critical friendly information, protect against espionage, sabotage, and other intelligence gathering activities, and communicate information about Air Force activities to the global audience."

p. 60: Applied Research Associates. For more information on Applied Research Associates, its activities, and its contracts, see the Top Secret America project page: http://projects.washingtonpost.com/top-secret-america/companies/applied-research-associates/.

p. 60: L-1 Identity Solutions. For more information on L-1 Identity Solutions, its activities, and its contracts, see the Top Secret America project page: http://projects.washingtonpost.com/top-secret-america/companies/l-1-identity-solutions/.

p. 60: SAIC. For more information on SAIC, its activities, and its contracts, see the Top Secret America project page: http://projects.washingtonpost.com/top-secret-america/companies/saic/.

p. 63: Olney, Maryland. An interesting photographic study of the underground Federal Support Center in Olney, Maryland, showing pre– and post–9/11 changes can be found at Cryptome: http://cryptome.org/eyeball/fsc/fsc-eyeball.htm.

p. 65: Global Response Staff. The CIA's Global Response Staff, aka the Global Response Service, is not publicly discussed by the government, though information on the CIA's own police, the Security Protective Service, for its various buildings in the Washington, DC, area can often be found on job sites advertising for CIA security positions.

p. 65: Blackwater/Xe Services LLC. For more information on Blackwater,

its activities, and its contracts, see the Top Secret America project page: http://
projects.washingtonpost.com/top-secret-america/companies/xe-services-llc/.

p. 68: Underground Facility Analysis Center (UFAC). For more information on the Defense Intelligence Agency (DIA, UFAC's parent organization),
its activities, and its contractors, see the Top Secret America project page:
http://projects.washingtonpost.com/top-secret-america/gov-orgs/dia/.

Created in 1997, UFAC is made up of elements of the CIA, the DIA, the
Defense Threat Reduction Agency, the National Geospatial-Intelligence
Agency (NGA), the National Security Agency (NSA), the U.S. Geological
Survey, and the U.S. Strategic Command (STRATCOM).

For more information on NGA, its activities, and its contractors, see the
Top Secret America project page: http://projects.washingtonpost.com/top
-secret-america/gov-orgs/nga/.

p. 68: Carahsoft Technology. For more information on Carahsoft, its activities,
and its contracts, see the Top Secret America project page: http://projects.washing
tonpost.com/top-secret-america/companies/carahsoft-technology-corp/.

p. 69: Defense Security Service (DSS). The DSS administers the Department of Defense Industrial Security Program. The official website is at http://
www.dss.mil/.

p. 71: Southern Command. For more information on Southern Command,
its activities, and its contractors, see the Top Secret America project page: http://
projects.washingtonpost.com/top-secret-america/gov-orgs/southcom/.

p. 72: Joint Use Intelligence Analysis Facility. The $62 million Joint Use
Intelligence Analysis Facility provides a secure intelligence facility for the
Defense Intelligence Agency (DIA) and the National Ground Intelligence Center
(NGIC) and allows the collocation of vastly expanded ground-forces technical
intelligence operations. The facility houses approximately 1,000 personnel: 800
from DIA and 200 from NGIC. More details on the new facility near Charlottesville, Virginia, can be found at http://www.nao.usace.army.mil/projects/military
%20projects/Rivanna%20Station/Rivanna_JointUse.asp.

For more information on the National Reconnaissance Office (NRO), its
activities, and its contractors, see the Top Secret America project page: http://
projects.washingtonpost.com/top-secret-america/gov-orgs/nro/.

pp. 73–75: National Security Agency (NSA). For more information on the
NSA, its activities, and its contractors, see the Top Secret America project page:
http://projects.washingtonpost.com/top-secret-america/gov-orgs/nsa/.

p. 74: Fort Meade, Maryland. The official website is at http://www.ftmeade
.army.mil/.

Information on the planned growth of Fort Meade and the National Security Agency can be found in:

- Department of the Army, Draft Environmental Impact Statement Addressing Campus Development at Fort George G. Meade, Maryland, July 2010.
- Fort Meade Briefing, Fort Meade Regional Growth Management Committee, "Working Within the Region to Transform Fort Meade Growth Impacts into Opportunities," May 2010.
- Fort Meade Briefing, Anne Arundel County and the Fort George G. Meade Region, 28 April 2008.

pp. 74–75: National Business Park. The Corporate Office Properties Trust (COPT) website for the National Business Park is at http://www.copt.com /propertyModule/park_detail.asp?parkid=108. A photographic study of National Business Park can be found at Cryptome: http://cryptome.org/eyeball/nsa-nbp /nsa-nbp.htm.

p. 75: L-3 Communications. For more information on L-3 Communications, its activities, and its contracts, see the Top Secret America project page: http://projects.washingtonpost.com/top-secret-america/companies/l-3 -communications/.

p. 75: Northrop Grumman. For more information on Northrop Grumman, its activities, and its contracts, see the Top Secret America project page: http://projects.washingtonpost.com/top-secret-america/companies/northrop -grumman/.

p. 76: Cyber Command, according to the Department of Defense, plans, coordinates, integrates, synchronizes, and conducts activities to direct the operations and defense of specified DoD information networks. It prepares for and, when directed, would conduct full-spectrum military cyberspace operations. On 23 June 2009, the secretary of defense directed the Commander of Strategic Command to establish CYBERCOM. Its Initial Operational Capability (IOC) was achieved on 21 May 2010.

Chapter 5: Supersize.gov
The specialized focus of the forty-five top-level government organizations of Top Secret America (e.g., counterthreat finances, cyber security, information operations) can be explored at http://projects.washingtonpost.com/top-secret -america/network/#/overall/most-activity/.

p. 86: Foreign Terrorist Tracking Task Force (FTTTF). The little-known FTTTF, operated by the FBI, was created pursuant to Homeland Security Presidential Directive 2 in August 2002. It is an interagency fusion center charged with using all sources of information (including data mining techniques) to discover potential domestic terrorism subjects. In addition to FBI and Justice

Department participation, the CIA; the National Security Agency (NSA); the Departments of Treasury, State, Defense, Homeland Security, Energy, and Health and Human Services; the Social Security Administration; and the Office of Personnel Management all have staff at the task force. The FTTTF has access to over forty sources of data containing lists of known and suspected foreign terrorists and their supporters through searches on a range of government and commercial databases.

p. 89: Strategic Command and information operations. For more information on Strategic Command, its activities, and its contractors, see the Top Secret America project page: http://projects.washingtonpost.com/top-secret -america/gov-orgs/stratcom/.

A change to the Unified Command Plan, signed by President Bush on 1 October 2002, assigned the global information operations mission to STRATCOM, including the Joint Task Force–Computer Network Operations (JTF–CNO) and the Joint Information Operations Center (JIOC).

p. 90: The $9 million propaganda program, the tip of the iceberg, was first reported by Walter Pincus, "Congressional Committees Raise Concerns over Pentagon's Strategic Communications," *Washington Post*, 28 July 2009.

pp. 91–92: JIEDDO and IEDs. The Joint Improved Explosive Device (IED) Defeat Organization (JIEDDO) was established in 2006 as an ad-hoc, high-level defense agency focused on leading, advocating, and coordinating all military actions to defeat IEDs. Headquartered in Crystal City, Virginia, JIEDDO has a network of research-and-development efforts, intelligence centers, and operational units engaged in counter–IED work in Afghanistan, Iraq, and other locations around the world.

p. 93: National Maritime Intelligence Center (NMIC). For more information on naval intelligence, its activities, and its contractors, see the Top Secret America project page: http://projects.washingtonpost.com/top-secret-america /gov-orgs/navy-intelligence/.

In January 2009, the new NMIC opened in Suitland, Maryland. It was created to serve as the national focal point for commercial maritime intelligence.

p. 94: 902nd Military Intelligence Group. For more information, see the official website: http://www.inscom.army.mil/MSC/Default902nd.aspx?text =off&size=12pt.

p. 94: Anwar Awlaki. Dana Priest first wrote about U.S. counterterrorism operations in Yemen and the search for Awlaki (Anwar al-Aulaqi). See "U.S. Military Teams, Intelligence Deeply Involved in Aiding Yemen on Strikes," *Washington Post*, 27 January 2010, p. A1, http://www.washingtonpost.com /wp-dyn/content/article/2010/01/26/AR2010012604239.html.

Priest also first reported on the November 2002 Predator strike in Yemen. See "CIA Killed U.S. Citizen in Yemen Missile Strike; Action's Legality, Effectiveness Questioned," *Washington Post*, 8 November 2002, p. A1, http://www .washingtonpost.com/ac2/wp-dyn/A25630-2002Nov7?language=printer.

p. 96: Intelligence Reform and Terrorism Prevention Act. The Congressional Conference Report establishing and discussing the act can be found at http://www.gpoaccess.gov/serialset/creports/intel_reform.html. The text of the act can be found at http://www.nctc.gov/docs/irtpa.pdf.

Chapter 6: One Nation, One Map

p. 105: Northern Command (NorthCom). For more information on NorthCom, its activities, and its contractors, see the Top Secret America project page: http:// projects.washingtonpost.com/top-secret-america/gov-orgs/northcom/.

The official mission statement is: "The Commander of USNORTHCOM is responsible for detecting, deterring and preventing threats to the people and territory of the United States; providing military support to Federal, State and local authorities in response to natural or man-made disasters or for other missions, as directed by the President or the Secretary of Defense; and executing theater security cooperation programs with Mexico, Canada and the Bahamas."

Three background studies of NorthCom are particularly useful:

- Jerry Cusic, "The Confusion of Homeland Security with Homeland Defense," Strategy Research Project, Army War College, 24 March 2009.
- Joseph Phillips, "Consequence Management of a Yield-Producing Nuclear Detonation INCONUS: Is NORTHCOM Ready," Naval War College, 4 May 2009.
- Steven C. Moe, "Efficacy of Regional Headquarters for National Guard Civil Support and Homeland Defense Missions" (master's thesis, Army Command and General Staff College, 11 December 2009).

p. 108: Homeland Security Infrastructure Program (HSIP). For more information on HSIP, see the National Geospatial-Intelligence Agency (NGA) Briefing, *Homeland Security Infrastructure Program (HSIP) Gold 2007 and Beyond*, 23 May 2007; and the NGA magazine *Pathfinder*, September/October 2008 issue.

p. 109: Federal Emergency Management Agency (FEMA). For more information on FEMA, its activities, and its contractors, see the Top Secret America project page: http://projects.washingtonpost.com/top-secret-america/gov-orgs /fema/.

p. 111: Mobile Consolidated Command Center (MCCC). Background information on the Northern Command (NorthCom) MCCC was found in:

- USNORTHCOM MCCC Integration Support, ENCORE Task Order (TO) Statement of Work (SOW) as of 8 November 2002.
- USNORTHCOM MCCC Secure Video Teleconferencing (VTC) System Security Authorization Agreement (SSAA), October 2003.

pp. 112–113: National Threat and Incident Database (NTIDB). The NTIDB is the Department of Homeland Security repository for intelligence analysis, the authoritative source of all U.S. government information concerning threats and incidents presenting danger to critical infrastructure and key assets.

p. 113: GIANT. GIANT is the GPS Interference and Navigation Tool. Background information was obtained in Air Force Space Command briefing (AFSPC/XOOI, Space Integration Branch), GPS Interference and Navigation Tool (GIANT) Way Ahead, July 2009.

p. 116: Coast Guard. For more information on Coast Guard intelligence, its activities, and its contractors, see the Top Secret America project page: http://projects.washingtonpost.com/top-secret-america/gov-orgs/coast -guard/.

p. 116: Banning armed Predator use in the United States. See Department of Defense Directive 3025.18, Defense Support of Civil Authorities (DSCA), 29 December 2010.

As of late 2011, the DoD has 146 unmanned aerial system (UAS) units based at 63 continental United States locations. By 2015, the Joint UAS Center of Excellence (JUAS COE) estimates, the DoD will have 197 units at 105 locations, a 35 percent increase in units and a 67 percent increase in number of locations. The Air National Guard (ANG) has operated unmanned systems since 2004. In 2011, five state National Guard units operated 9 Predator or Reaper unmanned aerial vehicles (UAVs) in combat air patrols in the Middle East. One of those units, the New York ANG's 174th Fighter Wing at Hancock Field ANG base in Syracuse, operated the MQ-9 Reaper in support of operations in Afghanistan, sending commands through satellite networks. This wing, which formerly had an F-16 flying mission, was the first Air Guard unit to operate MQ-9s.

p. 119: National Infrastructure Protection Plan (NIPP). Background information on the DHS–prepared NIPP (and the plan itself) can be found at http://www.dhs.gov/files/programs/editorial_0827.shtm.

p. 121: Paul McHale. The memorandum, obtained by the authors, is: Assistant Secretary of Defense (Homeland Defense) Paul McHale, Memorandum for Director Joint Staff, Assessment to Handle Multiple CBRNE (Chemical, Biological, Radiological, Nuclear, or High-Yield Explosive) Incidents Requiring Federal Assistance to State Authorities, 11 March 2003.

McHale's memo was supplemented by Defense Planning Scenario: Homeland Defense, 2010–2012 (U), 21 November 2003, a SECRET//NOFORN document, meaning that it cannot be shared with Canada, the only relevant country.

Chairman of the Joint Chiefs of Staff Instruction 3125.01B (CJCSI 3125.01B), Defense Support of Civil Authorities (DSCA) for Domestic Consequence Management (CM) Operations in Response to a Chemical, Biological, Radiological, Nuclear, or High-Yield Explosive (CBRNE) Incident, 19 October 2009, directed NorthCom to "form and employ as directed an additional two C2 JTF HQ, which (along with JTF-CS) are capable of deploying, planning, and integrating DoD's support to civil authorities for three near simultaneous CBRNE incidents. Confirm annually these three designated JTF headquarters' ability to deploy operationally and employ CCMRF [Chemical, Biological, Radiological, Nuclear, and High-Yield Explosive Consequence Management Response Force] elements."

p. 122: The Marine Corps Chemical, Biological Incident Response Force (CBIRF) in Indian Head, Maryland, provides the search-and-extract capability in nuclear-contaminated areas for the Chemical, Biological, Radiological, Nuclear, and High-Yield Explosive Consequence Management Response Force (CCMRF).

p. 126: Defense Support of Civil Authorities (DSCA). Department of Defense Directive 3025.18, Defense Support of Civil Authorities (DSCA), 29 December 2010, defines DSCA and the role of the Department of Defense.

The Chairman of the Joint Chiefs of Staff (CJCS) Standing DSCA Execution Order (EXORD), dated 14 August 2009, states, "Information collected on U.S. Persons by military personnel in a Title 10 USC status during [a DSCA] mission that indicates the existence of a threat to life or property or the violation of law will be turned over to civilian law enforcement official IAW [in accordance with] DoDD 5200.27, Acquisition of Information Concerning Persons and Organizations not Affiliated with DoD, and [Enclosure 2 to] DoDD 5525.5, DoD Cooperation with Civilian Law Enforcement Officials. However, before sharing foreign or counterintelligence, DoD personnel need to follow the requirements of Procedure 12 of DoD Regulation 5240.1-R on the types of permissible assistance."

The EXORD authorizes the use of traditional intelligence asset capabilities for "non-intelligence purposes" in the conduct of DSCA missions in seven cases:

- Situational awareness
- Damage assessment
- Evacuation monitoring
- Search and rescue

- Chemical, biological, radiological, nuclear, or high-yield explosives (CBRNE) assessment
- Hydrographic survey
- Dynamic ground coordination

See DSCA Handbook, Tactical Level Commander and Staff Toolkit, GTA 90-01-021, Expires 30 January 2012, pp. 5–18.

p. 126: Incident Awareness and Assessment. The Incident Awareness and Assessment quote comes from DSCA Handbook, Tactical Level Commander and Staff Toolkit, cited in the previous note. "This Defense Support of Civil Authorities (DSCA) Handbook was prepared by the Joint Test and Evaluation (JT&E) Command, Quick Reaction Test (QRT) team under the direction of the Office of the Secretary of Defense (OSD), Director Operational Test and Evaluation (DOT&E), Deputy Director, Air Warfare (DD, AW)."

See also:

- Northern Command, Incident Awareness and Assessment (IAA) Concept of Operations (CONOPS) for USNORTHCOM's Homeland Defense (HLD) and Defense Support of Civil Authorities (DSCA) Missions (Draft), N-NC/J23I, 3 October 2006.
- AFNORTH, Incident Awareness and Assessment (IAA) Concept of Operations, Tyndall AFB, FL: 1AF (AFNORTH)/A2, 19 January 2008. National Guard Bureau, Incident Awareness and Assessment Concept of Operations Information Paper, NGB/J2, 31 January 2008.

p. 127: *Geospatial Concept of Operations.* See Department of Homeland Security, Federal Interagency Geospatial Concept of Operations (GeoCONOPS), Version 2.0, July 2010, p. 95.

Chapter 7: *"Report Suspicious Activity"*

p. 128: Napolitano, "the threat facing us is at its most heightened state" since the attacks a decade ago. See Testimony of Secretary Janet Napolitano before the United States House of Representatives Committee on Homeland Security, "Understanding the Homeland Threat Landscape—Considerations for the 112th Congress," release date 9 February 2011.

p. 130: "an easygoing attitude toward different cultures." Cited in pamphlet obtained by the authors, from the Ohio–Kentucky–Indiana Regional Terrorism Early Warning Group (TEWG), "Terrorist Awareness, Recognizing Sleepers," 2005.

p. 130: FLIR Corporation. The official website is at http://www.flir.com/US/.

p. 137: Tennessee. For more information on Tennessee's homeland security and counterterrorism apparatus, see the Top Secret America project page: http://projects.washingtonpost.com/top-secret-america/states/tennessee/.

p. 144: Biometrics Identity Management Agency (BIMA). On 23 March 2010, Army General Order (DAGO) 2010-06, signed by the secretary of the army, redesignated the Biometrics Task Force (BTF) as BIMA.

p. 145: Suspicious Activity Reporting (SAR). The Nationwide Suspicious Activity Reporting (SAR) Initiative (NSI) is presented and explained by the government at http://nsi.ncirc.gov/.

p. 146: The $102,000 sole source contract and some of the intelligence reports were first discovered by the *Philadelphia Inquirer*. See Joelle Farrell and John P. Martin, "Rendell's Office Releases Content of All Bulletins on Planned Protests," 18 September 2010, http://articles.philly.com/2010-09-18/news/24976139_1_bulletins-rendell-homeland-security-office.

The Institute of Terrorism Research and Response website is at http://www.terrorresponse.org/.

p. 147: Guardian database. The FBI Guardian Program, which includes the Guardian and eGuardian (G/eG) applications, is a national program designed to record and share threat-related, Suspicious Activity Reports (SARs). Guardian is available to all FBI locations, Joint Terrorist Task Forces (JTTFs), fusion centers, and other government agencies located in shared facilities.

Chapter 8: 007s

pp. 165–168: National Center for Credibility Assessment. The website of the National Center is at http://www.daca.mil/.

p. 167: Defense Counterintelligence and Human Intelligence Center (DCHC). U.S. Department of the Interior Action Memo to the Secretary of Defense, Defense Counterintelligence and Human Intelligence Center Implementation Plan (approved by Secretary Rumsfeld 15 May 2008), established the DCHC and abolished the Counterintelligence Field Activity (CIFA), established after 9/11.

See also Department of Defense DTM 08-032, Establishment of the Defense Counterintelligence and Human Intelligence Center, 22 July 2008.

The cases of the Defense Office of Hearings and Appeals (DOHA) can be found online at http://www.dod.gov/dodgc/doha/industrial.

p. 175: Digital Realty Trust. For more information on Digital Realty Trust, its activities, and its contracts, see the Top Secret America project page: http://projects.washingtonpost.com/top-secret-america/companies/digital-realty-trust/.

Chapter 9: The Business Card

p. 176: General Dynamics. For more information on General Dynamics, its activities, and its contracts, see the Top Secret America project page: http://projects .washingtonpost.com/top-secret-america/companies/general-dynamics/.

p. 181: A 2008 study, published by the Office of the Director of National Intelligence, found that contractors made up 29 percent of the workforce in the intelligence agencies but cost the equivalent of 49 percent of their personnel budgets. The Chairman of the Joint Chiefs of Staff Operational Contractor Support Task Force, which started work in July 2009, concluded that contract work accounted for over 95 percent of logistic support and developmental projects in Afghanistan, employing more than 100,000 contractors, three-quarters of whom were Afghan nationals mostly hired by U.S. companies as subcontractors.

p. 181: Reduction of contractors. The implications in the reduction of the use of contractors can be seen in the efforts of the Joint Chiefs of Staff itself. Between fiscal year 2010–2012, the Joint Staff alone in-sourced 359 contractor full-time equivalents into civilian positions—that is, converted contractors to government employees. The number of civilians increased during the same time from 244 to 693, or by 449. See FY 2012 Budget Estimates, Joint Staff, Operation and Maintenance, Defense-Wide, TJS 851.

p. 186: SRA International. For more information on SRA, its activities, and its contracts, see the Top Secret America project page: http://projects .washingtonpost.com/top-secret-america/companies/sra-international-inc/.

p. 186: Berico Technologies. For more information on Berico, its activities, and its contracts, see the Top Secret America project page: http://projects .washingtonpost.com/top-secret-america/companies/berico-technologies/.

p. 189: Booz Allen Hamilton. For more information on Booz Allen Hamilton, its activities, and its contracts, see the Top Secret America project page: http://projects.washingtonpost.com/top-secret-america/companies/booz -allen-hamilton/.

p. 190: Michael Hayden. General Hayden's official biography can be found at http://www.af.mil/information/bios/bio.asp?bioID=5746.

p. 190: Anteon International. On 14 December 2005, General Dynamics Corporation announced that it would buy Fairfax, Virginia–based Anteon International Corporation for $2.1 billion in cash. The deal was the fifth for General Dynamics that year and was taken as a sign that the firm was shifting its attention to consulting on information technology and intelligence. The company became General Dynamics Information Technology (GDIT): http:// www.anteon.com/.

p. 190: United Technologies. The company website is at http://www.utc .com/Home.

p. 190: Behrman Capital. The company website is at www.behrmancap
.com/.

p. 191: BAE Systems. For more information on BAE Systems, its activities,
and its contracts, see the Top Secret America project page: http://projects
.washingtonpost.com/top-secret-america/companies/bae-systems-inc/.

p. 191: DynCorp International. For more information on DynCorp, its
activities, and its contracts, see the Top Secret America project page: http://
projects.washingtonpost.com/top-secret-america/companies/dyncorp
-international/.

On 12 April 2010, Cerberus Capital Management LP acquired DynCorp
International Inc. for about $1 billion.

p. 191: National Interest Security Company (NISC). For more information on NISC, an IBM company, its activities, and its contracts, see the Top
Secret America project page: http://projects.washingtonpost.com/top-secret
-america/companies/national-interest-security-company/.

p. 192: At least ninety senior officers who were in charge of various CIA
branches on 9/11 subsequently joined or became otherwise affiliated with corporations doing business with the intelligence community, according to the
Washington Post's Julie Tate. The article, "CIA's Brain Drain: Since 9/11, Some
Top Officials Have Moved to Private Sector," 13 April 2011, can be read at
http://www.washingtonpost.com/world/cias-brain-drain-since-911-some
-top-officials-have-left-for-private-sector/2011/03/25/AF3Nw1RD_story
.html.

pp. 192–193: The Chertoff Group. The company website is at http://cher
toffgroup.com/cgroup/.

p. 194: Cubic Corporation. For more information on Cubic, its activities,
and its contracts, see the Top Secret America project page: http://projects
.washingtonpost.com/top-secret-america/companies/cubic-defense
-applications-inc/.

p. 195: SkillStorm Government Integrated Systems (SGIS). For more information on SGIS, its activities, and its contracts, see the Top Secret America project page: http://projects.washingtonpost.com/top-secret-america/companies
/sgis/.

On 29 June 2010, SGIS, headquartered in San Diego, was acquired by
Salient Federal Solutions Inc., based in Fairfax, Virginia.

p. 197: McAfee. For more information on McAfee, its activities, and its
contracts, see the Top Secret America project page: http://projects.washingtonpost
.com/top-secret-america/companies/mcafee-secure-computing/.

p. 199: InTTENSITY. The company website can be found at http://inttensity
.com/.

On May 3, 2010, InTTENSITY announced that it had been awarded a Defense Intelligence Agency (DIA) contract to provide InTTENSITY software, the combined text extraction solution of Inxight and Attensity Software, for next-generation text extraction for mission elements at the DIA. InTTEN-SITY "combines both noun (Inxight ThingFinder) and verb (Attensity Server) extraction, providing the context for the connections between and among nouns of interest to government information analysts. This can make the critical difference in applications ranging from data triage to patterns of life analysis."

pp. 200–201: Intelligence and National Security Alliance (INSA). The organization website can be found at http://www.insaonline.org/.

Chapter 10: Managing the Battlefield from a Suburban Sanctuary

p. 203: Reaper. Because Predator has become synonymous with the lethal drone mission, the revolutionary quality of the Reaper has been overlooked. It was introduced in combat in October 2007. Reaper can fly faster, higher, and longer and carry more weapons and surveillance gear than Predator and has two global capabilities.

The spindly Predator has the ability to carry 700 pounds in flight, which means that when armed with its two laser-guided Hellfire missiles, it has only enough space for 450 pounds of additional sensors, including a limited eavesdropping capability.

Reaper, by contrast, can carry 3,750 pounds in flight and has better sensors and an integrated signals intelligence (SIGINT) capability. With that additional payload, Reaper carries four Hellfire missiles and two 500-pound laser-guided bombs. Reaper also has a 900-horsepower engine, compared with the Predator's 115-horsepower engine, giving Reaper a cruising speed of about 230 miles per hour, almost three times faster than the Predator. The Reaper fuselage is also wider—nearly the size of an A-10 fighter jet—and it carries more fuel, giving the Reaper a range of 3,682 miles compared with the Predator's 454 miles. Reaper also flies at a 50,000-foot ceiling, twice the height of Predator's, making it capable of quieter and stealthier operations.

p. 206: National Clandestine Service (NCS). The NCS is the CIA executive agent for all U.S. government and military clandestine human intelligence. Its former name was the Directorate of Operations.

p. 209: Drone use in the Obama administration. There were 167 unmanned aerial vehicles (UAVs) in the U.S. military inventory in 2002; 727 by 2004; 2,962 by 2006; and 6,191 by the time Obama became president, in January 2009. Research-and-development and procurement costs were averaging some $1.63 million annually. The total funding, which stood at about $350 million in 2001, ballooned to $4.1 billion in 2011. The government is set to spend somewhere around $49 billion overall for the next ten years for unmanned aerial systems. That would include production of approximately seventy to one hundred medium- and high-altitude aircraft each year. Author interviews with air force sources.

In 2002, the number of UAV systems (a ground station supporting a number of aircraft) deployed totaled sixteen. In 2008 the number of systems flying in the Middle East exceeded 1,000.

p. 209: Conflict Monitoring Center (CMC). The website of the CMC, which monitors drone strikes in Pakistan, can be found at http://cmcpk .wordpress.com/.

p. 210: Lockheed Martin. For more information on Lockheed Martin, its activities, and its contracts, see the Top Secret America project page: http:// projects.washingtonpost.com/top-secret-america/companies/lockheed-martin/.

p. 214: Collateral damage estimation. Background information on collateral damage estimation and the thresholds applied in the sensitive target approval and review process is contained in: CJCS Manual 3160.01A, Joint Methodology for Estimating Collateral Damage and Casualties for Conventional Weapons: Precision, Unguided, and Cluster, 30 December 2005; and CJCS Instruction 3125.01B, Sensitive Target Approval and Review (STAR) Process, 19 August 2009.

Chapter 11: Dark Matter

p. 226: Special Operations Command (SOCOM). For more information on SOCOM, its activities, and its contracts, see the Top Secret America project page: http://projects.washingtonpost.com/top-secret-america/gov-orgs/socom/.

Two SOCOM publications are useful: SOCOM, "History of SOCOM," 6th ed., 2008, http://www.socom.mil/Documents/history6thedition.pdf, and "USSOCOM Fact Book 2011," http://www.socom.mil/News/Documents /USSOCOMFactBook2011.pdf.

A clue about the Technical Operations Support Activity (TOSA) and its size came in the *Defense Manpower Requirements Report to Congress* (Defense Manpower Requirements Report Fiscal Year 2005, prepared by the Office of the Under Secretary of Defense for Personnel and Readiness ODUSD [PI] [RQ], March 2004), which stated (p. 74): "In FY 2005/06 INSCOM [Army Intelligence and Security Command] will complete the stand-up of the TIB/TIGs [Theater Intelligence Brigades and Groups (TIB/TIGs)] and transfer the Security Coordination Detachment (502 spaces) to Army SOCOM [USASOC]."

At the time, the Security Coordination Detachment was known as the unclassified cover unit for the Special Operations intelligence unit, sometimes known as Grey Fox and previously called the Intelligence Support Activity (ISA).

In February 2006, the government issued a particularly revealing contract solicitation that mentioned details about TOSA's activities: See Global Intelligence, Surveillance and Reconnaissance (ISR) Technical Operations Support Pre-Solicitation Industry Conference Solicitation Number: W9113M050018, Special Notice, USA-SNOTE-060209-007, 5 February 2006. Mysteriously, a notice was issued by the Army Space and Missile Defense Command on 20 March 2006, rescinding (and removing) the contract information: "Effective immediately the Army Space and Missile Defense Command (USASMDC) Solicitation W9113M050018, Global Intelligence, Surveillance and Reconnaissance Support, is hereby cancelled. The USASMDC, Technical Operations Support Activity, Army, DoD and/or U.S. Government are not liable for any costs incurred (or to be incurred) by interested vendors and/or prospective offerors in connection with Solicitation W9113M050018 and/or its cancellation."

p. 227: For background information on the Joint Special Operations Command (JSOC) in the early war in Afghanistan, see:

- *The 9/11 Commission Report,* p. 331.
- General Tommy Franks, *American Soldier,* pp. 273, 303 (see Notes on the Database and Written Source Material for complete publication information).
- General Richard B. Myers, *Eyes on the Horizon,* pp. 177, 192 (see Notes on the Database and Written Source Material for complete publication information).
- H. C. Von Sponeck, *A Different Kind of War: The UN Sanctions Regime in Iraq* (Berghahn Books, 2006), p. 118.

p. 231: General Tommy R. Franks, Commander in Chief, U.S. Central Command, AFA National Symposium, Orlando, Florida, 14 February 2002.

p. 228: Stanley McChrystal. In September 2003, Lieutenant General McChrystal became commander of the Joint Special Operations Command (JSOC), serving first as Commanding General, Joint Special Operations Command, from September 2003 to February 2006, and then as Commander, Joint Special Operations Command, and Commander, Joint Special Operations Command Forward, from February 2006 to August 2008. On 6 February 2006, the Department of Defense announced that JSOC Commander Army Major General McChrystal had been nominated to receive a third star and to continue in his job.

See Sean D. Naylor, "JSOC to Become Three-Star Command," *Navy Times*, 13 February 2006.

McChrystal's biography can be found at: http://www.cfr.org/afghanistan /biography-general-stanley-mcchrystal/p19396. His 2011 Technology Entertainment Design (TED) talk can be viewed at http://www.ted.com/talks /stanley_mcchrystal.html.

Michael Hasting's article "The Runaway General," in the 8–22 July 2010 edition of *Rolling Stone,* can be read at: http://www.rollingstone.com/politics /news/the-runaway-general-20100622.

p. 230: Title 10 and Title 50. Title 10 of the U.S. Code, Armed Forces, is that compilation of laws relating to the "armed forces," meaning the army, navy, air force, Marine Corps, and Coast Guard, and the "uniformed services," including the armed forces, the commissioned corps of the National Oceanic and Atmospheric Administration, and the commissioned corps of the Public Health Service. Military intelligence and Special Operations, or "preparation of the battlefield," though they may be clandestine in nature, are operations that, if discovered, could not be officially denied by the U.S. government.

p. 231: Pakistan and Oman operations. Musharraf's agreement to allow the Joint Special Operations Command (JSOC) to secretly run operations into Afghanistan from Pakistani bases is in *The 9/11 Commission Report*, p. 331.

Oman's permission to host AC-130 Spectre gunships and the JSOC's rear headquarters is in General Tommy Franks, *American Soldier*, p. 273 (see Notes on the Database and Written Source Material for complete publication information).

p. 232–233: "by the truckload." See H. C. Von Sponeck, *A Different Kind of War: The UN Sanctions Regime in Iraq* (Berghahn Books, 2006), p. 118.

The citations for Michael A. Longoria can be found at http://militarytimes .com/citations-medals-awards/recipient.php?recipientid=29168.

p. 234: William H. McRaven. McRaven's official biography is at http:// www.navy.mil/navydata/bios/navybio.asp?bioid=401.

On 19 August 2003, Rear Admiral William H. McRaven was assigned as the Deputy Commanding General for Operations, Joint Special Operations Command (JSOC), after having served as the director for Strategy and Defense Issues for the National Security Council at the White House. On 15 March 2004, *Newsweek* reported on the appointment of McRaven as commander of TF 121, "a covert, miniature strike force with a command structure so secretive that McRaven's role hasn't even been reported until now." See Michael Hirsh and John Barry, "The Hunt Heats Up: Man in Charge of Catching Osama Bin Laden 'Can Drive a Knife Through Your Ribs in a Nanosecond'; Inside the Search," *Newsweek*, 15 March 2004.

p. 234: The "wedding party incident" is described in:

- Department of Defense News Briefing, Tuesday, 2 July 2002, 12:30 PM EDT.
- Pamela Constable, "Sandals and Shrapnel Dot Attack Site; Afghan President Demands Closer Coordination with U.S. Military," *Washington Post,* 5 July 2002, p. A12.
- Central Command (CENTCOM), "Unclassified Executive Summary Investigation of Civilian Casualties, Oruzgan Province," released 16 September 2002.

pp. 236–237: EXORD. On 16 February 2003, the Chairman of the Joint Chiefs of Staff (CJCS) War on Terrorism Execute Order (EXORD), classified TS/Focal Point, was issued.

p. 236: Focal Point. Focal Point is a sensitive Special Operations umbrella for a set of compartmented programs, which, while not a "special access program" with its strict legal approval and reporting requirements, still requires use of Alternative Compensatory Control Measures (ACCMs) to maintain "SAP [Special Access Program]-like" security. For more information, see William M. Arkin, *Code Names: Deciphering U.S. Military Plans, Programs, and Operations in the 9/11 World* (Steerforth, 2005), chapter 1.

p. 237: Dell Dailey. For Dailey's official biography, see http://www.state .gov/outofdate/bios/87639.htm.

p. 244: National Media Exploitation Center (NMEC). The nationally funded, multi-agency initiative NMEC was created to support the war on terrorism and other high-interest operations in September 2003. It is a Director of National Intelligence (DNI) Center responsible for centralized management of all document and media exploitation conducted by the intelligence community and Department of Defense. Since its formation, it has transformed itself from a new thirty-person organization into the preeminent Document Exploitation (DOMEX) center with a workforce of over seven hundred employees, including personnel deployed to Iraq, Afghanistan, and Qatar.

Conclusion: Beyond the Fear of 9/11

pp. 262–263: "Let's stay calm." The transcript of the official interview with Gates appears at http://voices.washingtonpost.com/top-secret-america/2010 /07/dana_priest_interviews_sec_rob.html.

On 15 February 2011, Michael Vickers, now the undersecretary of defense for intelligence, stated, "The Taliban insurgency is in the tens of thousands. Al-Qaeda would be under 50 or so, 50 to 75, and that's on a part-time basis. Al-Qaeda is principally concentrated elsewhere, in Pakistan and then its affiliates in Yemen and elsewhere." See SASC, Hearing to Consider the Nominations of: Honorable Michael G. Vickers to Be Under Secretary of Defense for Intelligence; and Dr. Jo Ann Rooney to Be Principal Deputy Under Secretary of Defense for Personnel and Readiness, 15 February 2011.

On 2 March 2011, General James Mattis testified before Congress that "the senior leadership of AQ [al-Qaeda] and associated extremists groups—groups that are intent on carrying out attacks on innocent civilians worldwide—plan, prepare, and direct operations from this region, making it of critical interest to the security of the U.S. and our allies. Currently AQ in the border region is under the most intense pressure they have experienced since 2001." See Statement of General James N. Mattis, United States Marine Corps Commander U.S. Central Command before the House Appropriations Committee—Military Construction, Veterans Affairs, and Related Agencies Subcommittee on the Posture of U.S. Central Command, 2 March 2011.

p. 264: Tiversa. The company website can be found at http://www.tiversa .com/.

p. 267: Watchlists. On 9/11, the twelve different U.S. government terrorist watchlists contained 61,489 names, including 3,100 Americans on the FBI's watchlist.

By March 2004, when the Terrorist Screening Database (TSDB) was finally created, consolidating the separately maintained watchlists into one list of "individuals known or appropriately suspected to be or have been engaged in conduct constituting, in preparation for, in aid of, or related to terrorism," the 2001 number had doubled. By March 2004, according to intelligence sources, the National Security Agency (NSA) was also monitoring 19,000 people on its terrorism watchlist.

In September 2008, when the Terrorist Screening Center (TSC) celebrated its fifth anniversary, the watchlist had grown more than tenfold since 9/11. The list then contained more than 725,000 records, the vast majority representing international terrorists, but about 1 percent (some 7,000) were suspected domestic terrorists. Taking into consideration aliases and name variants, the number of individuals was estimated to be about half the total.

An organization that began with ten employees to create and manage a single watchlist of suspected terrorists had grown to a staff of more than 350 people. Approximately 270 million individuals were being screened by frontline law enforcement officers and agents each month. The database was also increasing by a monthly average of over 20,000 records.

By the time Barack Obama became president, the watchlist had grown to 1.1 million names, and the number of active terrorists was estimated to be approximately 400,000 individuals. U.S. persons (including both citizens and legal permanent residents) had grown to some 3 percent of the total (some 30,000). In 2008 alone, FBI field offices and joint terrorism task forces opened 471 cases for known or suspected terrorists previously unknown to be in the United States.

The Department of Justice inspector general conducted a full audit of the ever-growing watchlist in 2009 and found that as many as 35 percent of the nominations were outdated, many people were not removed in a timely manner, and tens of thousands of names were placed on the list without suitable cause. In the last year of the Bush administration, only 27,000 names were removed from the watchlist. People were captured or killed, or the intelligence and law enforcement agencies determined that they no longer met the criteria for inclusion. To stem some of the inflation, in February 2009 the Obama administration introduced new criteria for inclusion in the future, demanding that a "reasonable suspicion" standard be applied. The watchlist thereafter stabilized at about 600,000 names, made up of about 500,000 separate identities. U.S. persons (including both citizens and legal permanent residents) make up less than 5 percent of the listings (some 25,000). In 2009, some 10,000 individuals' names were removed from the watchlist based on the new criteria. See Department of Justice Office of the Inspector General Audit Division, the Federal Bureau of Investigation's Terrorist Watchlist Nomination Practices, Audit Report 09-25, May 2009.

Reasonable suspicion requires articulable facts that, taken together with rational inferences, reasonably warrant the determination that an individual "is known or suspected to be or has been engaged in conduct constituting, in preparation for, in aid of or related to terrorism and terrorist activities." The reasonable-suspicion standard is based on the totality of the circumstances to account for the sometimes fragmentary nature of terrorist information. Due weight must be given to the reasonable inferences that a person can draw from the available facts. Mere guesses or inarticulate "hunches" are not enough to constitute reasonable suspicion. See statement of Timothy J. Healy, Director, Terrorist Screening Center, Federal Bureau of Investigation, Statement before the House Judiciary Committee, 24 March 2010.

p. 271: Walid Shoebat. Shoebat's website is at http://www.shoebat.com/.

p. 272: Center for Security Policy's publication *Shariah: The Threat to America*. The publication can be found online at http://shariahthethreat.org/.

pp. 272–273: William G. Boykin. William M. Arkin first wrote about Boykin's religious activities in the *Los Angeles Times*. See "Commentary: The Pentagon Unleashes a Holy Warrior; A Christian Extremist in a High Defense Post Can Only Set Back the U.S. Approach to the Muslim World," *Los Angeles*

Times, 16 October 2003, http://articles.latimes.com/2003/oct/16/opinion/oe
-arkin16.

p. 276: CACI. For more information on CACI, its activities, and its contracts, see the Top Secret America project page: http://projects.washingtonpost
.com/top-secret-america/companies/caci-international-inc/.

INDEX

ABOUT THE AUTHORS

Investigative reporter Dana Priest has worked at the *Washington Post* for nearly twenty-five years, covering intelligence, the military, national health care reform, and local news. She has traveled overseas on various reporting assignments, including with Special Operations Forces on training missions, with army troops on peacekeeping deployments, and, in 2000, with the regional combatant commanders in charge of U.S. military operations around the world.

Priest has won every major journalism award, including the 2008 Pulitzer Prize for public service for "The Other Walter Reed" and the 2006 Pulitzer for beat reporting for her work on CIA secret prisons and counterterrorism operations overseas. Her 2003 book, *The Mission: Waging War and Keeping Peace with America's Military* (W. W. Norton), was named a finalist for the Pulitzer Prize for Nonfiction. She lives in Washington, DC.

William M. Arkin has been a columnist for the *Washington Post* and washingtonpost.com since 1998. He was an army intelligence analyst in West Berlin in the 1970s. Since Operation Desert Storm in 1991, he has conducted bomb damage assessments on the ground in Iraq, Lebanon, Yugoslavia, Afghanistan, and Eritrea, visiting more than eight hundred targets and briefing his findings to the Office of the Secretary of Defense, the CIA, the air force, and others.

Arkin was an adviser to a United Nations fact-finding mission to Israel and Lebanon and a consultant on Iraq to the office of the U.N. Secretary-General. He has worked for the Natural Resources Defense Council, Human Rights Watch, and Greenpeace. He has taught at the School of Advanced Air and Space Studies, U.S. Air Force, Maxwell AFB, Alabama; and been a fellow at both the Carr Center for Human Rights Policy at Harvard University and the Center for Strategic Education at the Johns Hopkins University School of Advanced International Studies (SAIS). He lives in Vermont.